Disease and Crime

Disease and crime are increasingly conflated in the contemporary world. News reports proclaim "epidemics" of crime, while politicians denounce terrorism as a lethal pathological threat. Recent years have even witnessed the development of a new subfield, "epidemiological criminology," which merges public health with criminal justice to provide analytical tools for criminal justice practitioners and healthcare professionals. Little attention, however, has been paid to the historical contexts of these disease and crime equations, or to the historical continuities and discontinuities between contemporary invocations of crime as disease and the emergence of criminology, epidemiology, and public health in the second half of the nineteenth century. When, how, and why did this pathologization of crime and criminalization of disease come about? This volume addresses these critical questions, exploring the discursive construction of crime and disease across a range of geographical and historical settings.

Robert Peckham is Co-Director of the Centre for the Humanities and Medicine at the University of Hong Kong, where he teaches in the Department of History.

Routledge Studies in Cultural History

Disease and Crime

A History of Social Pathologies
and the New Politics of Health

Edited by Robert Peckham

Routledge
Taylor & Francis Group

NEW YORK   LONDON

First published 2014
by Routledge
711 Third Avenue, New York, NY 10017

Simultaneously published in the UK
by Routledge
2 Park Square, Milton Park, Abingdon, Oxon OX14 4RN

*Routledge is an imprint of the Taylor & Francis Group,
an informa business*

Library of Congress Cataloging-in-Publication Data
Disease and crime : a history of social pathologies and the new politics of
     health / edited by Robert Peckham.
        pages cm. — (Routledge studies in cultural history ; 23)
     Includes bibliographical references and index.
   1. Crime—Sociological aspects.   2. Criminal behavior—Health aspects.
   3. Criminal behavior—Social aspects.   4. Diseases—Social aspects.
   5. Public health.   I. Peckham, Robert Shannan.
      HV6025.D56 2014
      364.2'4—dc23
      2013014171

ISBN13: 978-0-415-83619-7 (hbk)
ISBN13: 978-0-203-36195-5 (ebk)

Typeset in Sabon
by IBT Global.

Contents

Figures

Acknowledgments

I am grateful to the Lee Hysan Foundation for supporting a workshop on *Disease and Crime*, held under the auspices of the Centre for the Humanities and Medicine at the University of Hong Kong in April 2010. In particular, my thanks to Dr. K.S. Louie, former Executive Secretary of the Foundation. In developing the ideas for the book, I have benefited from numerous discussions with friends and colleagues and it is a pleasure to acknowledge them here: John Carroll, Didier Fassin, Sander Gilman, Brian Hurwitz, Sandra Teresa Hyde, Frédéric Keck, Jeff Martin, and Jin-kyung Park. Mark Seltzer owes some responsibility for inspiring the project in the first place. Thanks to Maria Sin for coordinating the project and assisting in the preparation of the manuscript. I am grateful to everyone at Routledge for their support and efficiency: Jennifer Morrow, Max Novick, Stacy Noto, and Laura Stearns. Thanks also to Eleanor Chan at IBT. Finally, my appreciation to the anonymous reviewers for their helpful comments and suggestions.

Introduction
Pathologizing Crime, Criminalizing Disease
Robert Peckham

BIOLOGY, SOCIETY, AND CRIME-DISEASE

This book maps the tensions, overlaps, and contradictions within and between social and biological understandings of disease and crime, tracking the discursive formation of the 'diseased' criminal from the mid-nineteenth century to the rise of biocriminology and the new biology of deviance and control in the twenty-first century. The aim is to not to rehearse oft-repeated social constructionist arguments, but to consider the continuities and discontinuities between biological and socio-cultural explanations of crime.[1] In so doing, the volume seeks to contribute to ongoing discussions about the extent to which contemporary biocriminological discourses remain rooted in a nineteenth-century determinism, even though the taxonomies of Victorian criminal anthropology (discussed in Chapter 2 of this volume by Chiara Beccalossi) may appear outlandish today. Expressed differently, *Disease and Crime* investigates, across different pathological sites, the shifting assumptions that have informed debates about where 'crime' is located, what factors produce it, and how it is managed. The book considers how and why disease—and, in particular, infectious disease—has come, reciprocally, to be framed as 'criminal.'

As Michael Berkowitz reminds us in his contribution to this collection, the rise of National Socialism in twentieth-century Germany underscores the lethal consequences of conflating disease with crime and implementing state policy around an absolute imperative to 'cure.' Although equations of Jews with 'parasites' and 'bacilli' antedated Nazism (with Jews being compared by one commentator to "cholera bacilli" in 1895), during the Third Reich, politics was progressively biologized, producing a 'new' politics of health.[2] While social problems were deemed to have a biological etiology, such problems could be treated with specific therapies. Adolf Hitler imagined himself to be the political incarnation of Robert Koch, the German bacteriologist celebrated for isolating the anthrax, tuberculosis, and cholera bacilli, as well as developing a set of scientific procedures—known as Koch's postulates—for confirming the causal relationship between specific microbes and diseases:

I feel I am like Robert Koch in politics. He discovered the bacillus and thereby ushered medical science onto new paths. I discovered the Jew as the bacillus and the fermenting agent of all social decomposition.[3]

This politico-bacteriological imaginary and the violent therapeutic interventions it implied rested on an organicist view of the homogenous nation conceived as a body (*Volkskörper*) susceptible to infection by parasites. Criminal pathogens fed off their hosts, impeding their 'efficiency in living' (*Lebenstüchtigkeit*). By extension, genocide was both preventative and curative: a form of mass immunization and a radical treatment of disease.[4]

The 'social' is invoked in two ways, here, with different implications for how the agencies of disease and crime are explained. First, in terms of the drive to identify, confine, and eliminate the biological criminal in order to maintain the integrity of the social order, since the pathologized criminal exposes the precariousness of the social body and its vulnerability to infection.[5] Second, in relation to a 'septic' society, which produces the criminal and thereby requires cleansing through radical intervention. The criminal is not the cause of disease but its symptom. Explanations are thus entangled: society is the pathologizing force that criminalizes the individual, while conterminously the biological criminal is the contaminating agent fermenting "all social decomposition." *Disease and Crime* investigates the ambivalence of this circular thinking and the contradictory motivations for disciplinary interpositions it entails: the gaze simultaneously turned inwards to probe the body of the criminal and directed outwards to examine the social pathologies of mass culture. As Mark Seltzer argues in his contribution to this book, a vicious cycle of reproduction constitutes the signature of an "antiseptic modernity." The compulsion to 'cure' through annihilation leads back to "bare life"—"the hunting and gathering stage of species life"—that necessitated the violent intervention in the first place.

But how did biopolitical assumptions travel in the other direction across the Führer's politico-bacteriological analogy, not only imbuing politics with scientific authority, but shaping how science was produced and how scientists viewed their work? In other words, if Hitler was Koch, who was Koch? As Laura Otis has shown, biological and political thinking were profoundly intertwined in the late-nineteenth and early-twentieth centuries:

If one believes that invisible germs, spread by human contact, can make one sick, one becomes more and more anxious about penetration and about any connection with other people—the same anxieties inspired by imperialism.[6]

The pathologist, biologist, and statesman, Rudolf Virchow, seized upon the political implications of the 'cell' as a fundamental unit of life that demarcated 'self' from 'non-self.' In an era of empire, when Europeans sought to control and extend their overseas dominions, the impetus to distinguish, protect, and defend this 'self' from the 'Other' was paramount. In 1881, Élie Metchnikoff, investigating how organisms defended themselves from attack by "intruders," demonstrated "immunity as a form of biological self-defense."[7] Koch, too, was conscious of the bacteriologist's latent political mission: to search out threatening parasites and eliminate them to allow for further expansion.[8] Biomedicine and politics became facets of the same political project. The doctor "was no longer merely a caretaker of the sick," but understood to be a "biological soldier."[9] As Virchow noted, "Medicine is a social science and politics is nothing but medicine writ large."[10]

Engaging with these broad themes, contributors to *Disease and Crime* present case studies that consider how, why, and when the pathologization of crime and the criminalization of disease came about. The essays explore whether crime in the modern era has always and necessarily been another way of talking about disease, and vice versa, and they consider the implications for policy of the contemporary "epidemic imaginary," which construes social phenomena (including crime) as forms of 'contagia.'[11] Finally, they inquire whether it is ever possible to disarticulate disease and crime. The chapters illuminate, from comparative perspectives and through different disciplinary lenses—from history to anthropology, and cultural studies—the discursive formation of crime-as-disease and disease-as-crime across a range of geographical and historical settings in Europe and Asia.

A theme linking many of the chapters is the role of state-sponsored institutions and agencies in regulating the 'life' of the state's citizens. Disease and crime are considered within a genealogy of biopolitics, where power is exerted through new modes of political knowledge.[12] The focus, in this context, as Carol Tsang reminds us in her chapter on the 'floating world' of prostitution in colonial Hong Kong, is on two apparently contradictory impulses discernible from the mid-nineteenth century, as states sought to govern increasingly mobile, urban, and diverse communities: on the one hand, a drive to aggregate citizens into 'populations,' and on the other, a counter-drive to disaggregate and categorize collectives into smaller and distinct sub-groups.[13] Both impulses were interdependent and involved the extrapolation of life from its actual contexts through a "technique of subjection" and its translation into forms of disciplinary knowledge.[14] As Michel Foucault would have it, life became "the target for new mechanisms of power."[15] Biology, statistics, epidemiology—and from the 1880s an emerging heterogeneous field called 'criminology'—abstracted experiences and behaviors into normative categories that were applied to manage populations.

The law played a critical role in this process of disassociation. Giorgio Agamben has explored the "point of intersection between the juridico-institutional and biopolitical models of power."[16] In a critique of Foucault, he argues that sovereign power has rested on a distinction between those recognized as 'persons' by the law and those excluded from the law's protection (including Jews in Nazi Germany, or as Hannah Arendt noted, the figure of the 'refugee') who existed only in a suspended condition that Agamben calls "bare life"—that is, their status was reduced to elemental biology bereft of the rights deemed intrinsic to human existence.[17] They had *zoē* (biological life) but were divested of *bios* (social life). Politics, for Agamben, continues to be predicated on this discrimination between sovereign rule and biopolitical exclusion, a distinction that found its ultimate expression in the concentration camp.[18] Indeed, the 'camp' functions as a paradigm for modern biopolitics, where, as Berkowitz suggests in Chapter 4 of this collection, the 'Other' is sequestered from the citizen and constrained in a liminal zone between life and death, being and non-being.[19] The spatial dimension of this biopolitics is the focus of many of the chapters in this volume: from Tsang's account of the 'peripheral' world of Chinese prostitution at the 'edge' of empire to Robert Peckham's investigation of the "warped space" of the London slum and the delineation of the 'crime scene,' Berkowitz's exploration of Nazi ghettos and concentration camps, Børge Bakken's interest in the *wangba*—or Internet bar—as a critical locus for crime-disease in contemporary China, and Frédéric Keck's description of the French suburbs as the site of 'contagious' violence.

A comparative study of the ways in which disease and crime have been conflated in different places and at different times serves both to ground and concretize such theoretical discussions, as well as to underline the ambiguity of the borders that define legal status in relation to biological existence. To analogize a criminal with a disease is, in one sense, to bestow a legal existence on disease, while framing the criminal as biology—that is, as "bare life" or *zoē*. A number of chapters in the book develop this theme and investigate the links between medicine and the law, tracing the shifting definitions of 'crime'—as an act punishable under criminal law—in relation to changing biomedical understandings of 'disease.'[20] As Charles E. Rosenberg has observed, 'disease' is "an elusive entity":

> It is not simply a less than optimum physiological state . . . disease is at once a biological event, a generation-specific repertoire of verbal constructs reflecting medicine's intellectual and institutional history, an occasion of and potential legitimation for public policy, an aspect of social role and individual—intrapsychic—identity, a sanction for cultural value . . . In some ways disease does not exist until we have agreed that it does.[21]

While eschewing a narrow, constructionist approach, this book is thus about the interplay of cultural, social, and political forces in shaping categories of 'disease' and 'crime.' And it is about the ways in which these categories have, in turn, been used to frame biological and social events, not only to serve particular ends, but to make sense of a world transformed by modern technology.

CASE STUDIES: EAST ASIA AND THE WEST

The approach adopted in *Disease and Crime* is genealogical, comparative, and cross-cultural. The emergent networks of disease and crime traced through the volume delimit the fault-lines of modernization.[22] The book suggests that sex crimes, bio-panic, and toxic modernity may be construed as the dark underside of modernization and its consequences. Modernity has involved the pasteurization of the modern zones of life with the imposition of clean lines, the espousal of the rational and hygienic, and the superseding of the natural by the technical and artificial. "Antiseptic modernity" was—and is—as Seltzer reminds us, premised on immunity and the conviction that crime, contagion, and eruptive nature are abnormal events or conditions that threaten to dissolve the borders of human identity, bringing the 'outside' in.[23] As this collection makes clear, however, there is a problem with this narrative of contagion.[24] In the book's charting of these emergent networks of crime and disease another account of modernity, or modernization, comes into view: one in which the concept of the 'boundedness' of modern life gives way to notions of inescapable 'connectedness.'[25]

Within the context of this 'connectedness,' a key theme of the book is the manner in which concepts, categories, and knowledge systems are translated from one setting to another through transnational, global flows in a process facilitated by empire and underpinned by novel technologies. Thus, Tsang, Bakken, and Paul Jobin, consider how pathologizing and criminalizing processes in Hong Kong, Mainland China, and Japan have been—and continue to be—shaped by 'Western' medical and criminal models. Conversely, they suggest that while 'Western' theories and practices have determined policy on 'crime' and 'disease' in Asia, Asia has also been—and continues to be—key to the formation of global models of 'disease' and 'crime.' In this sense, the book is concerned with "entangled history" and with challenging reductive arguments made about the homogenizing influence of (a largely US-led) West in 'medicalizing' indigenous cultures, replacing 'local' understandings of the human body and psyche with Western biomedical models.[26,27] On the contrary, 'globalization' creates new sites of the cosmopolitan, characterized by complex social interactions.[28] The emphasis in histories of medicine on the uni-directional diffusion of technology—from West to Rest—ignores the ways in which 'disease' identities and their 'treatments' are constituted across and between cultures. Today, as East Asia experiences rapid economic and technological development, with an attendant expansion of global influence, this process of reciprocal constitution deserves closer attention.

As Keck shows in Chapter 6 of this volume in his account of the preparedness plans elicited by fears of an anticipated highly pathogenic avian influenza A(H5N1) outbreak in France, Asia is conceived as the place from which infections emerge along the routes of animal (and human) migrations. Indeed, East Asia continues to be identified as a global hot-spot for emerging infections; a place, in the words of *Newsweek*, "that mixes people, animals and microbes from the countryside with travelers from around the world. You could hardly design a better system for turning small outbreaks into big ones."[29] Disease emergence is linked, here, as Priscilla Wald has noted, to global networks in which the "primitive farms" of Southern China gain a lethal new proximity to the super-cities of the West: New York, Toronto, and London. As Wald observes, such descriptions "exemplify how social interactions, spaces, and practices as well as the public understanding of a communicable disease are all conceptually reconfigured by their association with one another."[30] The study of this historical inter-action of spaces and practices in relation to understandings of disease and crime forms the central focus of this book.

Part I of *Disease and Crime* is overtly historical, with an emphasis on the nineteenth and early twentieth centuries. In Chapter 1, Tsang explores early attempts by the colonial state to crack down on prostitutes as agents of 'contagion' in Hong Kong, a British crown colony established as a mili-tary and trading foothold in East Asia. Tsang's interest is in the challenge posed to colonial authorities by a mobile Chinese population and particu-larly by female boatpeople who were invariably construed as 'loose women' living on the edge. The independence, resilience, and impenetrability of this 'floating world' fascinated colonial commentators. However, precisely because it was so untethered, this world was deemed to pose particular dangers, exerting a pernicious influence over colonial society. Within this context, Tsang considers representations of Chinese women as sexual pred-ators who dwell on the insalubrious peripheries of colonial society. The criminal female body is viewed as a socio-cultural artifact imagined and analyzed by colonial agents in the name of protecting and improving the social body. Tsang shows how, in this zone of "awkward engagement," legal and medical discourses converge, while the simultaneous criminaliza-tion and pathologization of Chinese women reflects underlying tensions, anxieties, and contradictions within the colonial imaginary about the state's ability to police its external and internal borders.[31]

As Mary Poovey has shown in the context of the formation of mass cul-ture in Victorian Britain, "concepts like that of 'population' took on some of the properties of material entities, largely as a consequence of the institu-tionalization of protocols for knowing and technologies of representation."[32] Underlying Tsang's argument and those of other contributors to this volume, is an interest in the asymmetries between 'disease' and 'crime' as categories with universal claims and their materialization in actual settings, through specific encounters. In other words, how have institutionalized abstractions ('crime' and 'disease') been mobilized in practise?[33] In what ways have they acquired "the properties of material entities"? And how have these abstrac-tions been modified and contested on the ground in the process?

In Chapter 2, Beccalossi addresses these questions from an altogether differ-ent perspective, by examining how 'disease' and 'crime' as 'scientific' catego-ries with universal claims were produced within a particular historical context. Focusing on the 'scientific' research of the Italian criminal anthropologist Cesare Lombroso, specifically in relation to his theories of sexual perversion, she tracks the overlaps between criminality, gender, and sexuality in relation to late nineteenth- and early twentieth-century definitions of the pathological.

This impulse to define and classify specific 'types' of human beings into the healthy and unhealthy, normal and pathological, law-abiding and criminal was perhaps most discernible in colonial settings. Paul Gilroy has argued that "camp-thinking"—which culminated in Nazi concentration camps—developed first in the colonies, where the colonial community came to be imagined in terms of a "biocultural kinship."[34] There, individuals were segregated along the lines of race, gender, and class into distinct populations with boundaries erected and policed to keep them apart. However, as Beccalossi reminds us, the "antinomies of modernity"[35] were also produced in the metropole through emergent scientific discourses of health and disease, as well as practices predicated on efforts to identify forms of 'perversion' in body and behavior.[36]

Beccalossi is particularly interested in the political and cultural implications of the disease-crime equation within Lombroso's theorizing. While his influence has often been disavowed, Lombroso's biopathologization of the criminal and the linkage of particular bodies with specific criminal traits persist to the present.[37] Thus, while the idea of 'criminology' as a set of discourses and practices developed from the 1880s, in part, as a reaction to criminal anthropology, a preoccupation with the body continues to be integral to the consolidation of criminology, in the biocriminology's focus on the criminal body. The development of neuroscience and genetics, as well as the shift from body measurements to novel technologies of visualizing internal "bodily economies" with computerized tomography (CT) and magnetic resonance imaging (MRI), reflect the extension of earlier preoccupations with "corporeal capturings," rather than their eclipse.[38,39]

'New' biological explanations of crime, which have superseded environmental and sociological criminology, stress the interrelationship between molecular neuroscience and environmental factors in producing criminality, seeking to move beyond the nature versus nurture binary.[40] Yet, as Peckham argues in Chapter 3, "Pathological Properties," the intertwining of science with environmental concerns was also central to late nineteenth- and early twentieth-century understandings of crime (and disease). The braiding of crime and disease articulates the logic of forensic medicine and of the forensic outlook more generally; it is this outlook which Peckham examines in relation to the history of a specific modern locale: the 'crime scene.'

The forensic outlook applied a typological framework for reading apparently random acts of violence as 'crime.' The locus of the criminal act was marked out as a 'scene,' temporarily suspended from the continuum of surrounding space in a process of sequestration akin to quarantining. In the words of Georg Simmel, the crime scene might be said to signify an endeavor to "cut a portion out of the continuity and infinity of space and arrange . . . this into a particular unity in accordance with a single meaning."[41] The turn-of-the-century photographs of Parisian crime scenes by the French criminologist Alphonse Bertillon exemplify the ways in which the 'scene' was produced with the application of 'scientific' protocols. Murdered victims—clothed, partially-clothed, or nude—lie on the floor of a furnished space, surrounded by a clutter of everyday artifacts and undisturbed by the presence of the photographer.[42] This is a mise-en-scène, wherein staged objects are converted into 'evidence' and made to tell a story. Indeed, the forensic outlook belongs to mass consumer culture; to the world of 'things,' which are endowed with an interiority and deciphered for their hidden meanings. Bertillon's images generalize quotidian objects into archetypes (door, table, chair, bed), at the same time as the objects acquire highly context-specific meanings, meanings that can be recuperated only through a careful analysis of their emplacement within a unique assemblage of other objects in the visual field. The striking angles, from which the supine postmortem subjects have been photographed—from under a draped table, obliquely, or looking down from above—as well as the irregular lighting, give the images an authenticity and dramatic quality. Bertillon constructed a purpose-made camera mounted on a tripod to document the scene (Figure 0.1), while he developed a system of "metric photography" to record the dimensions and configurations of specific spaces by deciphering spatial relations through a grid.[43] The marks of criminality are thus not only inscribed, as Lombroso held, on and in the body of the criminal; they are also discernible as traces in the places he moves through. Moreover, the crime scene is "established (and continually reestablished) through complex practices of marking, looking, calculating, interpreting, and rendering. It is actively made, not immediately given, a formation simultaneously material and symbolic."[44]

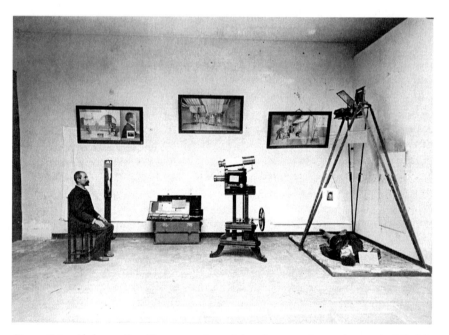

Figure 0.1   Alphonse Bertillon, overview of the photography section at the World's Columbian Exposition in Chicago, before 1893, National Gallery of Canada, Ottawa. Photo © NGC.

Against this background, Peckham shows how environmental and social explanations of disease—and, in particular, of cholera, "the classic epidemic disease of the nineteenth century"—merged with theories of crime; the pathological site was at once a body and a place.[45] Specifically, he reconsiders the Whitechapel murders of 1888 within two overlapping contexts: first, debates about slum dwellings and what Friedrich Engels called the "social murder" of the laboring class in industrial society; second, concerns about the arrangements of domestic space in relation to the diffusion of infectious disease and the 'contagious' properties of crime. Peckham demonstrates how spaces in the heart of the home came to be construed, not as passive settings, but as active agents complicit in the production of unhealthy conditions and violent crime. Data on houses were collated in surveys, reports, and statistical charts in a manner similar to the typological portraits of criminals assembled by criminologists.[46] Typological preoccupations in mass industrial Europe increasingly connected 'types' of dwellings with specific diseases, typical forms of wrongdoing, and types of bodies and behavior.

In Chapter 4, the book shifts its focus to the intertwined discourses of criminality and disease that were part of essentialist constructs of Jews in Nazi Germany. Berkowitz argues that "criminality, which was construed as inherent to Jewry, was perceived as a manifestation of disease, as well as a culturally conditioned, learned set of behaviors." He begins the essay by examining a passage from Thomas Mann's 1924 novel *The Magic Mountain* [*Der Zauberberg*] in order to underscore the interrelationship between morality, resistance to authority, and sickness. This reflection on the sanatorium, as a genre of 'camp,' introduces the key themes of his subsequent argument. As the converted Jew Leo Naphta articulates them in Mann's novel, the themes include "[the] idea of discipline and conformity, of coercion and compliance." Berkowitz explores the depictions of disease-crime in the concentration camps and ghettos, drawing on Howard Becker's notions of the "self-fulfilling prophecy" and the interpolations involved in stereotyping to suggest that the disease-crime charges brought against the Jews became self-fulfilling prophecies that mutually reinforced each other, especially in the Nazi ghettos and concentration camps. As Berkowitz notes, "Jews did turn to crime and became dependent on breaking the law for their survival. And Jews did contract infectious disease because the Nazis manufactured bizarre conditions that radically fostered ill health, contagion, and mass death."

In Part II of *Disease and Crime*, the emphasis is on the twentieth and early twenty-first centuries. In Chapter 5, Bakken considers categories of 'deviance' in the People's Republic of China, and in particular the ways in which moral panics have been framed as forms of 'contagion.' Drawing on extensive fieldwork, Bakken presents three illustrative case studies: first, what he calls "majority deviance," related to prejudices and dangers associated with the only child; second, what he calls the 'wayward girl' and the moral panic concerning so-called *zaolian* or 'premature love' among young girls; and, third, the new panic surrounding so-called 'Internet Addiction Disorder' or IAD. While the disco and the dance hall were the sites of disorder in the 1980s and 1990s, the *wangba*—or Internet bar—is now seen as the most dangerous site of crime and deviance.

Bakken shows how criminal activities have been pathologized in China, with consequences for how both 'crime' and 'disease' are understood. This entanglement came to the fore in 2003 as the Chinese government strove to make use of existing legislation in order to deal with social threats posed by the rapid diffusion of severe acute respiratory syndrome (SARS), which made its first 'appearance' in the fall of 2002 in Guangdong, reaching Hong Kong in February 2003, where it gained global media attention, spreading across the world with some 774 confirmed fatalities in 26 countries.[47] As then Premier Wen Jiabao asserted, the priority was to "bring fully into play legal weapons to win the war in preventing SARS."[48] In the absence of any provision dealing explicitly with the deliberate and 'criminal' spreading of infectious disease, in May 2003, the State Council issued "The Emergency Provisions in Dealing with Public Health Crises," which was followed by "The Explanations Concerning the Issues in the Application of Law Regarding Criminal Cases on the Prevention and Control of Outbreaks of Infectious Diseases." A host of new criminal activities were identified and defined, including—to the consternation of the WHO—the "deliberate spreading of infectious disease pathogens and virus [sic] and endangering public security."[49]

During the outbreak, and in its immediate aftermath, SARS was variously represented in the Chinese and international media in military terms as an armed onslaught. Alternatively, it was envisioned as a shadowy organization of terrorists or personified as a homicidal criminal. The reporting of SARS, and more specifically, the recurrence of a disease-as-war analogy in 2003, had different nuances in Mainland China, Taiwan, and Hong Kong, in much the same way as the language used in the coverage of SARS differed in the UK, Canada, and the US.[50,51] In the British media, for example, in contrast to Southeast Asia, military analogies were largely absent, although the coding of the virus as single killer was widespread.[52]

The 'mediatization' of infectious disease and the pervasive use of disease-crime analogies in reporting 'outbreaks' are themes explored in Chapter 6, "Contagious Wilderness: Avian Flu and Suburban Riots in the French Media." Keck's interest is in how an anticipated outbreak of avian flu in France in late 2005 was overtaken by an actual outbreak of urban violence in the form of suburban riots. Disease threat and riots were both conceptualized in terms of 'contagion.' The French debates are set in the context of post-9/11 equations of viral virulence and terrorism, since analogies between al Qaeda and viral threats were pervasive in the aftermath of the 2001 attacks on Washington and New York. In his remarks to the Council of Foreign Relations in October 2001, Richard N. Haass, Director of Policy Planning in the US State Department, for example, declared:

Another way of looking at the challenge is to view international terrorism as analogous to a terrible, lethal virus . . . Sometimes dormant, sometimes virulent, it is always present in some form. Like a virus, international terrorism respects no boundaries—moving from country to country, exploiting globalized commerce and communication to spread.[53]

On January 29, 2002, in his State of the Union Address, George W. Bush had further adumbrated his concept of the "axis of evil" and launched a plan for the counter-fight against terrorist cells lurking in "remote deserts and jungles" and hiding "in the center of large cities." The world had become a conflict zone for what Bush poignantly described as "terrorist parasites."[54] In an address to Congress in July 2003, no doubt influenced by SARS and drawing on the new discourse of 'emerging diseases,' the then British Prime Minister, Tony Blair, declared of fundamentalist Islam: ". . . a new and deadly virus has emerged. The virus is terrorism, whose intent to inflict destruction is unconstrained by human feeling."[55] Here, the criminal terrorists were biologized as pathogens. By the same token, security and the 'fight' against terror were conceived as medical and epidemiological interventions in the name of public health.

Drawing on this background, Keck is intent on tracking the convergence of two 'migrations': a discourse of security and terror from the US, and avian flu from Asia. He shows how the same metaphors were used in the French media (both press and TV) to cover these two events (violence and the threat of viral infection), and he provides an original and important riposte to critics of the 'mediatization' of disease who argue that the media serve to stoke fear and incite panic, in so doing exacerbating 'outbreak' situations. On the contrary, through close readings of news coverage in *Le Monde* and an analysis of a popular current affairs program on TV, *Mots croisés* [*Crossed Words*], Keck suggests that media representations of 'contagion' function as a novel way of articulating and making sense of 'new' emerging threats.

Many of the chapters in *Disease and Crime* engage with a growing secondary literature in history and sociology on the 'medicalization' or 'pathologization' of society: the processes through which 'badness,' or deviance, are transmuted to 'sickness.'[56] The emphasis is on how and why medical and health systems, as well as regulation, become tools for coercion and oppression sustaining a form of "therapeutic tyranny."[57] Contributors also consider the ways in which specific crimes have been re-conceptualized as treatable conditions or disorders, with profound implications for the victims of wrongdoing.

In Chapter 7, however, Jobin shifts the emphasis away from sociological and historical critiques of 'medicalization' to consider 'disease' and 'crime' from an altogether different vantage: that of victims of industrial pollution and occupational disease in contemporary Japan. In so doing, he examines how categories of 'disease' and 'crime' may be re-appropriated by 'victimized' social groups who take legal action against institutions. "In the case of asbestos lawsuits, where individuals and groups bring their charges to court in order to prove negligence," Jobin notes, "people are not treated *as* sick, they *are* truly sick. But they have an imperative to prove it. In their attempts to obtain formal apologies and compensation, they meet with tremendous difficulties in defining their affliction and then demonstrating that it results from corporate or state negligence." Jobin challenges social constructionist notions of 'disease' and crime' as elusive and contingent entities, detailing the victims' battles to be heard and recognized as 'victims.'

Finally, in Chapter 8, Seltzer resituates disease-crime in relation to the increasing intertwinement of social and biological orders: of history and natural history. Seltzer reads a number of 'experimental' novels by W.G. Sebald, Patricia Highsmith, Max Brooks, Cormac McCarthy, and Tom McCarthy to demonstrate how, in contemporary culture, "disease (the disorder of structure or function at the level of the organism) and crime (the disorder of structure or function at the level of social organization) [. . .] reciprocally index each other." For Seltzer, this reciprocity is a sign of "the official world": that is, a reflexive world, reminiscent of the "self-conditioned" life inside a laboratory. Disease and crime, he suggests, might be thought of as forms of violence generated by society against itself.

A 'NEW' POLITICS OF HEALTH?

Today, news reports proclaim 'epidemics' of crime, while politicians denounce terrorism as a lethal pathological threat. The language of epidemiology and the framing of social and political life in terms of infectious disease extend from discussions and analyses of street crime and mass incarceration to digital media bullying, alcoholism, and obesity.[58] Furthermore, epidemiological methods and approaches are increasingly being employed to analyze the multiple determinants of crime, elucidating "spatial patterns of violent crime risk."[59] The remit of the Centers for Disease Control and Prevention encompasses bio-violence and terrorism, youth violence, and crime. Recent years have witnessed the development of a new subfield, 'epidemiological criminology,' which merges public health with criminal justice to provide analytical tools for criminal justice practitioners and healthcare professionals.[60]

The subtitle of this book, "A History of Social Pathologies and the New Politics of Health," however, suggests a rupture between historical explanations of disease and crime, and contemporary theories, technologies, and practices. To be sure, the designation 'new' points to an emerging discourse of the 'diseased' criminal in the second half of the nineteenth century; a recognizably modern discourse in which, as the contributors to this volume show, biological explanations converged with socio-cultural and environmental accounts. The pathologizing gaze extended from body to society, with the state assuming increasing responsibilities for the promotion of health and the prevention and treatment of 'disease.' Yet, there are significant ways in which novel social configurations and technological developments, both in terms of biomedical interventions and media coverage, are giving rise to a 'new' public awareness of what 'health' and 'disease' accommodate. As medicine becomes increasingly expansive, pathologizing a range of 'conditions' hitherto deemed 'normal'—from shyness to obesity[61]—the nature of 'crime' itself is being reinterpreted within the context of a new norm and set of bodily practices.[62] In the words of Nikolas Rose, today crime has become a crucial site for the "biologization of the human soul."[63]

"If my prediction is correct," Nicole Rafter has observed, "we are on the threshold of a major shift that could lead to various genetic and other biological 'solutions' to criminal behavior." The outcome of this biologization of crime will depend, she notes, "on how well informed we are about the past and present biological theories of crime"—theories "which raise profound and inescapable issues about the nature of justice."[64] Despite the anxieties about "genetic essentialism and neurogenetic determinism," today there is a conspicuous turn away from social to integrative biosocial approaches to crime, which encompass such fields as molecular genetics, evolutionary psychology, and neuroscience in order to develop crime prevention policies that are "more effective than those strategies currently utilized within agencies of criminal justice, such as mass incarceration and capital punishment, that are based largely on ideological beliefs and 'common sense.'"[65,66]

Within the context of this wider debate about the social and the biological, *Disease and Crime* develops a much-needed new comparative and cross-disciplinary framework for investigating the different ways in which social groups have been categorized as criminal and diseased by legal, medical, and political authorities. In so doing, the book brings together and contributes to a number of important but hitherto disparate strands of contemporary scholarship, making connections between European and East Asian, metropolitan and (post-) colonial experiences. In different ways, each of the contributors elaborates on the theoretical insights of the new cultural criminology to investigate the overlaps between cultural and criminal practices. The focus throughout is on the interrelationship between marginality, illegality, and representation in modern societies.[67] The authors examine the complex intersections of culture and crime and inquire how these intersections have shaped social experience, particularly in relation to modern technologies that produce 'moral panic.'[68]

Although some attempt has been made to explore the "shared epistemological and ontological ideology" underlying, for example, pandemic preparedness and terrorism, little attention has been paid to the historical contexts of these disease and crime equations, or to the historical continuities and discontinuities between contemporary invocations of crime as disease and the emergence of criminology, epidemiology, and public health in the second half of the nineteenth century.[69] Drawing on a range of primary material, as well as on original fieldwork, each of the chapters in the volume questions key assumptions underlying constructionist approaches to disease and crime. Contributors examine the extent to which the current emphasis on medicine and law as regimes of discipline and punishment has tended to undermine notions of good care and justice. The chapters explore shifting ideas about causality and crime in relation to the development of scientific medicine.[70] They argue, on different grounds, that examining the ways in which disease and crime have been conflated historically can bring important new insights to the complex process whereby the 'natural' and the 'cultural' are co-produced.[71] At the same time, the volume contributes to recent work on biopolitics but, via its historical and comparative approach, makes it possible to reframe that account of life under the pressure of modernity. *Disease and Crime* thus fills a critical gap in existing scholarship, with relevance for those working across a range of disciplinary fields from history and anthropology to sociology and cultural studies, comparative East-West studies, and beyond.

ACKNOWLEDGMENTS

I would like to thank Mark Seltzer for commenting on an earlier draft of this essay. I am also grateful to Didier Fassin and to Jeff Martin, co-participants in the 'Humanitarian Violence' workshop held at the University of Hong Kong in May 2012, for their helpful suggestions on 'rethinking' violence.

NOTES

1. For a critique of the pervasive metaphor of 'social construction' in academic discourse, see Ian Hacking, *The Social Construction of What?* (Cambridge, MA: Harvard University Press, 1999).
2. Lucy S. Dawidowicz, *The War Against the Jews, 1933–1945* (New York: Bantam, 1975), 54; quoted in Robert Proctor, *Racial Hygiene: Medicine Under the Nazis* (Cambridge, MA: Harvard University Press, 1988), 379.
3. Richard Evans, *Telling Lies about Hitler: The Holocaust, History and the David Irving Trial* (London: Verso, 2002), 83–84.
4. The construal of a mass immunization program as a form of surreptitious genocide has been articulated in recent times, for example, in Nigeria where those opposed to the US promotion of polio immunization (including the president of Nigeria's Supreme Council for Sharia Law) contend that it is being conducted with genocidal intentions; see Arthur Allen, *Vaccine: The Controversial Story of Medicine's Greatest Lifesaver* (New York: W.W. Norton, 2007), 440. On the interrelationship between biological and medical developments and Nazi politics, see Paul Weindling, *Health, Race and German Politics Between National Unification and Nazism, 1870–1945*

(Cambridge: Cambridge University Press, 1989); on criminology as an aspect of political power in the Third Reich and the application of biological ideas to crime, see Nicole Rafter, "Criminology's Darkest Hour: Biocriminology in Nazi Germany," *Australian and New Zealand Journal of Criminology*, vol.41, no.2 (2008): 287–306.

5. On the social body, see, classically, Mary Douglas, *Purity and Danger: An Analysis of Concepts of Pollution and Taboo* (London: Routledge, 1991 [1966]).

6. Laura Otis, *Membranes: Metaphors of Invasion in Nineteenth-Century Literature, Science, and Politics* (Baltimore: Johns Hopkins University Press, 2000), 4–5.

7. Ed Cohen, *A Body Worth Defending: Immunity, Biopolitics, and the Apotheosis of the Modern Body* (Durham, NC: Duke University Press, 2009), 1–2.

8. Ibid., 31–32; see, also, Bruno Latour, *The Pasteurization of France*, trans. Alan Sheridan and John Law (Cambridge, MA: Harvard University Press, 1993 [1984]).

9. Robert Jay Lifton, *The Nazi Doctors: Medical Killing and the Psychology of Genocide* (New York: Basic Books, 1986), 30.

10. Michael Löwy, *The Theory of Revolution in the Young Marx* (Chicago: Haymarket, 2005 [2003]), 135.

11. John Nguyet Erni, "Epidemic Imaginary: Performing Global Figurations of 'Third World AIDS,'" *Space and Culture*, vol.9, no.4 (2006): 429–452; see, also, Chad Lavin and Chris Russill, "The Ideology of the Epidemic," *New Political Science*, vol.32, no.1 (2010): 65–82.

12. For a useful genealogy of biopolitics, see Thomas Lemke, *Biopolitics: An Advanced Introduction* (New York: New York University Press, 2011), 9–21.

13. For a study of the homogenizing and classifying features of nineteenth-century culture, see Mary Poovey, *Making a Social Body: British Cultural Formation, 1830–1864* (Chicago: University of Chicago Press, 1995).

14. See, Michel Foucault, *Discipline and Punish: The Birth of the Prison*, trans. Alan Sheridan (New York: Vintage, 1979), 155.

15. Ibid.

16. Giorgio Agamben, *Homo Sacer: Sovereign Power and Bare Life*, trans. Daniel Heller-Roazen (Stanford: Stanford University Press, 1998), 4.

17. Ibid., 126–135.

18. Giorgio Agamben, *Means without End: Notes on Politics*, trans. Cesare Casarino and Vincenzo Binetti (Minneapolis: University of Minnesota Press, 2000), 44.

19. Agamben, *Homo Sacer*, 131, 139.

20. Michael Clark and Catherine Crawford, eds. *Legal Medicine in History* (Cambridge: Cambridge University Press, 1994); and Katherine D. Watson, *Forensic Medicine in Western Society: A History* (London: Routledge, 2011).

21. Charles E. Rosenberg, "Introduction—Framing Disease: Illness, Society, and History," in *Framing Disease: Studies in Cultural History*, ed. Charles E. Rosenberg and Janet Golden (New Brunswick, NJ: Rutgers University Press, 1997), xiii.

22. This paragraph owes much to conversations and personal correspondence with Mark Seltzer.

23. Otis, *Membranes*; Cohen, *A Body Worth Defending*.

24. Priscilla Wald terms this "the outbreak narrative"; see *Contagious: Cultures, Carriers, and the Outbreak Narrative* (Durham, NC: Duke University Press, 2008), 2–3.

25. See Laura Otis, *Networking: Communicating with Bodies and Machines in the Nineteenth Century* (Ann Arbor: University of Michigan Press, 2001), 7.

26. On the methods of "entangled history" or *histoire croisée*, see Michael Werner and Bénédicte Zimmermann, "Beyond Comparison: Histoire Croisée and the Challenge of Reflexivity," *History and Theory*, vol.45, no.1 (2006): 30–50.

27. See the argument presented by Ethan Watters in *Crazy Like Us: The Globalization of the American Psyche* (New York: The Free Press, 2010).

28. On the "friction" produced by these complex interactions and the "awkward, unequal, unstable, and creative qualities of interconnection across difference," see Anna Lowenhaupt Tsing, *Friction: An Ethnography of Global Connection* (Princeton: Princeton University Press, 2005), 4.

29. Discussed by Wald in *Contagious*, 5–8.

30. Ibid., 7.

31. Tsing, *Friction*, xi.

32. Poovey, *Making a Social Body*, 4.

33. Tsing, *Friction*, 9.

34. Paul Gilroy, *Against Race: Imagining Political Culture Beyond the Color Line* (Cambridge, MA: Harvard University Press, 2000), 83–84.

35. Ibid., 71.

36. For an elaboration of Gilroy's thesis, see Rod Edmond, *Leprosy and Empire: A Medical and Cultural History* (Cambridge: Cambridge University Press, 2006). Edmonds argues that "the antinomies of modernity Gilroy sees at the colonial margin were simultaneously present, in muted and less extreme forms, in the metropole," 183.

37. See the argument made by Kevin Walby and Nicolas Carrier on Lombroso's influence—in particular his "bodily economies"—on subsequent analysts: ". . . looking at criminological biopathologizations from Lombroso onwards reveals the tremendous uniformity of biocriminology's 'solutions' as to what regards the criminal cum punishable body"; "The Rise of Biocriminology: Capturing Observable Bodily Economies of 'Criminal Man,'" *Criminology & Criminal Justice*, vol.10, no.3 (2010): 274.

38. See, for example, the essays on crime and molecular genetics, epigenetics, and evolutionary psychology collected in Anthony Walsh and Kevin M. Beaver, eds., *Biosocial Criminology: New Directions in Theory and Research* (New York: Routledge, 2009). For an overview of the social anxieties produced by the new biological 'criminology,' and in particular the discourse of 'neuroethics,' see Nikolas Rose, *The Politics of Life Itself: Biomedicine, Power, and Subjectivity in the Twenty-First Century* (Princeton: Princeton University Press, 2007), 224–251.

39. Walby and Carrier, "The Rise of Biocriminology," 275.

40. For the new biology of crime, see Debra Niehoff, *The Biology of Violence: How Understanding the Brain, Behavior and Environment Can Break the Vicious Circle of Aggression* (New York: The Free Press, 1999); Diana H. Fishbein, *Biobehavioral Perspectives on Criminology* (Belmont, CA: Wadsworth Publishing, 2001); and David C. Rowe, *Biology and Crime* (Los Angeles: Roxbury Publishing, 2002).

41. Quoted in Greg Siegel, "The Similitude of the Wound," *Cabinet*, vol.43 (2011): 96.

42. See Bertillon's "Album of Paris Crime Scenes" (1901–1908) in the online archive of the Metropolitan Museum of Art, New York: http://www.metmuseum.org/Collections/search-the-collections/190037970 (accessed January 28, 2013).

43. Alphonse Bertillon and Arthur Chervin, *Anthropologie Métrique* (Paris: Imprimerie Nationale, 1909); see, also, Teresa Castro, "Scène de crime: la

mobilisation de la photographie métrique par Alphonse Bertillon," in *Aux origines de la police scientifique: Alphone Bertillon, précurseur de la science du crime*, ed. Pierre Piazza (Paris: Karthala, 2011), 230–245.
44. Siegel, "The Similitude of the Wound," 96.
45. See, Charles E. Rosenberg, *The Cholera Years: The United States in 1832, 1849, and 1866* (Chicago: University of Chicago Press, 1987 [1962]), 1.
46. See, also, George Teyssot, "Norm and Type: Variations on a Theme," in *Architecture and the Sciences: Exchanging Metaphors*, ed. Antoine Picon and Alessandra Ponte (New York: Princeton Architectural Press, 2003), 150–151.
47. See Angela McLean, Robert M. May, John Pattison, and Robin A. Weiss, eds., *SARS: A Case Study of Emerging Infections* (Oxford: Oxford University Press, 2005).
48. Ronald C. Keith and Zhiqiu Lin, *New Crime in China: Public Order and Human Rights* (London: Routledge, 2006), 155.
49. Ibid., 157.
50. Wen-Yu Chiang and Ren-Feng Duann, "Conceptual Metaphors for SARS: 'War' between Whom?" *Discourse & Society*, vol.18, no.5 (2007): 579–602.
51. Robert J. Blendon, John M. Benson, Catherine M. DesRoches, Elizabeth Raleigh, and Kalahn Taylor-Clark, "The Public's Response to Severe Acute Respiratory Syndrome in Toronto and the United States," *Clinical Infectious Diseases*, vol.38, no.7 (2004): 925–931; Peter Washer, "Representations of SARS in the British Newspapers," *Social Science and Medicine*, vol.59, no.12 (2004): 2561–2571; and Patrick Wallis and Brigitte Nerlich, "Disease Metaphors in New Epidemics: The UK Media Framing of the 2003 SARS Epidemic," *Social Science and Medicine*, vol.60, no.11 (2005): 2629–2639.
52. Wallis and Nerlich, "Disease Metaphors."
53. Richard N. Haass, "The Bush Administration's Response to September 11th—and Beyond" (New York: Council of Foreign Relations, October 15, 2001): http://2001–2009.state.gov/s/p/rem/5505.htm (accessed January 28, 2013).
54. http://georgewbush-whitehouse.archives.gov/news/releases/2002/01/20020129–11.html (accessed January 28, 2013).
55. Quoted in Ronnie Lippens, "Viral Contagion and Anti-Terrorism: Notes on Medical Emergency, Legality and Diplomacy," *International Journal of the Semiotics of Law*, vol.17, no.2 (2004): 126.
56. Peter Conrad and Joseph W. Schneider, *Deviance and Medicalization: From Badness to Sickness* (Philadelphia: Temple University Press, 1992 [1980]).
57. Janet Katz and Charles F. Abel, "The Medicalization of Repression: Eugenics and Crime," *Contemporary Crises*, vol.8, no.3 (1984): 227–241.
58. Lavin and Russill, "The Ideology of the Epidemic," 68.
59. Corey S. Spark, "Violent Crime in San Antonio, Texas: An Application of Spatial Epidemiological Methods," *Spatial and Spatio-temporal Epidemiology*, vol.2, no.4 (2011): 301.
60. Mark M. Lanier, "Epidemiological Criminology (EpiCrim): Definition and Application," *Journal of Theoretical and Philosophical Criminology*, vol.2, no.1 (2010): 63–103; and Timothy Akers and Mark M. Lanier, "'Epidemiological Criminology': Coming Full Circle," *American Journal of Public Health*, vol.99, no.3 (2009): 397–402.
61. See, for example, Andrew Stark, *The Limits of Medicine: Cure or Enhancement* (Cambridge: Cambridge University Press, 2006); and Christopher Lane, *Shyness: How Normal Behavior Became a Sickness* (New Haven: Yale University Press, 2008).

62. See the arguments presented in Jonathan M. Metzel and Anna Kirkland, eds. *Against Health: How Health Became the New Morality* (New York: New York University Press, 2010).

63. Rose, *The Politics of Life*, 225.

64. Nicole Rafter, *The Criminal Brain: Understanding Biological Theories of Crime* (New York: New York University Press, 2008), 8.

65. Ibid.

66. Matthew Robinson, "No Longer Taboo: Crime Prevention Implications of Biosocial Criminology," in *Biosocial Criminology*, 243.

67. Jeff Ferrell, Keith Hayward, and Jock Young, eds. *Cultural Criminology: An Invitation* (London: Sage, 2008).

68. Stanley Cohen, *Folk Devils and Moral Panics* (Oxford: Blackwell, 1983 [1972]); and Judith Rowbotham and Kim Stevenson, eds. *Criminal Conversations: Victorian Crimes, Social Panic, and Moral Outrage* (Columbus: Ohio State University Press, 2005).

69. Nick Muntean, "Viral Terrorism and Terrifying Viruses: The Homological Construction of the 'War on Terror' and the Avian Flu Pandemic," *International Journal of Media and Cultural Politics*, vol.5, no.3 (2009): 199–216; Stefan Elbe, *Virus Alert: Security, Governmentality, and the AIDS Pandemic* (New York: Columbia University Press, 2009); and Andrew Lakoff and Stephen J. Collier, eds. *Biosecurity Interventions: Global Health and Security in Question* (New York: Columbia University Press, 2008).

70. Stephen Kern, *A Cultural History of Causality: Science, Murder Novels, and Systems of Thought* (Princeton: Princeton University Press, 2004).

71. Sheila Jasanoff, ed. *States of Knowledge: The Co-Production of Science and Social Order* (London: Routledge, 2004).

Part I

1 Hong Kong's Floating World
Disease and Crime at the Edge of Empire

Carol C. L. Tsang

The deep, sheltered waters of Victoria Harbour enthralled many British travelers to Hong Kong in the nineteenth century. Visitors were impressed by the vista of steep granite hills rising above the expanding city on the shoreline. And they were struck by the sight and sounds of innumerable Chinese boats teeming beside the jetties as they plied their wares and services. As Julius Berncastle remarked, typically, in *Voyage to China* (1850): "We were immediately, on our arrival, surrounded by a host of sampan boats, rowed and steered by women and children, the whole family generally passing all their lives in their boats."[1]

This waterworld and the boatpeople who dwelt in it were a salient feature of Hong Kong life that elicited contradictory responses from the British. On the one hand, they were construed in picturesque terms as a "healthy, happy, and contented" population engaged in legitimate small business, such as selling curry rice, omelets, and bananas. On the other hand, they were a dangerously mobile and ill-defined group comprised of a "low, poor and degraded" class of persons that hampered the colony's progress.[2] For many colonials the boatpeople were identified with criminality and deemed to be complicit in smuggling, piracy, and other illegal activities that undermined the social order.[3] Among the different social groups within the Chinese population, they were the most mobile and hence the most difficult for the authorities to understand and control.

Boatwomen, in particular, were singled out as a threat to British sailors. In 1845, Chief Magistrate William Caine, known for his unyielding treatment of the Chinese, wrote of an attempt by the government to curtail the activity of Chinese prostitutes in Tai Ping Shan, a poor Chinese area located in the western part of Hong Kong.[4] Caine noted that the women had all been "driven from the shore, but continued to exercise their calling in boats anchored in the harbour, where their freedom from Police surveillance gave birth to innumerable irregularities."[5] For Caine, this floating world represented an anti-social and nebulous sphere, beyond the purview of the nascent colonial state. In contrast to the 'flower boats' (*fa-shuen*)—ostentatious floating brothels that were a feature of the Canton waterscape—the alleged 'prostitutes' who plied their trade from smaller boats in Hong Kong were difficult to identify, blending into an amorphous, teeming population. This very anonymity rendered them at once a source of fascination, even desire, and an object of particular menace to be contained. In an inversion of salutary production, Caine envisioned the promiscuous boatwomen 'giving birth' to countless problems: "Accidents were of frequent occurrence, attended more than once with loss of life; robberies were committed on those who visited the boats with comparative impunity; and while the public morals were in no wise benefitted by the change, disease prevailed to a fearful extent." Among the social evils identified by Caine, the scourge of venereal disease, spread by Chinese prostitutes, worried him the most.[6]

Proposals to regulate prostitution in Hong Kong had been debated as early as the 1840s, soon after the territory's acquisition as a crown colony by the British. The danger posed by migrant women prompted a number of naval officers to urge the government to issue compulsory medical checks. Rear Admiral James Stirling argued that without such inspections, the government could not expect prostitutes to "seek the restraint and treatment requisite for their cure." He lamented that one-third of his men had contracted venereal disease from Chinese prostitutes in Hong Kong in the course of 1854. According to Stirling, these unruly women were draining the health and vigor of British forces, while ruining their own lives, and devastating "the whole population of China." Vice Admiral Sir Fleetwood Pellew concurred and urged the government to impose a medical examination on Chinese women, arguing that the system had worked effectively in places such as France, Gibraltar, Malta, and Macau.[7] Echoing Pellew, in 1854, Colonial Surgeon John Carroll Dempster cited the example of Gibraltar—one of the smallest British colonial possessions in the Mediterranean—as an island territory comparable to Hong Kong, concluding that the regulation of prostitution there furnished an applicable model for the crown colony. In Gibraltar, prostitutes were not allowed to stay in the garrison unless they had a permit.[8] All brothels were under close supervision of the police and civil surgeon. Even in Macau, the Portuguese colony close to Hong Kong, the system had proven to be effective in controlling the spread of venereal disease.[9]

Finally, in 1857, under the governorship of John Bowring, Hong Kong passed an Ordinance for Checking the Spread of Venereal Disease, anticipating the Contagious Diseases Act in the United Kingdom by seven years. Ordinance No. 12 required prostitutes who serviced European clients to be examined regularly and detained in the Lock Hospital until treated. However, despite this new legislation, prostitutes continued to be viewed as agents of contagion in government reports and official correspondence where there was a near-hysterical response to the perceived threat of an 'epidemic' of venereal disease.

In such narratives of contagion, Chinese prostitutes were invariably portrayed as sexual predators who dwelt on the periphery of Hong Kong society, from whence they preyed upon their unsuspecting European victims.[10] According to such narratives, prostitutes disguising themselves as boatwomen or washerwomen (the terms were used interchangeably) were especially construed as a "cunning" criminal class that threatened the colony's social stability and political order.[11] Anxieties about disease became intertwined with pervasive concerns about criminality, race, and gender. This chapter explores the ways in which migrant women in Hong Kong were imagined in colonial discourse in terms of a pathological and criminal body; 'imagined' first, in the sense that any threat posed by Chinese prostitutes to European men was exaggerated and, second, because colonialism is here understood as a deeply cultural process. As Nicholas Thomas suggests, colonialism's "discoveries and trespasses are imagined and energized through signs, metaphors and narratives."[12]

Notwithstanding the repeated emphasis on the dangers posed by local prostitutes, the Hong Kong government prosecuted only 37 women for infecting men with venereal disease between 1867 and 1887.[13] To be sure, there is a substantial literature exploring the ways in which conceptualizations of race, gender, culture, and space shaped the regulation of prostitution during the nineteenth century.[14] However, most historians of Hong Kong have ignored its floating world—a fluid domain that encapsulates colonial fears about migrancy and about illicit inter-racial relations in the early colony. My purpose, here, is to reappraise the testimonies of administrators, colonial agents, and journalists, in order to examine the shifting socio-political contexts within which the specter of the pathological and criminal female body was articulated from 1842 to the repeal of Ordinance No. 12 in 1887. In so doing, I elaborate on three major themes in *Disease and Crime*. First, I explore the extent to which the 'criminal' and 'pathological' were discursively constructed in relation to fears of migrancy and anxieties over the control of porous state borders. Second, I examine the contradictions and internal incoherencies that characterized the colonial imaginary of the 'diseased' prostitute. While Chinese women were condemned for preying on British soldiers, their image in colonial discourse as criminal perpetrators—in opposition to a 'feminized' and passive European masculinity—paradoxically re-inscribed them with an agency they were officially denied. Finally, I attribute the pathological and criminal, as abstracted categories, to the development of colonial knowledge about disease, race, and gender before the advent of 'germ theory'—which made visible the microbial, causative agents of disease—and the emergence of criminology as a distinct, albeit diffused, field.[15]

OPEN BORDERS, LOOSE WOMEN

Hong Kong's water-bound landscape and the fluid borders of its island topography intrigued foreign travelers. Writing as 'Old Humphrey,' the prolific English writer George Mogridge predicted in 1844 that Hong Kong would quickly surpass Macau because its water was "deep enough to float a first-rate man-of-war close to the land."[16] Above all, it was the "novelty" of Hong Kong's busy and distinctive waterworld that fascinated Mogridge: "the British war-vessels, clippers, and steamers; the Chinese junks, chop-boats, sampans . . . the deafening sounds of the tom-toms and gongs . . . firing of crackers, and burning of high-colored and tinseled paper . . . and scattered in a flaming shower on the water; altogether a stranger is absolutely bewildered with novelty."[17] Some two decades later, the peripatetic Isabella Bird recounted her impressions of the colony and noted that if "coasts usually disappoint," Hong Kong "exceeded all my expectations."[18]

Yet, if the sea and the novelty of its boisterous sea-life were lauded as particularly picturesque features of the colony, they were also seen by some as a threat to health and as a source of social evil. The lawyer and diplomat Henry Charles Sirr, known for his critical comments on the early colony, observed, for example, how "the exhalations arising from the water produce fever and ague," and "the successive inhabitants . . . were seized and died." Disease emanated from the water, which also provided a haunt for criminals. Hong Kong was "the resort of pirates, thieves, and depraved characters of every description." On account of its fractured geography and fluid borders, the colony attracted "a migratory or a predatory race" of criminal seeking refuge from the law. As Sirr concluded ominously, death was the colony's "presiding genius."[19]

The Chinese population of Hong Kong was often imagined as a floating world, epitomized by the din and confusion of the boatpeople: a world of drifters and a suspended frontier world of 'rootless' Chinese immigrant hordes, drawn to the colony to make their fortune in the 'freedom' and 'protection' afforded by British colonial institutions. They were inhabitants of a hybrid zone, at once within and outside the colonial order. Most of the Chinese who entered Hong Kong in the early years were members of the lower classes, including "labourers, artisans, Tanka outcasts, prostitutes, wanderers, and smugglers."[20] Women, too, made their way to the colony amidst the daily tide of workers flowing in across the border from the mainland. According to colonial administrators, many of these women came expressly to work as prostitutes or were kidnapped and brought over by their captors. Hong Kong was a transit hub in the inter-port trade of prostitutes, connected to other Chinese port cities, including Amoy (Xiamen), Swatow (Shantou), Shanghai, and Canton (Guangzhou). While many women stopped over in Hong Kong before being shipped off "by junks or steamers" to Singapore and further afield to California, some women stayed on to earn a living in the colony.[21]

Contemporary commentators saw in Chinese prostitution an exemplar of China's moral turpitude and decay. At the same time, in Hong Kong prostitution was considered a consequence of the colony's conspicuous gender imbalance, which nurtured and sustained the illicit trade. Mid-century Hong Kong was overwhelmingly male. According to the census of 1853, there were 876 European men and 28,928 Chinese men in the colony, but only 411 European women and 8,608 Chinese women.[22] This gender discrepancy was perceived as providing an incentive for prostitution that shocked many Chinese and colonials alike. Chinese women were invariably identified as prostitutes. In 1877, Police Magistrate Charles May declared that "only about one sixth of Chinese women in the colony live with one man either in marriage or concubinage, and all the rest come under the denomination of prostitutes to whom money being offered they would consent to sexual intercourse." Meanwhile, Pang Ui-shang, a Chinese traditional medicine practitioner, believed that nearly 75 percent of women in Hong Kong were prostitutes.[23]

While these figures may well have been exaggerations, the claims were not entirely unfounded. In 1844, brothels outnumbered private houses. Even after the government adopted a policy of deporting prostitutes to China, the number of known brothels increased from 32 in 1844 to 86 in 1854 and 137 in 1857. Moreover, colonial officials attributed the prevalence of venereal disease among government officers to prostitutes, who were considered the chief source of contagion. In 1845, venereal disease accounted for 36 out of a total of 501 disease cases, although it was only in 1855 that the Colonial Surgeon proposed specific prophylactic measures for checking the spread of venereal infections from brothels and prostitutes who solicited clients on the streets.[24]

Given the extreme difficulty of identifying and pursuing Chinese prostitutes among the migrant, water-born population, the government focused its activities on policing more visible and easily identifiable groups and, in particular, targeted the brothels. In 1857, Ordinance No. 12 was ratified, and a system of mandatory medical examination was instituted in brothels servicing the Europeans (and not the Chinese) as a measure to safeguard soldiers from venereal infection. Chinese prostitutes who were proven by the Colonial Surgeon to have infected European soldiers and sailors would either be fined or detained in the Lock Hospital.[25] Under the new legislation, brothels were classified as Chinese and 'foreign,' licensed and unlicensed, and divided into 'first-class,' 'middle-class,' and 'lower-class' establishments. Although in theory the foreign brothel owners catered solely for European men, many were willing to service Indian troops and Malay 'coolies.'[26] Wealthy Chinese men usually frequented the first-class brothels where they obtained their concubines, who were generally free from disease. In most cases, these women were not prostitutes but rather entertainers who performed musical offerings.[27] Chinese prostitutes working in foreign brothels, as the commissioners who inquired into the Contagious Diseases Ordinance of 1867 pointed out, belonged to a "decidedly inferior class of women" who were either the castoffs of brothels serving the Chinese or former patients of the Lock Hospital. While the wealthier Europeans preferred kept women to Chinese prostitutes in foreign brothels, the lowest class of foreign men in Hong Kong, primarily British soldiers, visited these brothels most frequently.[28]

Although a number of scholars have examined the regulation of prostitution in Hong Kong's licensed and unlicensed brothels during the nineteenth century, what remains unclear are the reasons for the discrepancy between, on the one hand, the government's persistent and vociferous identification of the threat posed to colonial residents by diseased Chinese prostitutes, and, on the other hand, the few women who were actually prosecuted under the new legislation for infecting men with venereal disease.

Prostitution underscored anxieties about Hong Kong's open borders and the challenges that these posed for security, particularly given that the colony was dependent on cheap migrant labor from China. Hong Kong had been a center for the regional and international trafficking of women since its acquisition by Britain, and prostitutes were among the first women to enter the colony.[29] If migrant women were associated with promiscuity, immorality, and criminality,[30] Hong Kong was extoled for its open, 'laissez-faire' regime in opposition to the closed-door policy of the Qing Empire. This very openness, then, which contributed to Hong Kong's growing status as a global hub raised issues about effective control and about moral order.[31] It also underlined Hong Kong's ambiguous state as a crown colony which was "politically under British rule and influence," and thus clearly distinct from China proper, and yet had a population that was indistinguishable from those of neighboring provinces on the mainland.[32]

In the words of Registrar General Cecil C. Smith, nearly 80 percent of all Chinese prostitutes in Hong Kong were migrant women from Canton and neighboring regions.[33] As epitomized by the boatpeople, such migrants inhabited a murky world outside the scope of government surveillance.[34] Unlike the prostitutes working in licensed and unlicensed brothels, the women of this illicit waterworld provided sexual services in a 'non-place' beyond the state's reach. The crenulated coastline and complex waterways of Hong Kong and the Pearl River Delta were understood to promote stealth, providing cover for smuggling and piracy: "The numerous islands, creeks, and bays are most favourable for the hiding-places of these rovers, who, 'hydra-headed,' appear again as fast as they are destroyed."[35] Although some travelers stressed that, unlike the British, the Chinese were not "a seafaring people," they invariably conceded that the Chinese had a history of navigating "large rivers" and—as the artist Thomas Allom put it—of "creep[ing]" along the seashore.[36]

Boatpeople made up a sizable population, particularly in the early years of the colony. The census of 1863 indicates that the number of boats in Hong Kong amounted to 4,019 with a population of 30,537 boatpeople, constituting around one-fourth of the total population.[37] However, these figures are likely to be underestimates, given the high mobility of the Chinese seafaring people.[38] Early Hong Kong's economy relied heavily on these boatpeople. The British traveler Francis M. Norman, who paid a visit to the colony between 1856 and 1860 (at precisely the moment that Ordinance No. 12 had come into effect), commented that "the floating population" encapsulated "native life, features, and habits" of the Hong Kong working Chinese population. He observed the "immense number" of people who lived in junks and sampans across Hong Kong and the waters of Canton, and made a living by selling basic foodstuff such as rice and fruits. Sometimes a big family of "three generations" crowded into one small boat because of their extended family structure and extreme poverty. Women "born, marry, and die afloat," and it was commonplace to see them rowing small junks with their babies strapped to their backs. Their husbands, on the contrary, played only a supporting role by overseeing the business or pulling a short row.[39] At a time when many Chinese women were confined to the domestic sphere, their feet bound according to tradition, women in the waterworld occupied a comparatively prominent social position.[40]

WOMEN ON THE EDGE

Chinese boatwomen expressed their independence, not only through their engagement in business and their performance of conventionally 'male' tasks: they also exercised control over their bodies in ways that could threaten the colonial establishment (and, for that matter, sections of the 'Chinese' community). Although historically it might be argued that there were two discourses on prostitution in China—upper-class and lower-class prostitution—both forms involved the exploitation of female domestic service, a disruption of social order, and a threat to physical and social health.[41] The boatwomen enjoyed relative freedom, in contrast to the status of women in traditional Chinese society and to the plight of female slaves, concubines, and prostitutes who had been bought and sold "legally or illegally" for centuries.[42]

Most British colonials viewed the business of prostitution as being dominated entirely by brothels, and they assumed that the women working there had been coerced into prostitution.[43] However, Chinese female migrants, including those who worked as boatwomen and washerwomen, led very different lives from the prostitutes in the licensed and unlicensed brothels. Yet, to date, scant attention has been paid to the lives of these early Chinese migrants to Hong Kong (and across East Asia, more generally), in part, because of the absence of archival material. What little information there is, must be gleaned from oral history, from limited Chinese sources, and from the colonial archive where fear of Chinese immigrants dominates the discourse of illicit prostitution, disease, and crime.[44]

The Englishman Augustus Frederick Lindley, an officer in the Royal Navy and later a supporter of the Taiping Rebellion (1850–1864), described how, on his arrival in Victoria Harbour in 1859, he was "startled by the appearance of amphibious creatures, the Chinese boat and laundry women." Lindley noted that the Tanka boat-girls were "strong and well-figured" on account of their "aquatic life" and "incessant labour." Indeed, his description lingers on the prowess and alluring physical appearance of these "wicked little gipsies," whose characteristics are accentuated in the accompanying lithograph, where a bare-footed boat-girl gazes into a mirror, while another exerts herself rowing (Figure 1.1):

Figure 1.1   "Hong-Kong Boat Girls" (London: Day & Son, 1866).

Their long and intensely black hair, brilliant and merry though oblique black eyes, light-yellowish brown and often beautifully clear complexion, and lithe robust figures, constitute a charming and singular variety of feminine attraction. . . . Through constant exposure to the sun, they are mostly tanned to a regular olivaster gipsy hue.[45]

Four decades after Lindley, writers in English-language newspapers were describing the boatwomen in similar terms, the insouciance of the boatwomen contrasted with the condition of their counterparts in the 'West,' who were then pressing for emancipation:

The boatwomen of China have no need to agitate for women's rights— they possess them . . . . whether she be a single woman, a wife, a widow, is the head of the house, that is to say, of the boat. If she is married, the husband takes the useful but subordinate place of deck hand or bow oarsman. She does the steering . . . and in general, lords it over everything.[46]

Boatwomen are characterized, here, by their "considerable freedom in attire." They "let nature alone" and know nothing of "pinched feet and waists." As a result, they usually go around "barefooted and barelegged." Boatwomen are in "fine physical condition," since the hard work on the boats keeps their muscles "magnificently developed."[47] The boatwomen are depicted in terms of a sexualized physique, strength, and independence, qualities also identified by a turn-of-the-century American observer in Canton. While the "gaudily painted flower boats" on the Pearl River intrigue American tourists, the foreigners' fetishizing gaze is drawn specifically to the bodies of the "lusty boatwomen" who "rapidly sculled ashore."[48]

Many colonial commentators in the mid-century found these "lusty" Chinese boatwomen threatening. To many, Victoria Harbour teemed with 'loose' women. According to Colonial Surgeon John Ivor Murray "almost every boat" in Hong Kong was "more or less a sailor's brothel." Dr. William Stanley Adams, Health Officer and Medical Inspector of Emigrants, confirmed Murray's claim when he commented that "a great amount of disease" spread among European seamen came from the washerwomen.[49] He specified that men preferred washerwomen to prostitutes in the brothel houses, since the former were more "attractive" and "much better looking." Colonial Surgeon Philip B. C. Ayres argued that the boatwomen were more susceptible to venereal disease, especially gonorrhea, because they were young and had relatively little sexual exposure. Gonorrhea, Ayres maintained, developed easily with excessive friction during sexual intercourse. While older women used medicinal plants such as arnica and oak bark to reduce the abrasion from sex, young washerwomen took "no precautions" and were thus prone to disease.[50] Despite the threat of contagion suggested by such reports, Acting Registrar General John Gerrard conceded in 1879 that there had not been a "single instance" in which soldiers had caught disease from women in the floating brothels.[51] In other words, the peril of contagion was a hypothetical or imagined threat.

Underlying many accounts of these women was a presumption that they masqueraded as boatwomen and washerwomen to evade the law. By the same token, it was held that 'loose' women, disguised as grass-cutters, dwelt on the hillsides where they lured men to commit indecent acts. Acting Captain Superintendent of Police Charles Vandeleur Creagh noted that European soldiers preferred associating with these grass-cutters rather than with the prostitutes in the brothels.[52] From the colony's establishment, migrant women were often associated with the open hillsides. As one British newspaper reported in 1841, although it was impossible to estimate the number of inhabitants in Hong Kong, it was not uncommon to see "a large group of females descending from the hills, whither they had been either to cut grass or to till some favored spot amid the varieties of hill or dale."[53] This is a pseudo-bucolic and implicitly sexual vision of females cavorting in the landscape. Yet, like boatwomen, the 'women of the hillside' were marginal, elusive, and beyond the law.[54] In short, they remained at once objects of desire, inhabitants of a world unconstrained by rigid convention, and objects of revulsion, evoking the dangers of transgressive inter-racial contact. And while these subterfuge prostitutes were liable to prey on European men, colonial commentators frequently portrayed such men—and, in particular, soldiers—as innocent, passive victims. While they may have traveled extensively in Asia, the soldiers were nonetheless "rarely intimately acquainted with" Hong Kong.

MALE INFORMANTS AND CHINESE AGENTS

Against the backdrop of scandalous stories circulating about wanton female migrants, the government stamped down hard on prostitution. Because the colonial officers were unable to police the predatory women on the fluid borders of the colony, and notably the boatwomen, they turned instead to the prostitutes in the supposedly 'fixed' brothel houses. Between 1857 and 1877 in order to build their case against prostitutes and ensure convictions, the colonial state employed a group of paid male informers, ranging from European constables to Chinese manual workers, who performed their duties by sleeping with the suspected women. The majority of these convictions involved women in the unlicensed brothels rather than the floating brothels not because of the government's lack of interest in tracking down the boatwomen, but largely because of the state's inability to trace their location and identify the women amidst what appeared—at least from the colonial administrators' perspective—to be a formless, floating world.

During prosecution, male informers usually "prepared a disguise of false whiskers and mustaches" and sometimes pretended "to be sick and intoxicated" so that the prostitutes would not suspect them.[55] Empowered by both Ordinance No. 12 of 1857 and 1867, and assisted by these male informers, police officers in Hong Kong possessed extraordinary power to break into houses and arrest any woman without a warrant. A police officer could also charge women who were found to have received marked money from male informers after having sexual intercourse. In 1864, when the Contagious Diseases Act was passed in Britain, the government began using public money to employ male informers to arrest prostitutes. While initially most informers were European constables and inspectors, Chinese men also began to serve as witnesses and informers. These Chinese men, who frequented the brothels and often lived closest to them, were usually members of the working-class, such as cooks, servants, or tailors. Most were well-acquainted with the prostitutes and could provide more accurate evidence, making them particularly useful as government agents, enabling the state to probe into the 'unknowable' lifestyle of Chinese prostitutes, intervening in their activities, and hunting down those who sought to evade the law. Although some informers contracted venereal disease after having sexual relations with the defendants, a few still remained exceptionally active and were employed many times. This was because the prosecution system guaranteed valuable cash and material rewards such as diamond rings to the informers. In 1873, the system of detection had already developed with European inspectors beginning to supply their Chinese informers with money. This mode of cooperation yielded an even higher success rate in capturing illegal prostitutes.[56]

According to the government, such prosecution practices were proven to be effective in apprehending women working in unlicensed brothels. At the same time, they reaffirmed and amplified colonial fears about the threat posed by Chinese prostitutes. The police inspectors often broke into the premises and arrested the women without warrant when they considered the house a brothel or saw men enter the premises accompanied by women. Many prosecutions were thus based on assumptions rather than on any concrete evidence. Furthermore, in 1868 reports attested that women were increasingly attempting to evade prosecution. While some succeeded, many women broke their limbs after jumping out of windows to escape arrest. Some even died. But a few teenage girls were found innocent and proven to be virgins only after being medically examined. Meanwhile, using public money, some male informers took advantage of the prostitutes. One man engaged in sexual intercourse with a 15-year-old girl, while another raped the 'prostitute' to collect his reward. The woman in question was eventually fined $100 and had her child taken away. The prosecution procedures endorsed by the ordinance thus created a good deal of embarrassment for the government.[57]

In 1877, a gruesome accident brought the prosecution system to a halt. A Chinese prostitute and a female servant, who resided in an unlicensed brothel at 42 Peel Street, Central, fell off the roof and died after being chased by John Lee, Inspector of Brothels.[58] After a lengthy trial, the jurors concluded that both women had died "accidentally, casually and by misfortune" but conceded that Inspector Lee had "exceeded his powers" by entering the brothel, which was neither a sly brothel nor a house that had been under suspicion for any length of time.[59] The prosecution procedures laid down by the ordinance in convicting Chinese prostitutes, as the jurors strongly argued, were "illegal and immoral" and should be "thoroughly revised."[60] This event prompted Governor John Pope Hennessy, who had just assumed office and was known for being more accommodating towards the Chinese, to formally inquire into the Contagious Diseases Ordinance of 1867. Criticizing the prosecution procedures on moral grounds, Hennessy blamed the registrar general for using "the money of the State" to employ the police force to "commit adultery with unlicensed Chinese women." Some of these policemen, Hennessy stressed, were married and lived with their wives in Hong Kong.[61] His unwavering attitude prompted other British colonials to question the prosecution procedures' legitimacy. Police Magistrate H. E. Wodehouse, for instance, strongly denounced the measures taken to obtain "evidence against suspected houses." He also reassured Hennessy by stating that he would stop employing male informers in "the remaining three weeks" of his tenure in office.[62]

Such problematic prosecution procedures highlighted British colonial anxieties about infection and the need to protect their soldiers from 'contamination' by Chinese women. Some defended the system by saying that many Chinese prostitutes, as migrants, moved from dwelling to dwelling and left Hong Kong when they had saved enough money. Although some returned, most did not consider Hong Kong to be their permanent home.[63] This made it extremely difficult for the police to trace the activities of the diseased women. Some colonials resorted to using male informers because they failed to impose regular medical checkups on Chinese prostitutes. Chief Inspector William Whitehead, who visited the Chinese brothels licensed for foreigners once or twice a week, stated that it was only possible for him to call the women's names from the board during inspection. Out of courtesy, he did not go through the rooms if he saw the women sitting inside. Women could therefore evade the checkup easily.[64] Even when the soldiers complained to the chief magistrate about women from whom they claimed to have contracted disease, they invariably failed to identify the female 'culprits.' Between 1867 and 1887, the government successfully prosecuted fewer than 40 Chinese prostitutes for infecting soldiers. While Acting Registrar General Alfred Lister suggested that the men refused to indicate the diseased women out of "a principle of honor," the majority of the plaintiffs stated that they were "drunk at the time" and did not know the woman who infected them.[65,66] Even when the men indicated the correct brothels, they often pointed out the wrong women.

DEFINING AND KNOWING THE CHINESE

There were some attempts to differentiate and classify the migrant population with a view to a more systematic management of the population. The boatwomen, while they were often referred to as 'Chinese,' were also identified as belonging to a separate race. Thus, Berncastle on his approach to Macau noted the good-looking Tanka girls: "The bay is covered with a small boat, called Tanka-boat, rowed by Tanka girls, a distinct race, who live all their lives in their little craft, plying for hire and going backwards from the ships to the shore at modest fares."[67] In 1879, the missionary and sinologist Ernest J. Eitel explicitly identified Tanka girls as prostitutes:

> These Tan-ka people of the Canton river [Pearl River] are the descendants of a tribe of aborigines pushed by advancing Chinese civilisation to live on boats on the Canton river, being for centuries forbidden by law to live on shore . . . . They invaded Hong Kong the moment the Colony was opened, and have ever since maintained here a monopoly . . . of the trade in women for the supply of foreigners and of brothels patronized by foreigners. Almost every so-called 'protected woman,' i.e. kept mistress of foreigners here, belongs to this Tan-ka tribe, looked down upon and kept at a distance by all the other Chinese classes . . . They form a class of their own, readily recognised at a glance. They are disowned by Chinese society, whilst they are but parasites on foreign society. The system of buying and selling female children and of domestic servitude with which they must be identified is so glaring an abuse of legitimate Chinese domestic servitude that it calls for corrective measures entirely apart from any considerations connected with the general body of Chinese society.[68]

Less than 20 years later, Elizabeth Wheeler Andrew and Katherine Caroline Bushnell asserted in *Heathen Slaves and Christian Rulers* (1907), that the Tanka were a "saltwater people" living in the coastal waters of Guangdong, Fujian, and Guangxi; an "aboriginal tribe" who were regarded as inferior by the 'Chinese,' although they spoke Cantonese. Tanka women (*ham-shui-mui* or 'salt water girls' in Cantonese), Andrew and Bushnell declared, had been "grossly corrupted by contact with the foreign voyagers and sailors" and traded "in women and girls brought from the mainland to meet the demands of profligate foreigners."[69]

Although the 'Tanka' may be "readily recognized at a glance" and are depicted as inferior by the Chinese population, in actual fact the differences between 'Chinese' and 'Tanka' were blurred. For the British, the 'parasitic' and 'criminal' nature of the Tanka women epitomized a degenerate tendency within Chinese culture more generally. Moreover, colonial administrators found Tanka women especially threatening because of their 'floating' existence. Indeed, given the difficulties in categorizing the transitory and heterogeneous working population, which comprised a vast range of occupations—including prostitutes, washerwomen, servants, skilled workmen, hawkers, and laborers—colonial officials tended to aggregate local residents, conceptualizing the 'Chinese' as an undifferentiated social group. This process of abstraction and homogenization was a feature of nineteenth-century metropolitan mass culture, wherein populations were represented as singular 'social bodies.' Meanwhile, novel institutions and technologies, including statistical thinking, helped to define and standardize modes of knowing. As Mary Poovey has argued:

> the aggregation of distinct populations, and the conceptual disaggregation of a social domain—were intimately connected, for identifying the problems that afflicted the nation involved isolating the offending populations, abstracting from individual cases the general problems they shared, and devising solutions that would not contradict the specific rationalities of those domains by which British social relations had traditionally been organized.[70]

In Hong Kong, although colonial administrators acknowledged the laboring population's role in sustaining the economy, they were concerned about the potential menace that this 'rootless' population posed.[71] In formulating and implementing legislation designed to regulate mobility, disease and crime were frequently evoked as interchangeable rationales for intervention. Laborers were deemed to loiter, while their unsanitary habits and unhealthy dwellings incubated filth-diseases. Among these laborers, who were overwhelmingly male, Chinese prostitutes prompted additional anxieties since they presented the prospect of miscegenation and the diffusion of lethal infections.[72]

In both official and popular discourses, Chinese migrant workers—male and female—were frequently 'aggregated' into a single social body. According to the presiding colonial narrative, Hong Kong had been a 'barren rock' serving as a den for marauding pirates and other criminals until the British took control of the island. Many officials and travelers reiterated such views. While they recognized the advances made in 'taming' the wild terrain, they also perceived continuities in cases of murder and robbery. Chinese migrants were frequently lumped together as "quarry-men, smugglers, fishermen, or pirates." The 'Chinaman' was indistinct from the crowd. And Chinese crowds invariably "divided their whole time between eating, smoking, and gambling."[73] As reflected in the metropolitan press, the Chinese migrant was a close companion of "Canton mandarins, ladies, boatwomen, and prostitutes," engaging in Chinese gambling games such as *fantan*.[74]

The complexities of 'Chinese' society made it difficult for the colonial state to penetrate. Migrants not only organized themselves "according to kinship and native-place links," but they also united "along class lines when common interests were threatened."[75] Intricate social networks made it virtually impossible for British colonials to infiltrate or understand the society of the governed. Faced with this impenetrable 'mass,' British administrators sought to organize the population around imported categories of 'crime' and 'disease.' The 'Chinese' were viewed as a source of corruption. Prostitution, in particular, was considered to be "essentially Chinese and radically un-English."[76] Even before Ordinance No. 12 came into effect, syphilis was known as the "Hong Kong Disease," and a 'racial identity' was bestowed on a looming disease threat.[77] Through creating categories and oppositions between the British and Chinese, colonial administrators constructed knowledge about an amorphous, 'floating' community aiming to regulate the lives of the colony's migrant population upon which it depended.

By the 1880s, however, disease itself was being re-conceptualized as bacteriology shed light on the causative micro-agents of infection. It was established, for example, that the most lethal type of syphilis came from Japan, rather than Hong Kong.[78] As early as 1869, Staff Surgeon George Birnie Hill had declared that syphilis had been brought to the colony by seamen from Yokohama.[79] Less than a decade later, Chief Inspector Whitehead reaffirmed Hill's comment by identifying European seamen as carriers of syphilis.[80] Meanwhile, Acting Registrar General M. S. Tonnochy suspected that many men contracted disease from European women rather than Chinese women but were afraid to acknowledge their source of infection.[81] He noted that there might be "one or two loose women in the Garrison, among the soldiers' wives," who would allow any man to have connection with them with just half a dollar. If the men caught disease, they would either deny it or point to the first woman they saw in the licensed brothels in Ship Street, because they were "unwilling to betray the woman who gave it to them."[82] Tonnochy's claim was not entirely unfounded. In one incident, disease was directly traced to a French woman, rather than a Chinese prostitute.[83]

The construction of the wanton, predatory Chinese migrant obscured the situation of many women who were kidnapped and forced into prostitution, with many women abused by their keepers.[84] Li-Ho, who contracted gonorrhea from a foreigner, was beaten until her body was "covered with bruises." She was more fortunate than others: some were beaten to death, while others committed suicide.[85] A number of women found solace and support in European men. Ho-A-Ho, for instance, fell in love with a European seaman and "did not stipulate for any money." She even took the man to her father's house without telling her parents in advance.[86] Another Chinese prostitute, Wong-A-Tsoi, specified that she found Englishmen attractive and thought she "should have men of this kind" if she became a prostitute.[87] Some European men also reciprocated the women's affections. James Allison, for example, testified in the courtroom that he agreed to "take care" of his woman, Ho-A-Yow, after she had been beaten by her brothel keeper.[88]

CONCLUSION: CRIME, DISEASE, AND COLONIAL DESIRE

In September 1887, Hong Kong put an end to Ordinance No. 12 following the repeal of the Contagious Diseases Acts in Britain.[89] The abolition of compulsory medical examination meant that prostitutes reserved the right to apply for medical examination at the Registrar General Office at their own will. When interviewing the women, the registrar general would make sure that they met him voluntarily without being forced by the brothel keepers. The women were also free to leave or stay in the Lock Hospital. Although Colonial Surgeon Philip Ayres maintained that the prostitutes were all satisfied with the current voluntary system, the European, Japanese, and Chinese brothel keepers strongly petitioned for a continuance of the examinations. Chinese keepers, in particular, hoped the ordinance would be restored, arguing that a single outbreak of disease would be enough to ruin their business.[90]

However, suspicion against Chinese female migrants persisted long after the repeal. A discourse of contagion, which conflated the pathological with the criminal and located the source of infection in the female Chinese body, became a means of differentiating the colonizer from the colonized, avoiding inter-racial mixing, and exerting control over the inscrutable but querulous 'coolie' population. From this perspective, it may be argued that disease prevention was never their first priority. In 1877, the commissioners appointed by Governor Hennessy to inquire into the working of the Contagious Diseases Ordinance of 1867 remarked that "the number of women caught under sanitary regulations has always been, as compared with those left unregulated, insignificant." They further asserted "there is no sufficient evidence to show that the spread of venereal disease has been checked or prevented, or its type modified, by the operation of the Brothel Laws."[91] Not only had the ordinance proven to be ineffective in stamping down venereal disease, but it also left a budget deficit of over $40,000.[92]

In this chapter, I have explored the racialized assumptions that underpinned representations of the prostitute as a purveyor of disease and a perpetrator of crime in nineteenth-century Hong Kong; and I have suggested that this pathological-criminal equation reflected colonial anxieties about the transgression of borders and the flows of migrant labor upon which the colony was dependent. Given this shifting and predominantly 'Chinese' population, colonial administrators sought to create fixed and stable boundaries within which to manage the colony's residents. 'Crime' and 'disease' were objects of formalized knowledge that enabled a heterogeneous population to be identified, differentiated, and abstracted. However, ambiguities of class, race, and gender—epitomized by the floating world of prostitution—problematized the categories within which the 'Chinese' were viewed. They revealed the contested nature and fictive dimensions of a colonial British identity, which, far from being homogenous and stable itself, was haunted by visions of inter-racial transgressions.

NOTES

1. Julius Berncastle, *A Voyage to China: Including a Visit to the Bombay Presidency; the Mahratta Country; the Cave Temples of Western India, Singapore, the Straits of Malacca and Sunda and the Cape of Good Hope*, vol.2 (London: Shoberl, 1850), 33–34.
2. Francis Martin Norman, *"Martello Tower" in China, and the Pacific in H. M. S. "Tribune," 1856–60* (London: G. Allen, 1902), 86–87; William Charles Milne, *Life in China* (London: Routledge, Warnes, & Routledge, 1861), 440; and Henry Charles Sirr, *China and the Chinese: Their Religion, Character, Customs and Manufactures* (London: Orr, 1849), 3.
3. Norman, *"Martello Tower" in China*, 86–87.
4. Christopher Munn, "William Caine," in *Dictionary of Hong Kong Biography*, ed. May Holdsworth and Christopher Munn (Hong Kong: Hong Kong University Press, 2012), 57–58.
5. *China Mail*, May 22, 1845, 2.
6. Ibid.
7. "Prostitution in the Colony," May 18, 1855, Great Britain, Colonial Office, Series 129, CO129/50, 80–83, 85–86, 89–90, 92, Public Record Office, Kew, London (hereafter PRO).
8. In 1883 Governor Sir George Bowen described Hong Kong as the "Gibraltar of the East" because he saw Hong Kong as a garrison town rather than a colony; see Frederick Madden and David Fieldhouse, eds., *The Dependent Empire and Ireland, 1840–1900: Advance and Retreat in Representative Self-government* (Westport, CT: Greenwood Press, 1991), 495. On prostitution regulation in the British Mediterranean, see Philip Howell, *Geographies of Regulation: Policing Prostitution in Nineteenth-Century Britain and the Empire* (Cambridge: Cambridge University Press, 2009).
9. "Prostitution in the Colony," May 18, 1855, PRO CO129/50, 82–83.
10. For a discussion of the ways in which anxieties about 'contagion' drove nineteenth-century plot lines and provided metaphors for different kinds of destabilizing transmissions, see Allan Conrad Christensen, *Nineteenth-Century Narratives of Contagion: "Our Feverish Contact"* (London: Routledge, 2005).
11. *Report of the Commissioners to Enquire into the Working of the "Contagious Diseases Ordinance, 1867"* (Hong Kong: Noronha, 1879), 31.
12. Nicholas Thomas, *Colonialism's Culture: Anthropology, Travel and Government* (Cambridge: Polity, 1994), 2.

13. *Report of the Commissioners*, 40.
14. On prostitution in Hong Kong, see, for example, Philippa Levine, "Modernity, Medicine and Colonialism: The Contagious Diseases Ordinances in Hong Kong and the Straits Settlements," *Positions*, vol.6, no.3 (1998): 675–705; Philippa Levine, *Prostitution, Race, and Politics: Policing Venereal Disease in the British Empire* (New York: Routledge, 2003); Philip Howell, "Prostitution and Racialized Sexuality: The Regulation of Prostitution in Britain and the British Empire before the Contagious Diseases Acts," *Environment and Planning D: Society and Space*, vol.18, no.3 (2000): 321–339; Howell, *Geographies of Regulation*; Kerrie L. MacPherson, "Conspiracy of Silence: A History of Sexually Transmitted Diseases and HIV/AIDS in Hong Kong," in *Sex, Disease, and Society: A Comparative History of Sexually Transmitted Diseases and HIV/AIDS in Asia and the Pacific*, ed. Milton Lewis, Scott Bamber, and Michael Waugh (Westport, CT: Greenwood Press, 1997); and Elizabeth Sinn, "Chinese Patriarchy and the Protection of Women in 19th-Century Hong Kong," in *Women and Chinese Patriarchy: Submission, Servitude and Escape*, ed. Maria Jaschok and Suzanne Miers (Hong Kong: Hong Kong University Press, 2001).
15. For a nuanced account of 'germ theory' in practice in nineteenth-century Britain, see Michael Worboys, *Spreading Germs: Disease Theories and Medical Practice in Britain, 1865–1900* (Cambridge: Cambridge University Press, 2000). The term 'criminology' was coined in 1885 by Italian law professor Raffaele Garofalo, a student of the criminologist Cesare Lombroso. On Lombroso's criminal science, generally, see Daniel Pick, *Faces of Degeneration: A European Disorder, c.1848–c.1918* (Cambridge: Cambridge University Press, 1989).
16. Old Humphrey, *Points and Pickings of Information about China and the Chinese* (London: Grant and Griffith, 1844), 14.
17. Ibid., 17.
18. Isabella L. Bird, *The Golden Chersonese and the Way Thither* (New York: G.P. Putnam's Sons, 1884), 29.
19. Sirr, *China and the Chinese*, 3, 5.
20. John M. Carroll, *A Concise History of Hong Kong* (Lanham, MD: Rowman & Littlefield, 2007), 36.
21. *Report of the Commissioners*, Appendix, 125, 151, 161. See James Francis Warren, *Ah Ku and Karayuki-San: Prostitution in Singapore 1870–1940* (Singapore: Singapore University Press, 2003), 68, 70. As Warren notes, "Shanghai and Hong Kong were recognized centres of prostitution and used as depots for the supply of Japanese prostitutes to other parts of China in the 1870s and 1880s," 70; on migrations across Asia, see Sunil S. Amrith, *Migration and Diaspora in Modern Asia* (Cambridge: Cambridge University Press, 2011).
22. "Hong Kong," *Hong Kong Government Gazette* (Hong Kong: Government Printer), December 31, 1853, 89.
23. *Report of the Commissioners*, 11–12, 31.
24. *China Mail*, January 29, 1846, 199; "Hong Kong," *Hong Kong Government Gazette* (Hong Kong: Government Printer), April 1, 1854, 103; ibid., May 12, 1855, 358, ibid., March 28, 1857, 2.
25. *Report of the Commissioners*, 29.
26. Howell, *Geographies of Regulation*, 215–216.
27. "Supervision and Personal Inspection of Brothels," January 18, 1869, PRO CO 129/142, 297.
28. Howell, *Geographies of Regulation*, 216; *Report of the Commissioners*, 6–7.
29. Christopher Munn, *Anglo-China: Chinese People and British Rule in Hong Kong, 1841–1880* (Richmond, UK: Curzon, 2001), 322; Elizabeth Sinn, *Pacific Crossing: California Gold, Chinese Migration, and the Making of Hong Kong* (Hong Kong: Hong Kong University Press, 2013), 227.

30. For a comparative discussion of how migrants have been identified by government administrators as the root of crime and disease, see the essays collected in Alison Bashford, ed., *Medicine at the Border: Disease, Globalization and Security, 1850 to the Present* (London and New York: Palgrave, 2006).
31. On the tension within the crown colony between an impulse to keep networks open for trade, and a counter-impulse to close off pathways of disease, see Robert Peckham, "Infective Economies: Empire, Panic, and the Business of Disease," *Journal of Imperial and Commonwealth History*, vol.41, no.2 (2013): 211–237.
32. *Report of the Commissioners*, 3, 5.
33. Ibid., Appendix, 1.
34. Ibid., 7, 14.
35. Berncastle, *A Voyage to China*, 43.
36. Thomas Allom, *China, in a Series of Views, Displaying the Scenery, Architecture, and Social Habits of the Ancient Empire* (London: Fisher, Son, & Co., 1843), 40.
37. Norman, *"Martello Tower"* in China, 84–87; George Allgood, *China War, 1860: Letters and Journal* (London: Longmans, Green, & Co., 1901), 21.
38. Chinese boatpeople traveled as far as California. In this connection, see Sinn, *Pacific Crossing*.
39. Norman, *"Martello Tower"* in China, 84–87; George Allgood, *China War, 1860: Letters and Journal* (London: Longmans, Green, & Co., 1901), 21.
40. On Chinese women who were allegedly never seen out of doors in China, see Berncastle, *A Voyage to China*, 38.
41. Gail Hershatter, *Dangerous Pleasures: Prostitution and Modernity in Twentieth-Century Shanghai* (Berkeley: University of California Press, 1997), 9.
42. *Report of the Commissioners*, 3.
43. Levine, *Prostitution, Race, and Politics*, 53.
44. An exception is Warren, *Ah Ku and Karayuki-San*.
45. Augustus Frederick Lindley, *Ti-Ping Tien-Kwoh: The History of the Ti-Ping Revolution, Including a Narrative of the Author's Personal Adventures* (London: Day & Son, 1866), 4–5.
46. This report on Chinese "boatwomen" was widely circulated in English-language newspapers, where it was included amongst miscellaneous news; see, for example, *Church Weekly*, January 14, 1898, 8; *Silver Lake Record*, January 13, 1898, 6; *The Perry Daily Chief*, January 14, 1898, 4.
47. Ibid.
48. *Postville Review*, June 8, 1906, 8.
49. *Report of the Commissioners*, 30.
50. Ibid., Appendix, 36.
51. "Sir J. P. Hennessy's Statements Respecting Lock Hospital," October 17, 1882, PRO CO129/203, 127.
52. *Report of the Commissioners*, Appendix, 11, 36a.
53. *Belfast News-letter*, April 23, 1841, 4.
54. *Report of the Commissioners*, Appendix, 11, 36a.
55. Ibid., Appendix, 48.
56. Ibid., 11–12, 17–18, 27.
57. Ibid., 13–16, 18–21.
58. Ibid., iii–iv.
59. PRO CO129/203, 114.
60. *Report of the Commissioners*, vii–viii, x–xi.
61. PRO CO129/203, 79.
62. Ibid., 123.
63. *Report of the Commissioners*, Appendix, 2.
64. Ibid., 41.
65. Ibid., 40.

66. Ibid., Appendix, 248–249.
67. Berncastle, *A Voyage to China*, 182.
68. Ernest J. Eitel, "Report on Domestic Servitude in Relation to Slavery," October 25, 1879, *Correspondence Respecting the Alleged Existence of Chinese Slavery in Hong Kong: Presented to Both Houses of Parliament by Command of Her Majesty* [C.-3185] (London: HMSO, 1882), 55.
69. Elizabeth Wheeler Andrew, and Katherine Caroline Bushnell, *Heathen Slaves and Christian Rulers* (Oakland, CA: Messiah's Advocate, 1907), 10–11.
70. Mary Poovey, *Making a Social Body: British Cultural Formation, 1830–1864* (Chicago: University of Chicago Press, 1995), 8.
71. Munn, *Anglo-China*, 78–79.
72. Ibid., 322–324.
73. Milne, *Life in China*, 440; Rev. George Smith, *A Narrative of an Exploratory Visit to Each of the Consular Cities of China and to the Islands of Hong Kong and Chusan in Behalf of the Church Missionary Society in the Years 1844, 1845, 1846*, 2nd ed. (London: Seeley, Burnside, & Seeley, 1847), 70.
74. *Leeds Mercury*, September 12, 1888, 3; *Sheffield Evening Telegraph*, September 14, 1888, 4.
75. Munn, *Anglo-China*, 71.
76. *Report of the Commissioners*, 6.
77. Ibid., Appendix, 280, 282.
78. Ibid., 40–41.
79. Ibid., Appendix, 277.
80. Ibid., 41.
81. Ibid., Appendix, 244.
82. Ibid., Appendix, 246–247, 250.
83. Ibid., Appendix, 7.
84. Ibid., Appendix, 128, 162.
85. Ibid., Appendix, 127–128.
86. Ibid., Appendix, 33.
87. Ibid., Appendix, 34.
88. Ibid., Appendix, 112.
89. The successful repeal in Britain owed much to the unyielding effort of the Ladies' National Association for the Repeal of the Contagious Diseases Acts (LNA) headed by Josephine Butler. As a devout Christian concerned about the welfare of prostitutes, Butler criticized the acts for their sexual double standard and oppression of female individual liberty.
90. "Hong Kong," *Annual Report of the Director of Medical Services* (Hong Kong: Government Printer, 1887), 222–223.
91. *Report of the Commissioners*, 52.
92. Ibid., Appendix, 308.

2 Sexual Deviancies, Disease, and Crime in Cesare Lombroso and the "Italian School" of Criminal Anthropology

Chiara Beccalossi

Cesare Lombroso is often mentioned as the founder of modern criminal anthropology, the thinker who shifted the focus from the crime to the criminal by changing 'Western' notions of individual responsibility. His influence extended beyond the frontiers of Italy and Europe, with followers in the US, Latin America, and Asia, making him one of the most influential intellectuals at the turn of the nineteenth century. Indeed, Lombroso's work is crucial to understanding how late nineteenth-century medical writers and social scientists came to conflate disease with crime. To use a Foucauldian term, Lombroso employed a "medical gaze" when observing the criminal. This is hardly surprising, since he had trained as a doctor and practiced as a psychiatrist for many years.[1] He viewed criminals as sick individuals and believed that "the anti-social tendencies of the criminals [were] the result of their physical and psychic organization, which differs essentially from that of normal individuals."[2] In his own words, crime was "an unfortunate natural production, a form of disease."[3]

Rejecting the still dominant juridical doctrines, developed by the Italian philosopher and jurist Cesare Beccaria in the second half of the eighteenth century, which relied on the principle that the individual could exercise free will, Lombroso argued throughout his career that crime was caused by biological, psychological, and social factors. In contrast to Beccaria, he also advocated that punishment be commensurate with the danger that the criminal posed to society, rather than with the crime itself. Influenced by German materialism, English evolutionism, and French and Italian positivism, Lombroso drew in his work on authors such as Herbert Spencer, Jacob Moleschott, Ernst Haeckel, Bénédict Augustin Morel, and Pierre Paul Broca. It was Lombroso's staunch faith in biological determinism that led him to question how far individuals were responsible for their criminal acts, as well as their insanity or, for their so-called 'sexual psychopathologies.' Such a stance had a significant impact on contemporary social scientists, as well as influencing a broader readership. As the distinguished British literary critic John Addington Symonds noted in 1891, Lombroso had precipitated a "revolution of ideas," a new way of thinking about human behavior and individual responsibility.[4]

In the same years as Lombroso was conducting his observations on individual responsibility in relation to criminality, a number of European and North American medical writers were increasingly paying attention to what they regarded as sexual pathologies. As Richard von Krafft-Ebing and Havelock Ellis were only too willing to acknowledge, Lombroso was a pioneer in this new field of inquiry.[5] The basic assumption underlying much early sexological research was that individuals were not responsible for their sexual drives. In other words, sexual inclinations, far from being a matter of free choice, were innate.[6] While arguing that sexual drives were inborn, medical writers pathologized some non-reproductive sexual behaviors, such as male same-sex practices, hitherto treated as pertaining to the domain of the law. Yet the association between same-sex desire and crime did not disappear. On the contrary, in Lombroso's work, this association persisted, although it acquired a new and modern meaning. Crime, like homosexuality, became a pathological condition.

Focusing on Lombroso's work on same-sex desires, this chapter examines the ways in which Lombroso, through his use of atavism and degeneration theories, conflated disease with crime. My aim is to illustrate just how this entanglement of disease and crime became possible and to demonstrate how, at the very moment Lombroso and the criminal anthropologists shifted their focus from the crime to the criminal, they medicalized the criminal by employing medical theories of the time which explained the behavior of the insane. Thus, psychiatrists such as Henry Maudsley, who had studied individual responsibility in cases of violent crime, anticipated the idea that criminality might have a biological origin. My objective in what follows is not to offer an exhaustive study but rather to provide an overview of the development of this equation between disease and crime as it is articulated in Lombroso's writings on sexual psychopathologies. Some of the main difficulties in approaching Lombroso's work derive from the sheer extent of his oeuvre, the continuous modifications he made to his theories, and his shift from a strong biological determinism in his early writings to a more environmental and sociologically oriented position in his later work.[7] Exploring Lombroso's sexological research can help us understand how disease and crime became intertwined in Western medical and criminological thinking during the later part of the nineteenth and early twentieth centuries. At the same time, it furnishes an important historical context for the rise of contemporary biocriminology, where techniques from biomedicine and the life sciences are increasingly being used to re-define the 'criminal.'

PARALLELISM BETWEEN HOMOSEXUALITY AND CRIMINALITY

In 1906, Lombroso presented a paper entitled "Du parallélisme entre l'homosexualité et la criminalité innée" ["Parallelism between Inborn Homosexuality and Criminality"] at the Sixth International Conference of

Criminal Anthropology in Turin.[8] This was not the first time that a criminal anthropologist had given a paper on homosexuality at an international conference. In 1896, the Viennese physician Luzenberger had attended the Ninth Conference of the Società di Freniatria in Florence, presenting a paper on sexual perversions.[9] In 1901, Arnold Aletrino, a Professor of Criminal Anthropology at Amsterdam University, gave a paper on the topic of sexuality at the Fifth International Conference of Criminal Anthropology in Amsterdam.[10] Despite these antecedents, however, the significance of Lombroso's intervention in 1906 should not be underestimated. Lombroso was already generally considered to be the founder and leading proponent of criminal anthropology, although by that date his methods were being censured by a number of criminal anthropologists keen to promote new trends within the discipline. The fact that Lombroso had decided to give a public lecture on homosexuality is indicative of the importance this topic had acquired within the criminological discourses of the time.

The parallelism upon which Lombroso based his paper did not draw on the assumption that same-sex practices were to be regarded as a crime. Instead, Lombroso, who since the early 1880s had argued that same-sex desires constituted a form of mental illness, assumed that crime, like homosexuality, was itself a phenomenon akin to a pathological condition. The association posited by Lombroso between homosexuality and criminality was based on the premise that both criminality and homosexuality were grounded in biology.

In his paper, Lombroso asserted that a number of studies on sexual psychopathologies, such as those conducted by Albert Moll, Benjamin Tarnowski, Pasquale Penta, Guglielmo Cantarano, Carl Westphal, and von Krafft-Ebing, had shown that there existed different types of homosexual. These, Lombroso suggested, shared a number of characteristics with various types of criminal. He argued that in the same way as there existed a form of temporary criminality in childhood, even in those men who would eventually become honest and upstanding, so too there existed a temporary homosexuality in all men who would subsequently develop a "normal" sexual life. As all children were liars, thieves, immoral, and cruel towards weaker creatures, so, according to Lombroso, in their childhood all men experienced strong friendships that had the characteristics of a homoerotic attraction. All children were jealous of and attracted to a particular mate.[11]

Moreover, Lombroso explained that in the same way as there existed "occasional criminals" and "born criminals," so too there existed "occasional homosexuals" and "born homosexuals." "Occasional homosexuals" were able to experience "normal" relationships, that is, those formed with a view to reproduction, but when they were compelled to live in single-sex environments, such as prisons, colleges, or asylums, they would readily engage in "obsessive" homosexual relationships. Conversely, "born homosexuals" were sexually attracted to those of their own sex from childhood and could not maintain "normal" sexual relationships. Thus, congenital homosexuality was different from "temporary homosexuality" in its exclusive element, but, as Lombroso stressed, "temporary homosexuality" was a normal phenomenon in childhood, especially in single-sex schools.[12]

Lombroso also suggested other analogies between different types of criminal and homosexual. In the same way as 40 percent of born criminals belonged to a "special type" displaying a specific physiognomy, so too did a large number of homosexuals evince physical characteristics of the opposite sex: they displayed a feminine physiognomy and could be identified by such features as a lack of facial hair, a large pelvis, hypertrophic breasts (sometimes even secreting milk), an asymmetric face, mongolism, and macrocephaly. These physical characteristics were due to the effects of degeneration.[13] However, Lombroso conceded that there existed a large number of born criminals, about 60 percent, who did not display any "special type," but only a few anomalies due to factors such as alcoholism and syphilis. Following this same line of inquiry, he also acknowledged that a large number of homosexuals did not display any distinctive physical features. Yet all these categories shared a characteristic: both criminals and homosexuals were "immoral." All homosexuals had certain psychological traits in common: they were frivolous, vain, selfish, jealous, and mendacious, given to acting on impulse, and disposed to gossip. In the nineteenth century, all these traits were generally associated with women. More specifically, congenital homosexuals, Lombroso explained, had sexual drives since early childhood, were prone to feigning madness, were immodest, and tended to be aesthetes, which is why artists, musicians, and actors were often sexual inverts. Criminals, on the other hand, were prone to sexual orgies and to zoophilia, were vindictive, demonstrated a propensity for evil in general, and were likely to have tattoos. In other words, they displayed atavistic tendencies. The causes of inborn criminality and congenital homosexuality were similar: both criminals and homosexuals were epileptics or neurotics, or had parents who were "old" and "odd." Both criminals and homosexuals were consequently ill, naturopathic, and incurable. Lombroso concluded that regardless of the similarities between the two groups, different social and legal solutions were required for each, since homosexuals were less dangerous than criminals. Whereas criminals would continue to be socially dangerous for the rest of their lives, the sexual activity of homosexuals would eventually come to an end.[14]

In his 1906 paper, Lombroso did not spell out what strategies would have to be deployed to treat homosexuality and to neutralize the threat that it posed. However, he believed that society had to be defended from sexual perverts, and he indicated that interning homosexuals in special institutions, such as asylums, might be one practical solution. There is also historical evidence indicating that Lombroso treated female homosexuals using invasive techniques, such as the removal of the ovaries or, more often, through cliterodectomies.[15]

Lombroso's 1906 paper on the parallels between homosexuality and criminality is significant in a number of ways. First, Lombroso argued that transitory same-sex desires were normal in childhood, the implication being that a kind of universal latent homosexuality could be found in each and every 'normal' individual, at least during childhood. This belief was shared by a number of Italian psychiatrists at the turn-of-the-century who had moved away from studying homosexuality in asylums and prisons to focus on 'normal' environments, such as schools.[16] Second, Lombroso's paper reveals the importance of homosexuality within criminal anthropological research at the beginning of the twentieth century. On the occasion of the Sixth International Conference of Criminal Anthropology, the actual founder of the "science of deviance" discussed homosexuality, which thereupon ceased to be merely a footnote referring to a peculiar sexual perversion and became a central chapter within the discipline of criminal anthropology. Finally, Lombroso drew an explicit parallel between criminality and a form of mental pathology, homosexuality. While the association between crime and homosexuality was not new, the premises of such an association in Lombroso's argument were relatively original. The homosexual was similar to the criminal in that biological determinism could account for both phenomena. The following two sections will focus on this parallel between criminality and homosexuality as conceptualized by Lombroso, illustrating how it was possible for the Italian criminal anthropologist to posit such an association.

CRIME AS DISEASE

Lombroso was not the first to believe that crime had a biological, often hereditary, explanation, yet such a notion was nonetheless relatively recent. Historians have shown the extent to which phrenology, between the late eighteenth and the beginning of the nineteenth century, associated a certain criminal propensity with the innate faculties of the brain. As Nicole Rafter has noted, "phrenology encouraged articulation of the so-called medical model of criminality, which portrays criminality as a sickness and hence properly part of medicine's jurisdiction. It encouraged the belief that criminals, because sick, are not therefore responsible for their behavior."[17] For example, Johann Gaspar Spurzheim's work, *Physiognomical System* (1815), included a chapter on the "Organ of the Propensity to Destroy, or of Destructiveness," which illustrated how phrenology approached criminality. Spurzeheim argued that the "propensity to kill" was independent of social factors, and that it originated in an organ of the brain.[18]

Other historians have observed that, from the early nineteenth century, a number of psychiatrists working on the problem of individual responsibility in cases of violent crime anticipated the idea that criminality could have a biological origin. For example, Etienne-Jean Georget's (1795–1828) study of "homicidal monomania" and James Cowles Prichard's (1786–1848) investigation of "moral insanity" had introduced the idea that some persons possessed an irresistible drive to commit certain acts, including criminal acts.[19] In 1857, in his *Traité des dégénérescences physiques, intellectuelles et morales de l'espèce humaine* [*Treatise on Physical, Intellectual and Moral Degenerations of the Human Species*], Bénédict Augustin Morel famously argued that conditions such as insanity and criminality were symptoms of degeneration, an underlying constitutional condition that was inherited. Morel argued that mental illness was essentially a deviation from—or "degeneration" of—an ideal type.[20] In European psychiatry, degeneration came to be viewed as a progressive decline culminating in self-extinction: physical and mental qualities were understood to deteriorate from one generation to the next, until they reached a final stage of sterility. Mental pathologies were induced by hereditary predispositions, which, in combination with certain determining factors such as alcoholism, syphilis, and so on, caused the degenerative process to manifest itself more severely with each successive generation. A tendency towards insanity or perversion could be congenitally inherited from a 'tainted' family whose history was characterized by mental illness, syphilis, or debauchery; in a word, degeneration. During the second half of the nineteenth century, degeneration became associated with a wide range of human deviancies: from sexual deviance to criminality. By employing degeneration to explain virtually any form of human deviance, psychiatrists came to believe that any abnormal behavior had organic causes.

Within this explanatory framework, in the mid-nineteenth century a number of psychiatrists and prison officers developed similar ideas to those put forward by early nineteenth-century phrenologists and suggested that some individuals were criminal by constitution. For instance, in the 1860s and 1870s, a handful of medical officers working in the British prison system conceptualized the criminal as belonging to a relatively homogeneous group with distinctive physical and mental traits, which was precisely the kind of assumption underlying Lombroso's later conception of a "born criminal" type.[21] In the early 1870s, the *Journal of Mental Science* published a series of articles by prison physicians and surgeons concerned to describe the physical and psychological characteristics of criminals. For instance, in 1870, a physician at Perth prison in Scotland by the name of James Bruce Thomson argued that many criminals were born as such.[22] In 1872, Maudsley, whose work was read widely in Italian medical circles, wrote in his *Responsibility of Mental Disease* of "instinctive criminals," observing that the "criminal class constitutes a degenerate or morbid variety of mankind, marked by peculiarly low physical and mental characteristics."[23] Indeed, Maudsley maintained that crime was often hereditary and asserted that "the true thief" was "born not made."[24] By relying on constitutional explanations of deviance, Maudsley conflated crime with disease; as far as he was concerned, they were one and the same phenomenon. This conflation emerged in Europe and Britain as psychiatrists began to focus on the criminal responsibility of the insane, that is, when they began to reflect on the extent to which the insane were to be considered responsible for any criminal acts they might happen to commit.

The above examples serve to show how Lombroso was anticipated by other psychiatrists; indeed, he was by no means alone in thinking that crime had biological causes. Yet prior to the first edition of Lombroso's *L'uomo delinquente* [*The Criminal Man*], published in 1876, the study of criminals had been somewhat fragmented and episodic.[25] Lombroso systematized the available knowledge about the criminal and, after assembling whatever physical, sociological, and psychological observations of criminals he could lay his hands on, formulated a general theory. He accumulated a wide range of data—analyzing skulls and the physical anomalies of criminals, using for this purpose both cadavers and living subjects. In the latter case, Lombroso documented every detail from the height, weight, and strength of the individual to the shape of their nose, ears, forehead, and even feet. Along with detailed measurements of the body, Lombroso used tattoos, underworld poetry and jargon to provide a portrait of the criminal. Lombroso sought out correlations between criminality and age, marital status, sex, profession, diet, and environment.[26] Since the first edition of *L'uomo delinquente*, Lombroso had argued that crime was rooted in multiple causes, ranging from the biological and psychological organization of the individual to social factors such as urbanization or education. However, in the first edition itself the influence of biological factors prevailed over environmental explanations; while a small part of criminality was due to social conditions, most criminals had been destined to become such for strictly constitutional reasons.[27]

Lombroso adopted a number of other theories to support his claim that criminality was an inborn condition. In the first two editions of *L'uomo delinquente*, published in 1876 and 1878, criminality was explained through the theory of atavism. The latter was concerned with the tendency of plants and animals to reproduce ancestral types, and, in the case of humanity, to resemble one's grandparents or great-grandparents more than one's parents. Atavism was a reversion, a 'throw back,' so to speak. The notion of atavism used by biological writers certainly referred to Darwin, but its origin lay in earlier botanical studies.[28] The atavistic criminal man represented an earlier stage of human evolution. Lombroso identified this ancestral type through several stigmatized physical characteristics, including the length of ear lobes and fingers, and the osseous structure of the skull. Atavism was also associated with moral corruption, which produced deviant behaviors. It became manifest in the criminal, in the insane person, and in other human deviations, but generally speaking any white civilized "normal" man was at risk of reverting to the ancestral type.[29] Inspired by the German biologist Haeckel and his recapitulation theory, Lombroso believed that normal civilized men were liable to return to a primitive condition because individuals, in their development, recapitulate the whole course of human evolution.[30]

While atavism formed the main theoretical aspect of the first two editions of *L'uomo delinquente*, from the third edition (1884) on, Lombroso increasingly drew on the concept of degeneration and introduced the term "born criminal." Developed by the French physician Morel in *Traité des dégénérescences physiques*, by the 1880s the notion of degeneration had become the dominant framework for understanding mental disorders. If Lombroso owed his use of the theory of degeneration to Morel, it was from the Italian criminologist Enrico Ferri that he had borrowed the term "born criminal." Ferri, Lombroso's student, had coined the term in 1880, and it had subsequently made its way into the third edition of Lombroso's *L'uomo delinquente*.[31]

In every edition of Lombroso's *L'uomo delinquente,* the conflation of crime with disease is a recurrent theme. For example, Lombroso believed that, like a disease, "crime is rooted in multiple causes."[32] Similar comments directly comparing disease and crime can be found throughout his oeuvre: "crime is like an illness that requires a specific remedy,"[33] or "insanity and criminality are so closely linked as to be nearly identical."[34] In *L'uomo delinquente*, of all the forms of disease, mental illness in particular was repeatedly compared to crime. According to the Italian criminal anthropologist, the born criminal was constitutionally "morally insane," had psychological characteristics that belonged to the primitive stage of humankind, and lacked any moral sense. Formulated in the 1830s by the British physician and ethnologist Prichard, the notion of "moral insanity" indicated a disorder of the emotions, instincts and will, but one that left most of the intellectual faculties unaffected. This same notion was still widely used by Italian psychiatrists and criminal anthropologists like Lombroso in the second half of the nineteenth century.[35]

One cannot help but suppose that Lombroso, having trained as a medical doctor and then as a psychiatrist, applied his clinical eye to the criminal. In short, Lombroso employed a "medical gaze" to re-define the criminal, viewing him as a diseased being, since "aetiology can be established for crime just as it can for illness."[36] Lombroso medicalized the crime as well as the criminal body; his assiduous measurements of the criminal, and his increasingly complex classifications of the different criminal types, drew on his clinical approach:[37]

> In general, thieves are notable for their expressive faces and manual dexterity, small wandering eyes often oblique in form, thick and close eyebrows, distorted noses . . . and sloping foreheads. Like the rapist they often have jug ears.[38]

Indeed, rapists "nearly always have sparkling eyes, delicate features . . . and some are hunchbacked."[39] "Habitual murderers have a cold, glassy stare," he noted, "the nose is often hawk-like and always large; the jaw is strong, the cheekbones broad . . . and the canine teeth developed."[40] Thus, the body could reveal inclinations and propensities, and in Lombroso it was used as a means of diagnosing particular criminal inclinations.

SAME-SEX DESIRE AS DISEASE

There is now an extensive historical literature that shows how psychiatrists constructed same-sex desires as mental disorders in the last decades of the nineteenth century. Before this period, medical writers had occasionally included same-sex desires in their observations.[41] Medical forensic writers conventionally associated same-sex practices with pathological anatomy. For example, Tardieu's study *Étude Médico-Légale sur les Attentats aux Mœurs* [*Medico-Legal Study of Crimes against Morals*] (1857) claimed that it was possible to identify individuals devoted to same-sex practices by inspecting the individual's genitals and anus. He found that male prostitutes arrested in Paris had penises displaying certain specific signs of physical change and shape through repeated acts of anal sex. Some male prostitutes had pointy penises, while individuals who typically enjoyed passive, anal sex had an "infundibuliform" anus.[42]

According to Arnold I. Davidson, in the course of the nineteenth century, psychiatrists moved away from understanding sexual perversion as a result of anatomical-pathological dysfunction to a view of sexual perversion as a result of functional deviations of the sexual instinct. In other words, an anatomical understanding of sexual perversions was replaced by a psychological one.[43] In the 1860s, continental psychiatrists, grounding their arguments in deterministic theories of hereditarian degeneration, increasingly subscribed to the new view that sexual deviance in many cases was not the result of immoral choices, but rather symptomatic of innate characteristics. In 1869, a German psychiatrist, Carl Westphal, published the first psychiatric article on what he coined *conträre Sexualempfindung* [contrary sexual feeling], focusing on a case history of a woman who, from an early age, had desired other women, was repelled by men, and felt herself to have "a man's nature."[44] Subsequently, the term *conträre Sexualempfindung* was adopted by Krafft-Ebing in 1877, by the Italian forensic doctor Arrigo Tamassia in 1878, and finally by the French neurologist Jean-Martin Charcot and the French psychologist Valentin Magnan in 1882.[45] Following Westphal's text, European doctors began collecting case studies of sexual inverts (or homosexuals), whose main psychological characteristic was gender discordance (the feeling of having the nature and characteristics of the opposite sex).[46] Historians have interpreted these analyses as a decisive shift in medical thinking about same-sex behavior: from an emphasis on physiological characteristics as entailed by the same-sex practices involved to an emphasis on same-sex behaviors as a manifestation of a biological and psychological predisposition.[47] In this sense, homosexuality as a psychological innate condition is a nineteenth-century medical invention.

Such a construction owed much to Lombroso, as eminent sexologists, Krafft-Ebing and Havelock Ellis among them, were the first to recognize. Lombroso began to publish his work in the field of sexual inversion in 1881, with a pioneering article entitled "L'amore nei pazzi" ["Love in the Insane"] appearing in *Archivio di psichiatria*.[48] This article tacitly followed Krafft-Ebing's earlier attempt to classify various forms of non-procreative sexual behavior. Lombroso identified five main types of pathological love: "necro-filomanie" (broadly speaking, necrophilia); "eroto-maniaci" (a form of mystical love); "amore zoologico" (love for statues or animals); "amore paradosso" (paradoxical love; broadly speaking, fetishism and exhibitionism); and finally "amore invertito" (inverted love).[49] The section dealing with "amore invertito" included eight case histories of sexual inversion, two of which were the result of Lombroso's original observations.[50] Lombroso's two case histories consisted of a list of physical stigmata that confirmed that the subjects in question were degenerate, followed by a catalogue of illnesses or anomalies drawn from their family trees. Lombroso recorded only a single psychological trait in his subjects: the tendency to display feminine behavior, such as dressing up as women or preferring to work at home. He also noted that many sexual inverts presented anomalies such as sparse beards or narrow intelligence, which were taken as evidence of an impediment in cerebral development. Interestingly enough, while Lombroso subscribed to the view that same-sex desires were mental pathologies, he provided detailed descriptions of the physical characteristics of sexual inverts. In subsequent observations he continued to stress the physical characteristics of sexual inverts. For example, in 1885, when describing a female homosexual he highlighted her "nearly martial" masculine appearance, the anomalous shape of the skull, her marked mandibular prognathism, "badly implanted" ears, dark skin, and atrophic breasts; her genitals were abnormal.[51]

Observations on sexual psychopathologies were also included in his major works, *L'uomo delinquente* and *La donna delinquente* [*The Female Offender*], published in 1893. The inclusion of sexual inversion in *L'uomo delinquente* reveals how Lombroso was able to conflate sexual psychopathologies with crime. Since the first edition of *L'uomo delinquente*, Lombroso had paid attention to same-sex practices. However, the main emphasis, up until the fourth edition, published in 1889, had been on pederasty, that is, on same-sex practices from a legal point of view. Following a tradition established by Ambroise Tardieu, Lombroso was initially more interested in identifying the physical signs of same-sex practices. In part, this was because, despite the fact that since the early 1880s Lombroso had subscribed to the view that same-sex desires were a form of mental pathology and not a crime, in the North of Italy same-sex practices were still punishable by law until 1889.[52] As such, same-sex practices had legal implications that Lombroso could hardly avoid discussing. However, in the fourth edition of *L'uomo delinquente*, by addressing both "pederasty" and "sexual inversion," Lombroso approached same-sex desires from both a legal and a psychiatric point of view. The fourth edition of *L'uomo delinquente* consisted of two volumes: one focused on the legal aspects of criminality, the other on the pathological. Many forms of criminality were deemed to have their parallel in forms of mental pathology. In the second volume, Lombroso explored psychiatric categories that had "parallels" in the criminal sphere, such as the pyromaniac and the arsonist or the kleptomaniac and the thief.[53] Sexual inversion had its parallel in pederasty and rape. What distinguished sexual inversion from pederasty was the violent behavior of some individuals engaging in same-sex acts: to a certain extent, the pederast was a rapist who engaged in same-sex acts. Pederasty was a legal category, sexual inversion a psychiatric one.

What was the basis of Lombroso's claim that psychiatric categories had "parallels" in the criminal sphere? In Lombroso's work, as in much late nineteenth-century criminal anthropology, the common feature between the pederast and the sexual invert, as between the criminal and the insane person, was the medicalization of their behavior through theories such as atavism and degeneration theory. According to Lombroso, degeneration triggered sexual perversion in general and same-sex desires in particular. Physical degeneration itself was caused by a "tendency to return to a stage of hermaphroditism," entailing a closing of the gap or even a confounding of the two sexes.[54] As a result, not only sexual inverts, but also male criminals could exhibit the kind of "feminine infantilism that leads to pederasty," which was mirrored by masculinity in female criminals. In both men and women, this tendency to hermaphroditism often set in before puberty, with many men dressing as women and vice versa. Lombroso was therefore able to draw a parallel between mental diseases like homosexuality and criminality, because both of these manifestations were thought to be biologically grounded. It was atavism and degeneration that provided the biological link. Criminals, like the insane, were driven to act in a certain way because they were atavistic and degenerate beings. By dint of their innate degenerate nature, they were not free to act in any other way.

CONCLUSION

Although Lombroso had recognized that in some cases homosexuality and criminality could be explained through environmental causes, by the time he came to deliver the paper on the "parallels" between homosexuality and criminality at the Sixth International Conference of Criminal Anthropology, held in 1906, the idea that a biological predisposition could explain both phenomena had become central in his work. The medicalization of the criminal had been implicit in Lombroso's project from the outset, inasmuch as he believed that the criminal was not free to act in any other way. Historians have often pointed out that while previous thinkers, such as Jeremy Bentham and Cesare Beccaria, relied on the principle that the individual could exercise free will, Lombroso's theories were opposed to this view. As I have sought to show, atavism and degeneration theories allowed Lombroso to explain crime and homosexuality as biologically driven. At the very moment in which some thinkers began to question free will in criminal acts, biomedical explanations accounted for criminal behavior. The implications for medicalizing criminal and sexual acts went further: medical and legal thinkers placed the idea of individual responsibility at the very heart of criminal anthropological and sexological discourses. By arguing that both criminal and sexual behaviors could, to a very considerable extent, be construed as biologically determined, Lombroso contributed to the introduction of a new way of thinking about individual responsibility, which allowed criminal conduct and sexual drives to be conceived, not as choices, but as innate propensities. This novel conceptualization of criminal inclination and sexual desires was integral both to the emerging medical discipline of sexology and to criminal anthropology.

In Lombroso's work, the equation between disease and crime was the result of a process in which a medical way of thinking was employed in the study of the criminal. In his studies of sexual inversion and criminality, one can discern the process—well described by historians with Foucauldian sympathies—by which medicine was re-defining other fields, becoming linked, in so doing, to the exercise of power and control. As this chapter has shown, Lombroso looked at the criminal body with a "medical gaze." This was possible because medical writers—and, once again, one should not forget that Lombroso had trained as a physician and kept practising, even as he became a criminologist—were able to encroach upon the domains of legal and sexual knowledges. In the final analysis, a deeper understanding of this same process may shed light on the growing influence of medical thought in the late nineteenth century. Crime and forms of 'deviant' sexual behavior were reframed as diseases at the very moment when medical thought became a dominant framework within which to understand phenomena that had hitherto lain outside the sphere of medicine.

NOTES

1. Michel Foucault developed the concept of "medical gaze" to denote the power of modern medicine to define and re-define the human body. See Michel Foucault, *The Birth of the Clinic: An Archaeology of Medical Perception* (London: Tavistock, 1976).
2. Gina Lombroso-Ferrero, *Criminal Man according to the Classification of Cesare Lombroso* (New York: G.P. Putnam's Sons, 1911), 5; see, also, David G. Horn, *The Criminal Body: Lombroso and the Anatomy of Deviance* (New York: Routledge, 2003), 10–11.
3. Cesare Lombroso, "Prefazione del traduttore" in Jacob Moleschott, *La Circolazione delle vita: lettere fisiologiche* (Milan: G. Brigola, 1869), x–xi, cited in Horn, *The Criminal Body*, 8–9.

4. John Addington Symonds, *A Problem in Modern Ethics Being an Inquiry into the Phenomenon of Sexual Inversion. Addressed Especially to Medical Psychologists and Jurists* (London: Charles R. Dawes ex Libri, 1896), 67. This book was originally published privately in 1891.

5. Richard von Krafft-Ebing, *Psychopathia Sexualis with Special Reference to Contrary Sexual Instinct: A Medico Legal Study* (Philadelphia: F.A. Davis, 1893); and Havelock Ellis and John Addington Symonds, *Sexual Inversion* (London: Wilson and Macmillan, 1897).

6. Gert Hekma, "A History of Sexology: Social and Historical Aspects of Sexuality," in *From Sappho to De Sade: Moments in the History of Sexuality*, ed. J. Bremmer (London: Routledge, 1989), 173–193; and Harry Oosterhuis, *Stepchildren of Nature: Krafft-Ebing, Psychiatry, and the Making of Sexual Identity* (Chicago: University of Chicago Press, 2000).

7. Silvano Montaldo and Paolo Tappero, eds., *Cesare Lombroso Cento Anni Dopo* (Turin, Italy: UTET, 2009), ix.

8. Cesare Lombroso, "Du parallélisme entre l'homosexualité et la criminalité innée," *Archivio di psichiatria, antropologia criminale e scienze penali*, vol.27 (1906): 378–381.

9. A. Luzenberger, "Sul meccanismo dei pervertimenti sessuali e la loro terapia," *Archivio delle psicopatie sessuali*, vols.19–20 (1896): 265–271.

10. Arnold Aletrino, "La situation sociale de l'uraniste," *La scuola positiva*, vol.11 (1901): 481–496.

11. Lombroso, "Du parallélisme," 378.

12. Ibid.

13. As historians have frequently pointed out, Lombroso believed that the inborn criminal displayed certain 'typical' physical characteristics: their heads were asymmetrical, their upper lips thin, their ears large, their bushy eyebrows met over the nose, their eyes were deep set, and their toes were pointy. Indeed, such physical characteristics demonstrated the biological basis of criminality; see Mary Gibson, *Born to Crime: Cesare Lombroso and the Origins of Biological Criminology* (Westport, CT: Praeger, 2002); Horn, *The Criminal Body*; and Daniel Pick, *Faces of Degeneration: A European Disorder, c.1848–1918* (Cambridge: Cambridge University Press, 1989).

14. Lombroso, "Du parallélisme," 378–381.

15. Chiara Beccalossi, *Female Sexual Inversion: Same-Sex Desires in Italian and British Sexology, c.1870–1920* (Basingstoke: Palgrave Macmillan, 2012), 134–135.

16. Ibid., 73–78.

17. Nicole H. Rafter, *Creating Born Criminals* (Urbana: University of Illinois Press, 1997), 76–77.

18. Nicole Rafter, *The Criminal Brain: Understanding Biological Theories of Crime* (New York: New York University Press, 2008), 49–50.

19. Richard F. Wetzell, *Inventing the Criminal: A History of German Criminology, 1880–1945* (Chapel Hill: University of North Carolina Press, 2000), 17–20.

20. Ian A. Dowbiggin, "Back to the Future: Valentin Magnan, French Psychiatry, and the Classification of Mental Diseases, 1885–1925," *Social History of Medicine*, vol.9, no.3 (1996): 383–408.

21. Neil Davie, *Tracing the Criminal: The Rise of Scientific Criminology in Britain, 1860–1918* (Oxford: Bardwell Press, 2005), 22.

22. See, for example, J. Bruce Thomson, "The Psychology of Criminals," *Journal of Mental Science*, vol.16 (1870): 321–350.

23. Quoted in Havelock Ellis, "The Study of the Criminal," *Journal of Mental Science*, vol.36 (1890): 5.

24. Rafter, *Creating Born Criminals*, 81.
25. Lombroso published five editions of *L'uomo delinquente*: 1876, 1878, 1884, 1889, 1896–1897.
26. Renzo Villa, *Il deviante e i suoi segni: Lombroso e la nascita dell'antropologia criminale* (Milan: Franco Angeli, 1985), 156.
27. Ibid., 155.
28. Ibid., 144–149.
29. Pick, *Faces of Degeneration*, 109–152.
30. For a history of the idea of 'recapitulation' and the connection between individual development (ontogeny) and the evolution of species (phylogeny), see Stephen Jay Gould, *Ontogeny and Phylogeny* (Cambridge, MA: Harvard University Press, 1977).
31. Villa, *Il deviante e i suoi segni*, 169, 188. For an overview of the changes in the different editions of Lombroso, *L'uomo delinquente*, see Cesare Lombroso, "Introduction," in *Criminal Man*, trans. and with an Introduction by Mary Gibson and Nicole H. Rafter (Durham, NC: Duke University Press, 2006), 1–41.
32. Lombroso, *Criminal Man*, trans. Gibson and Rafter, 114, quoted from the second edition of Lombroso's *L'uomo delinquente* (1878).
33. Ibid., 341, quoted from the fifth edition of Lombroso's *L'uomo delinquente* (1896–1897).
34. Ibid., 271, quoted from the fourth edition of Lombroso's *L'uomo delinquente* (1889).
35. Villa, *Il deviante e i suoi segni*, 157–158. On the relationship between moral insanity and sexual perversions in nineteenth-century European psychiatry, see Chiara Beccalossi, "Nineteenth-Century European Psychiatry on Same-Sex Desires: Pathology, Abnormality, Normality and the Blurring of Boundaries," *Psychology & Sexuality*, vol.1, no.3 (2010): 228–229.
36. Lombroso, *Criminal Man*, trans. Gibson and Rafter, 114, quoted from the second edition of Lombroso's *L'uomo delinquente* (1878).
37. Horn, *The Criminal Body*.
38. Cesare Lombroso, *L'uomo delinquente studiato in rapporto alla antropologia, alla medicina legale ed alle discipline carcerarie* (Milan: Hoepli, 1876), 31.
39. Ibid., 32.
40. Ibid., 32.
41. See, for example, Kenneth Borris and George Rousseau, eds., *The Sciences of Homosexuality in Early Modern Europe* (London: Routledge, 2008).
42. Ivan Crozier, "The Medical Construction of Homosexuality and its Relationship to the Law in Nineteenth-Century England," *Medical History*, vol.45, no.1 (2001): 79; see, also, Ivan Crozier, "'All the Appearances Were Perfectly Natural': The Anus of the Sodomite in Nineteenth-Century Medical Discourse," in *Body Parts: Critical Explorations in Corporeality*, ed. Christopher E. Forth and Ivan Crozier (Lanham, MD: Lexington Books, 2005), 70; and Sean Brady, "Homosexuality: European and Colonial Encounters," in *A Cultural History of Sexuality in the Age of Empire*, ed. Chiara Beccalossi and Ivan Crozier (Oxford: Berg, 2011), 46.
43. Arnold I. Davidson, "Closing up the Corpses: Diseases of Sexuality and the Emergence of the Psychiatric Style of Reasoning," in *Meaning and Method: Essays in Honor of Hilary Putnam*, ed. George Boolos (Cambridge: Cambridge University Press, 1990), 295–326.
44. Carl Westphal, "Die conträre Sexualempfindung: Symptom eines neuropathischen (psychopathischen) Zustandes," *Archiv für Psychiatrie und Nervenkrankheiten* vol.2 (1869): 73–108, trans. in Michael A. Lombardi-Nash, *Sodomites and Urnings: Homosexual Representations in Classic German*

Journals (London: Harrington Park Press, 2006), 87–120. The importance of this case and its effects on psychiatric writing about homosexuality is discussed in Ivan Crozier, "Pillow Talk: Credibility, Trust and the Sexological Case History," *History of Science*, vol.46, no.4 (2008): 375–404.

45. Richard von Krafft-Ebbing, "Über gewisse Anomalies des Geschlechtstriebs und die klinisch-forensich Verwertung derselben als eines wahrscheinlich funktionellen Degenerationszeichens des centralen Nervensystems," *Archiv für Psychiatrie und Nervenkrankheiten*, vol.7 (1877): 291–312; Chiara Beccalossi, "The Origin of Italian Sexological Studies: Female Sexual Inversion ca. 1870–1900," *Journal of the History of Sexuality*, vol.18, no.1 (2009): 109–111; and Vernon A. Rosario, *The Erotic Imagination: French Histories of Perversity* (Oxford: Oxford University Press, 1997), 69, 83–89.

46. See Jennifer Terry, *An American Obsession: Science, Medicine, and Homosexuality in Modern Society* (Chicago: University of Chicago Press, 1999).

47. Claude François Michéa, "Des deviations de l'appétit vénérien," *Union Medicale* (July 1849): 338–39; Johann Ludwig Casper, "Ueber Nothzucht und Päderastie und deren Ermittelung Seitens des Gerichtesarztes," *Vierteljahrschrift für gerichtliche öffentliche Medizin*, vol.1 (1852): 21–78. On the importance of these texts, see, for example, Hekma, "A History of Sexology," 173–193; Hekma, "'A Female Soul in a Male Body': Sexual Inversion as Gender Inversion in Nineteenth-Century Sexology," in *Third Sex, Third Gender: Beyond Sexual Dimorphism in Culture and History*, ed. G. Herdt (New York: Zone Books, 1994); Oosterhuis, *Stepchildren of Nature*, 39; Ivan Crozier, "Introduction," in *Sexual Inversion: A Critical Edition: Havelock Ellis and John Addington Symonds*, ed. Ivan Crozier (Basingstoke: Palgrave Macmillan, 2008), 18–19. Phrenologists linked sexual function to the cerebellum and occasionally observed same-sex desires, see, for example, Philipp Gutmann, "On the Way to Scientia Sexualis: 'On the Relation of the Sexual System to the Psyche in General and to Cretinism in Particular' (1826) by Joseph Häussler," *History of Psychiatry*, vol.17, no.1 (2006): 45–53; Michael Lynch, "'Here Is Adhesiveness': From Friendship to Homosexuality," *Victorian Studies*, vol.29, no.1 (1985): 67–96; and Michael Shortland, "Courting the Cerebellum: Early Organological and Phrenological Views on Sexuality," *British Journal of the History of Science*, vol.20, no.65 (1987): 173–199. Recently, historians of the early modern period have shown that science attributed same-sex desires to inborn temperament and dispositions well before the nineteenth century, see Borris and Rousseau, *The Sciences of Homosexualities*.

48. Cesare Lombroso, "L'amore nei pazzi," *Archivio di psichiatria, antropologia criminale e scienze penali*, vol.2 (1881): 1–32.

49. Krafft-Ebing, "Über gewisse Anomalies."

50. Lombroso, "L'amore nei pazzi," 24, 26–27.

51. Cesare Lombroso, "Del tribadismo nei manicomi," *Archivio di psichiatria, scienze penali ed antropologia criminale*, vol.4 (1885): 218–221. For an analysis of this case, see Beccalossi, *Female Sexual Inversion*, 133–135.

52. Before the unification of Italy (1861), different punishments were meted out for male same-sex practices in the different states. In the Papal States, for example, male same-sex acts were punished with life imprisonment; in the Lombardo-Veneto region (Trentino-Alto Adige, Friuli-Venezia-Giulia, Istria, and Fiume), which was under Austrian rule, sodomy was punished with custodial sentences from six months to one year. In the Kingdom of Sardinia, under the Savoy monarchy, male same-sex acts could land a man in prison for up to 10 years. The rest of Italy adopted the Napoleonic Code, which was silent on the issue of homosexuality, meaning that there was no legal

framework for censoring same-sex acts. With the promulgation of the 1889 Penal Code (also known as the Zanardelli Penal Code), private homosexual behavior between consenting adults ceased to be a punishable offense.

53. Cesare Lombroso, *L'uomo delinquente in rapporto all'antropologia, giurisprudenza ed alle discipline carcerarie. Delinquente nato e pazzo morale,* vols.1 and 2 (Turin: Bocca, 1889).

54. Cesare Lombroso and Guglielmo Ferrero, *La donna delinquente, la prostituta e la donna normale* (Turin: Roux, 1893), 416.

3 Pathological Properties
Scenes of Crime, Sites of Infection

Robert Peckham

Dank roofs, dark entries, closely-clustered walls,
Murder-inviting nooks, death-reeking gutters.

Punch, September 29, 1888

INTRODUCTION: HOMESICK IN THE CITY

The photographs of Eugène Atget taken from the late 1890s depict a city all but emptied of its inhabitants: a haunted topography of deserted, poster-plastered streets, dark cobbled alleyways, entrances, courtyards, and derelict squares (Figure 3.1). The images, elegiac in their emptiness and ominously staged, suggest a forensic gaze, reminding us of Susan Sontag's observation that the preeminent function of photographs is to "furnish evidence."[1] Paris is opened up for inspection by the camera even as it appears closed down, the dereliction suggesting mass exodus or quarantine. For the cultural critic Walter Benjamin, Atget's pictures recall a crime scene: they bear evidence of a wrongdoing. In his 1931 essay "Little History of Photography" [*Kleine Geschichte der Photographie*], Benjamin notes, "It is no accident that Atget's photographs have been likened to those of a crime scene. But isn't every square inch of our cities a crime scene?"[2]

In what sense, though, is the modern city a crime scene? Who is the perpetrator of the alleged crime and who the victim? This chapter seeks to address these questions by exploring how, in the course of the nineteenth century, the criminal body became inseparable from broader environmental debates about the pathologizing effects of particular urban loci. As the century progressed, disease and crime came increasingly to be located through the visualization of unsettled and unsettling metropolitan places and spaces. As Anthony Vidler has suggested, the 'uncanny'—a sensation of estrangement and a condition of anxiety—became linked to the expanding city.[3] The 'unhomeliness' of the modern cityscape gave rise to a host of newly identified psychopathologies, which were held to be endemic to the industrialized urban environment, producing a sick, enervated, and unruly populace.[4] In Vidler's words, by 1914 the 'metropolis' implied "both a physical site and a pathological state which, for better or for worse, epitomized modern life."[5]

Figure 3.1   Eugène Atget, Rue Hautefeuille, Paris (VIème arrondissement), 1898 © Eugène Atget/Musée Carnavalet/Roger-Viollet.

More specifically, this chapter reconsiders the pathological dimension of the modern city by returning to a series of crimes committed in the autumn and winter of 1888 in London's East End. "The real significance of the sequence of crime lies in the locality of the murders," Peter Ackroyd has written of the Whitechapel murders, where five women were butchered in what appeared to be 'serial' killings.[6] As Alexandra Warwick has argued, "as well as forming an origin for the construction of the identity of the serial killer," the murders "initiate certain ideas about the relationship of subjects to spaces and the existence of the self in the modern urban land-scape that continue to underpin contemporary discourses."[7]

Coverage of the killings in 1888 suggests the extent to which, by the late century, bodily economies had become intertwined with spatial economies, crime interwoven with disease. Homicide was framed in terms of infection and specifically identified as a form of 'contagion': a communicable 'fever' of crime, which threatened to diffuse westwards from "the kitchen middens of humanity" in the East End.[8] Prevalent metaphors of crime-as-disease accentuated a spatial continuity (crime and disease traveled through space), at the same time as they drew attention to the specificities of place and time: Whitechapel as the crime scene.

The aims of this chapter, then, are threefold: first, to suggest ways in which late nineteenth-century commonplaces about the morbid nature of certain places and spaces in the industrialized city had roots in earlier responses to epidemic disease. From the 1830s, the threat of cholera, an 'alien' and highly infectious bacterial disease associated with the urban poor, fueled bourgeois insecurities about the disaffecting and pathological nature of the city, leading to intensifying municipal and state-sponsored urban interventions by the mid-century. Second, the chapter investigates how these interpositions gave rise to anxieties about the consequences of the violence that they entailed, as well as "the landscapes of fear and topographies of despair" produced by industrial capitalism.[9] Third, the essay considers reiterations of the 'slum' as the disruptive and "warped" space of an alienated and criminal subject: "murder-inviting nooks" characterized by displacement, fracture, and void.[10]

There is a substantive literature showing how cholera epidemics in the nineteenth century brought to the fore social tensions and made visible competing value systems, while furnishing the state with opportunities for regulating the bodies of its citizens and inculcating new models of behavior.[11] However, the argument made in this chapter is that the experience of epidemic disease and preoccupations with locating it in the city's insalubrious corners, 'opened up' a new way of thinking about—and acting upon—'crime.' Conversely, a criminological outlook fed back into medico-scientific and sanitary approaches. The 'crime scene,' which developed as a crucial locale in the 1880s and 1890s, marked this conceptual and disciplinary convergence, and represented the extension of the laboratory's operational modes into the city.

A critical focus in this volume is on how categories of 'disease' and 'crime' have been promoted as universals, even as their contingency is manifest in the ways they have been re-configured in highly context-specific situations. This chapter seeks to contribute to this discussion by tracking the equivocal nature of the 'crime scene,' which came increasingly to be understood by contemporaries in its modern sense as a space sequestered from the public gaze, where material evidence was gathered and documented by professionals for methodical processing. However, the 'crime scene' was also conceived as a site for public debate, a space in which the anonymous urban poor were recast as 'subjects' whose lives were legible in new ways. In this sense, as in Atget's streetscapes, the 'crime scene' connoted a closing off and an opening up: a calculated detachment and a subjective immersion.

Similar tensions characterize the laboratory, a space in which the 'self' of the investigator is systematically effaced, his invisibility a precondition for the visibility of the disease-agent under observation. As Lorraine Daston and Peter Galison have noted, during the nineteenth century, 'objectivity'—understood as the suppression or erasure of the 'self'—became an "epistemic virtue," or scientific ideal. However, if one aim of objectivity was to maintain a critical distance between self and object of study, objectivity also involved striving for an unmediated knowledge of the world. A paradox arose: in the endeavor to achieve such proximity, the barrier between subjectivity and objectivity collapsed.[12] It is precisely here, in the dissolving space between onlooker and the object of his contemplation, that fears of 'contagion' took shape: an apprehension that in his dispassionate inspection of the criminal, the onlooker might himself be exposed to infection and transmute into the pathological object of his study. Running through this chapter, then, is an interest in how—even as they strove to make visible the hidden 'horrors' of urban destitution—sanitarians, social reformers, and journalists worried that the new visibility they were bringing to the 'sick' and tawdry homes of the poor was acting as a novel source of criminal contagion. Supposing these compulsions to open up poor dwellings for inspection in order to expose "the rotten core beneath the bloom of ripe fruit"—or, as George Gissing put it in *The Nether World* (1889), "the intimacies of abomination"—were contributing to the 'problem,' facilitating contagion in the name of enforcing health?[13,14]

CHOLERA AND "SOCIAL MURDER"

By the 1890s, much of the cityscape of old Paris had been destroyed to make way for Baron Haussmann's wide boulevards and open spaces. From 1898, institutions such as the Bibliothèque Historique de la Ville de Paris had begun acquiring Atget's photographs of Paris as documents of a vanishing world.[15] Haussmann's remodeling of the city from the 1860s had entailed a mass program of expropriating land and clearing working-class districts to make way for development.[16] In part, the project had been a response to the threats posed by epidemic disease and notably cholera, as Victor Hugo observed in *Les Misérables*.[17] Indeed, the re-planning of European cities, such as Paris and London from the mid-nineteenth century, had been prompted by a sanitarian impetus to 'disinfect' dilapidated and disease-ridden districts of the metropolis.

The threat of infection gave rise to a "generalized fear" directed "not only against epidemic but against possible riot" and citywide crime.[18] In the wake of cholera, sanitary proposals were put forward involving, as one contemporary put it, "round-the-clock vigilance to ensure that calm and order are not disturbed and by enforcement of health regulations in repairs and new construction."[19] Outbreaks of cholera from 1832, when 18,000 Parisians perished, highlighted the dangers posed by overcrowding and insanitary conditions in the capital.[20] Drawing on miasmic explanations of disease, sanitary reformers emphasized healthy circulations and sought to 'open up' the dank, fetid corners of the capital.

Disease, then, while it afflicted the poor, also incited increasingly intrusive state intercessions and surveillance strategies aimed at regulating the lives of the poor, as well as their dwellings. As Alain Corbin has noted, "The flood of discourse on the habitat of the masses and its stifling atmosphere revealed the new preoccupation after the 1832 cholera morbus epidemic."[21] The focus shifted to the working-class dwelling as the 'home' of disease; there was a drive "to inspect the habitat of the masses . . . District commissions were set up when it was announced that the scourge was imminent; their function was to visit every house, detect the causes of insalubriousness, and force the landlord to comply with police rules."[22] New beliefs about the etiology and transmission of disease created new norms and assumptions about domestic space: "new anxieties generated and governed innumerable descriptions of interiors"—from the damp walls to closet recesses and corner cupboards, to the particular dangers posed by corridors and staircases.[23] This 'disinfection' of the working-class went hand-in-hand with a moral mission: "to rid the masses of their animal fetidity, to keep them at a distance from excrement, was part of the therapeutic strategy deployed against social pathology."[24] Efforts to 'treat' social pathology by violent excision thus entailed a new focus on "domestic atmospheres" and an invasive supervision of poor houses, which required their exposure for inspection.[25] Thus, while the bourgeois retreated from the masses, they simultaneously sought to enter the habitats of the poor to ensure healthy configurations of space, the appropriate layout of furniture, and the optimal orientation of windows, doors, and stairs.

The post-cholera emphasis on the enumeration of space and the scrutiny of poor dwellings was not, of course, confined to France. In *The Condition of the Working-Class in England in 1844*, Friedrich Engels threw open the houses of the poor in Manchester for critical inspection. Engels acknowledged that his interest in working-class dwellings had been motivated by recent epidemic episodes, and he likened the city explicitly to a crime scene.[26] The slums of the "Great Towns" were evidence, he alleged, of a "social murder" perpetrated against the poor:

> When one individual inflicts bodily injury upon another, such injury that death results, we call the deed manslaughter; when the assailant knew in advance that the injury would be fatal, we call this deed murder. But when society places hundreds of proletarians in such a position that they inevitably meet a too early and an unnatural death, one which is quite as much a death by violence as that by the sword or bullet . . . [this] deed is murder just as surely as the deed of the single individual, disguised, malicious murder, murder against which none can defend himself, which does not seem what it is, because no man sees the murderer, because the death of a victim seems a natural one.[27]

For Engels, industrial capitalism is the invisible "assailant," producing the unsanitary conditions it claims to loathe. Engels inverts the association of the poor with crime to suggest that poverty is the outcome of a culpable system that inflicts structural violence on the workers; a "murder" that passes undetected since the death of its victims appears "natural." The pervasive crime of the system, in other words, produces the criminal. "Capital," Karl Marx observed in a celebrated metaphor that conflated murder with filth-disease (the first volume of *Das Kapital* appeared in English in 1887), "comes dripping from head to toe, from every pore, with blood and dirt."[28]

The idea of the "social murder" was articulated in different guises and with increasing fervor as the century progressed. In the 1840s, the physician Thomas Southwood Smith—along with Edwin Chadwick a leading sanitary reformer—observed before a committee of the House of Common that the poor were "victims that are sacrificed. The effect is the same as if twenty or thirty thousand of them were annually taken out of their wretched homes and put to death."[29,30] And over four decades later, William Booth was to write: "Every year thousands of children are killed off by what is called defects of our sanitary system. They are in reality starved and poisoned."[31] The city is once again imagined as a crime scene: the willful disregard for the poor is tantamount to a criminal act. Infectious disease is generated by 'offending' living conditions and might thus be understood as a lethal "poison" administered with premeditation in an act of "social murder."

If poverty was akin to murder, the poor were themselves driven to murder by their squalid surroundings. As George Godwin, editor of *The Builder*, commented in 1856:

> The localities that are the nurseries of sickness and death are almost invariably found to be the haunts of immorality and crime. Filth and squalor are as productive of moral debasement as of physical depravation; the two natures of man are so intimately connected, that the defilement of the one is generally associated with pollution of the other.[32]

According to this "exorbitant analogism," crime was understood to be both the starting point and end point in a recurrent feedback system.[33] If crime was the outcome of a physical condition produced by disease in an act of "social murder," disease itself encouraged immoral tendencies that, in turn, induced crime: "Bad air produces feelings of exhaustion and lowness of spirits, and these tempt to the use of stimulants, the fruitful parents of all crime."[34] In the words of *The Morning Post*, reporting on the Whitechapel killings, crime and squalor were "mixed and matted together."[35] And as the Reverend Thomas Beames asserted in 1850, crime was also highly contagious. The fevers generated in slums invariably dispersed to distant parts of the city, triggering disorder.[36]

In describing this loop effect, nineteenth-century commentators made use of convoluted biomedical analogies wherein distinctions between disease and crime blurred in a compounded disease-crime imaginary that confused diagnosis with symptom and therapy. Thus, the Reverend William Tuckniss writing on "the suppression of crime and vices" in the preface to Henry Mayhew's *London Labour and the London Poor*:

> We have been dealing with effects rather than with first causes, and in our zeal to absorb, divert, or diminish the former, the latter have generally escaped detection. When too late, we have discovered that mere palliatives will not suffice and that they are powerless to resist the steady growth of crime in all its subtle developments.[37]

In short, the degradation of the 'rookeries' was tantamount to a form of "social murder," while deadly diseases incubated in districts where the "houses represent every conceivable aspect of filth and wretchedness."[38] By the same token, disease caused crime, which was conceptualized as a form of fever, highly contagious in nature. The conflated etiologies of crime and disease, and the construction of the city as a crime scene, were to persist into the twentieth century with the 'No-Rent' campaign run by the anarchists Frank Kitz and Charles Mowbray who framed the abuse of the poor as a form of 'murder' and the city slum as the crime scene. As one campaign poster proclaimed:

MURDER!

> —WORKMEN, why allow yourselves, your wives, and children to be daily murdered by the foulness of the dens in which you are forced to live?[39]

WRECKED LIVES, BROKEN HOUSES

Between August and November 1888, the streets of Whitechapel were scenes of crime. Five women were murdered in a district of London's East End characterized by its "brutality," where "the houses were as broken down and deplorable as the unfortunate inhabitants."[40] Over a period of four months, newspapers reiterated gruesome details of the homicides and drew attention to the "hideous conditions" of the capital. As *The Morning Post* proclaimed, the Whitechapel murders underscored "the daily sins, the nightly agonies, the hourly sorrows that haunt and poison and corrupt the ill-fated tenants . . . in those homes of degradation and disease."[41]

The moral injunction to represent these noxious spaces—to bring light to the darkness of the slums—was pervasive in the 1880s. The trope of "lifting the veil" on the darkness of the East End recurred in media coverage of the Whitechapel murders. Thus, characteristically, *The Morning Post* wrote:

> The veil has been drawn aside that covered up the hideous condition in which thousands, tens of thousands, of our fellow-creatures live, in this boasted nineteenth century, and in the very heart of the wealthiest, the healthiest, the most civilized city in the world.[42]

In 1889, Charles Booth published the first volume of his survey of London, which focused on the East End and incorporated extensive maps that made visible new relations between types of dwellings, 'criminal' populations, and poverty. Booth's project was framed from the outset in terms of a tension between the visible and the hidden, the real and the phantasmagoric.[43] The murders had torn away the veil obscuring the "pestilential" slums, and with the help of new technology, notably photography, "the plague spots where all these evils flourish and whence they spread" could be "mapped out."[44] As *The Star* announced:

> The cry of the East End is for light—the electric light to flash into the dark corners of its streets and alleys, the magic light of sympathy and hope to flash into the dark corners of wrecked and marred lives.[45]

Wrecked lives in broken homes: the association of dysfunctional tenants with inadequate dwelling-places was a conspicuous feature of the news reporting during and in the aftermath of the killings. As George Sims had earlier put it in *How the Poor Live* (1883): "The walls are damp and crumbling, the ceiling is black and peeling off, showing the laths above, the floor is rotten and broken away in places, and the wind and the rain sweep in through gaps that seem everywhere."[46] Houses were classified as "bad" (meaning unsanitary and structurally unsound), just as classes of people were deemed to evince "badness," tarring the districts in which they lived, such as Whitechapel, with a "bad" name. While crime was associated with a certain norm of deviant behavior, disease was understood to reside in—and to emanate from—the fabric of unwholesome houses. Articulated as a question, the issue was this: did the wrecked residents poison their dwellings, or did the slum dwellings break their inhabitants? In other words, where was 'badness' located?

Booth sought to address this question in his survey of London's poor. There, he repeatedly noted the "bad," "broken" streets and houses, implicitly attributing the criminal tendencies of their residents to the deleterious environment. At the same time, however, he deemed "the badness of the houses [to be] due primarily to the insanitary and dirty habits of the occupants."[47] An environmental determinism overlapped with—and undermined—a theory of moral agency to produce a contradictory but influential discourse of crime, disease, and poverty. The 'house' was understood as more than the bricks-and-mortar backdrop to criminal action. Slum dwellings were imagined in terms of an active agency: houses could kill. Properties, like people, had criminal profiles and 'pathological' propensities. Like people, houses could be infectious, seeping in and damaging the dark corners of human lives. Thus, while crime and disease were framed in terms of contagion, human agency and its material contexts became entangled in complex ways.

On Saturday, September 8, Annie Chapman's body was discovered in the backyard of 29 Hanbury Street, "a fair example of a large number of houses in the neighbourhood."[48] The murder prompted a detailed analysis of the building (doors, rooms, passages, and yard) by the coroner at the inquest, as well as a description of the occupants and their social backgrounds, occupations, and habits. The body of Mary Jane Kelly was subsequently discovered on the morning of Friday, November 9, inside the dingy space she rented in Miller's Court, a furnished single room at the back of 26 Dorset Street, Spitalfields. As *The Globe* announced on November 10, this murder marked the monster's "move indoors" and his familiarity with "every local twist and corner."[49]

The media provided a detailed inventory of the contents of the room, which was described as being between 12 to 15 square feet, with two windows, and furnished with a bed, two tables, and a chair. A broken wine bottle held a candle.[50] The wall above the fireplace was decorated with a print of 'The Fisherman's Widow.' As Kelly's door key was lost, she had bolted and unbolted the door from the outside by inserting a hand through a window, which was curtained by a piece of muslin. As Inspector Frederick G. Abberline noted at the inquest: "An impression has gone abroad that the murderer took away the key of the room . . . it has been missing some time, and since it has been lost they have put their hand through the broken window, and moved back the catch."[51] The broken window, emphasized in subsequent reports, is a detail that recurs in descriptions of the East End, underscoring the single-room dwelling as an indeterminate, ambiguously bounded space. The police photographed the room's interior and Kelly's eviscerated body sprawled on the bed, with bodyparts scattered across the room.[52] The front page of *The Illustrated Police News* of November 17, 1888, depicted various episodes from the murder in a graphic montage, including a sketch of the police photographing the body, views of the "scene of the murder" ("the murderer's chosen spot"), and a map of the locality of the crimes, with the window into the victim's room featuring as a prominent detail (Figure 3.2).

The dispersal of the murdered woman's flesh and the inventory of the room were obscenely conflated in subsequent reports, as if body and room were inseparable and part of some grisly 'economy of the makeshift.' Here, bodyparts are transformed into 'things,' while 'things' (bed, tables, and chair), as silent witnesses of crime, become part of an unintelligible universe.[53] As Bill Brown has noted in his study of 'things' in

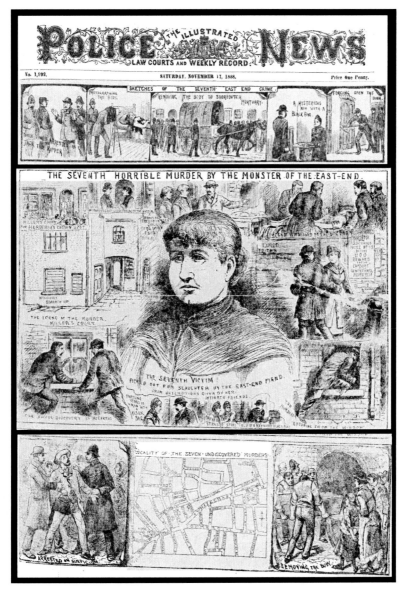

Figure 3.2 "Sketches of the Seventh East End Crime," *The Illustrated Police News*, November 17, 1888.

turn-of-the-last-century America, there is a "slippage between *having* (possessing a particular object) and *being* (the identification of one's self with that object)."[54] As in the 'fragmented,' modernist photographs of Paul Strand, inanimate objects are "transformed into both something less (fragments) than the objects they were, but also something more (forms)," acquiring an "indeterminate ontology where things seem slightly human and humans seem slightly thing-like."[55] Motifs of dissolution and disappearance pervaded reports of the Ripper murders, even as the killer was repeatedly described as possessing a capacity to materialize and dematerialize at will in the city.[56]

The 'crime scene' figures as a space cordoned off from the surrounding environment. It is a site, beyond the public gaze, where everyday objects, including the body of the postmortem victim, are reassembled and re-contextualized to acquire specific new meaning as 'objective' evidence of a crime. As the coroner reported, mulling over the identity of the killer: "There were no meaningless cuts."[57] At the same time, however—as the page of *The Illustrated Police News* suggests with its central portrait of Kelly framed by illustrations that narrativize her violent demise—the 'crime scene' functions as a site for making visible an obscure life and in so doing reconstituting the scattered fragments of a body in a distinctly modern subject.

ABJECT SPACE: INSIDE THE SLUM

In its original sense, used in the early 1800s, the word 'slum' signified little more than a room. By the 1820s, however, the word had become a slang term for a "room in which low goings-on occurred." Later—and certainly by the 1840s—it had come to include whole houses and districts.[58] Earlier associations were overlaid with new meanings and by the 1880s the 'slum' room stood in for whole districts of the city, while districts were defined in relation to singular, abject spaces. In 1883, the Reverend Andrew Mearns had published his impassioned (but anonymous) plea for housing reform, *The Bitter Cry of Outcast London*, drawing on Sims' serialized descriptions in *The Pictorial World*. Based on "home to home visitations," Mearns' tract gave the British reading public a bleak picture of the "abject" living conditions of the capital's poor. In it, he detailed the interiors of lodging houses and single-room dwellings, where he claimed incest was rife; his tract is, in effect, an inventory of dilapidated rooms, on average eight square feet, characterized by flimsy, filthy walls, ceilings, and furniture: "a broken chair, the tottering relics of an old bedstead, [or] the mere fragment of a table."[59]

Another view of the 'slum' room—more than a decade later, but looking back to the 1880s—is the series of paintings (the so-called "Camden Town Murder" paintings) produced by the British artist Walter Sickert, who had taken a keen interest in the Whitechapel murders. The artist was convinced that the crimes had been committed by a veterinary student who had lodged in the house where he was living in Mornington Crescent, and he painted a picture of the murderer's room, entitled "Jack the Ripper's Bedroom."[60] In this work, the slum is pictured as a dark, brooding, semi-intelligible space. The indefinite forms in the painting, rendered in a limited tonal range, compel the viewer to actively decipher space. The furniture is indistinct, blurring into the background. The room is no longer "a stable container of objects" but reflects "the psychological disturbances of an alienated subject."[61] As David Peters Corbett has observed of the Camden Town paintings, murder "is the medium through which the labile nature of knowledge is given substance":

> The mysteries of identity and the impenetrability of action in the city find a home there. Murder is the distillation of everything that runs counter to the imposition of knowledge onto the city—it stands for what lacks system, for what is unmotivated, unpredictable, violent, and intense in a way that the rationalized systems of the city, smoothly running, can never be. It is the embodiment of the city as opaque, of the terrors and phantasms that crawl out of the uncertainties of city spaces and haunt the streets.[62]

Sickert's slum room is a psychologized space of hidden recesses or "spectral eruptions" (to use Sharon Marcus' evocative phrase) in which objects bear a multiplicity of meanings and where the irrational cannot be subordinated.[63] Mearn's broken slum rooms with their "rude substitute" tables and chairs are here broken down further. Sickert's work registers the dispersal of distinct, 'realistic' forms; the human shape merges unsettlingly with the semi-choate space of the room, intimating both a dispersal of identity and the subject's entrapment within a space he cannot control.[64]

As the journalist George Sala had remarked in 1859: "Subdivision, classification, and elaboration are certainly distinguishing characteristics of the present era of civilisation."[65] However, the confusion of the 'slum' as an improvised, makeshift, and unstable space, elides such elaboration. As *The Architect* put it: using a bedroom for a function other than sleeping was "unwholesome, immoral, and contrary to the well-understood principle that every important function of life required a separate room."[66] The 'slum' room is a space that is "unwholesome" precisely because it doubles up for use as something other than its intended purpose; in so doing, the room is marked by a fundamental instability of personal and social boundaries, conducive to immoral, criminal behavior, such as incest.[67]

In March 1888, Gissing described the discovery of his estranged wife's body, Margaret (a prostitute), in a Lambeth slum room, some six months before the first of the Whitechapel murders took place:

> Let me describe this room. It was the first floor back; so small that the bed left little room to move . . . On the door hung a poor miserable dress and a worn out ulster; under the bed was a pair of boots. Linen she had none; the very covering of the bed had gone save one sheet and one blanket. I found a number of pawn tickets, showing that she had

pledged these things during last summer . . . I drew out the drawers. In one I found a little bit of butter and a crust of bread.[68]

Gissing proceeds with a detailed inventory of the slum, which is much more than a room, since it bears the traces of an entire life, but it is also much less, recalling the murderous slums in popular Victorian literature, of the kind alluded to by H. G. Wells in *Tono-Bungay* (1909), where an "interminable succession of squalid crimes" take place, with "women murdered and put into boxes, buried under floors."[69] For Gissing, the room is testimony to a "savage" crime inflicted by an "accursed social order." If the slum is the "poverty trap"—as Charles Booth called it—it is also, always and inevitably, as Gissing would have it, the scene of a crime.

A few years after the Whitechapel murders, in 1892, the Portuguese historian, economist, and social critic Oliveira Martins went on a guided tour of the East End, accompanied for his protection by a police detective. He took in a Chinese opium den, the Jewish quarter, and the sites where Jack the Ripper's victims were found. Martins' description of the crime scene moves from dark exterior, heaped with mud and populated by "queer-looking men," to the interior of the room where Mary Kelly had been found eviscerated:

> The door opened and we entered, going down from the level of the street, for the tenement was partly underground. It was an enclosure that was at most double the size of the little iron bedstead placed on one side of it. A petroleum lamp, without screen, gave an uneasy light over the room, if such a place wherein we were could be called . . . You might have cut the air of the room with a knife. There was also a broken chair, some remnants of clothes hung up on a line, and in a corner, in the dark shade, something that appeared to me to stir . . . The mother grunted, the father breathed with difficulty, and the detective, as we went out, said to us: 'It was on that bed that Jack the Ripper mutilated another woman. Did you not see on the wall at the side some dark splashes? It was the blood that gushed upon it, and it is there still.'[70]

The slum room merges into the yard and alley: the homes of the poor are never private since they cannot exclude the literal refuse from the streets. "Gaining access to the poor main's stinking dwelling [almost] amounts[ed] to an underground expedition."[71] Inside, the room itself feels murderous—"you might have cut the air of the room with a knife"—as if the physical setting is complicit in crime. Like other 'Ripper' narratives, this account of the crime scene seeks to render intelligible a space that eludes intelligibility. Even the identity of the killer ('Jack the Ripper'), as the epitome of a particular type of killer (the 'serial killer'), "reflects exactly the incoherences [sic] that it is constructed to overcome."[72]

The locale of the horror narrative, of course, is the haunted house: the building where bodies lurk in the dead spaces of roofs, ceilings, and walls, and where fresh blood threatens to seep out of the frayed wallpaper as a sign of past violence and deaths to come. A place where corridors, windows, doors, and cupboards open on to dark places where the protagonists would rather not go but where they are compelled to go: they *need* to see. This is the crime scene; a crime that is past and a crime that is about to take place (again). It is a scene which came to visibility in London in the 1880s with the Whitechapel murders and against the backdrop of a renewed debate about the condition of London's working-class properties—lodging houses and single-room dwellings—as well as 'model dwellings' and the Artisans' and Labourers' Dwellings Improvement Act 1875, which permitted local authorities to purchase land for slum clearance.

In Conan Doyle's short story "A Case of Identity," set in 1888, Sherlock Holmes confides to Watson his desire to "fly out of that window hand in hand, hover over this great city, gently remove the roofs, and peep in at the queer things which are going on."[73] The house is a cover for dubious action, and detection become synonymous with a compulsion to unhinge facades and lift off roofs: to make visible the hidden. The preoccupation with prizing open suspect dwellings in order to peer in at the "queer things" inside was, of course, nothing new in the 1880s. As we have seen, epidemic episodes from the 1830s had prompted a shift of focus onto the dark, dirty, and malodorous dwellings of the poor. The working-class 'slum' was continually on view. As one commentator declared, in an injunction to prize open the hidden spaces of the poor: "We will enter these streets and peep into those dark, close, unhealthy, and forbidding looking rooms."[74]

In 1866, Florence Nightingale had bemoaned "the evil in house construction." Old papered walls, carpets, furniture, and sinks were all sources of dangerous impurity as bad as the "dung-heap in the basement" or the sewer under the house which was "nothing but a laboratory from which epidemic disease and ill health is being distilled into the house."[75] "A dark house," Nightingale wrote, "is always an unhealthy house, always an ill-aired house, always a dirty house."[76] There was a latent tension in this discourse of the "dark house" between, on the one hand, the jerry-built house as a passive setting of disease, where agency belonged to the 'criminal' contractors and money makers, the negligent housekeepers, and poisonous vapors, and, on the other hand, the house itself as an active agent imbued with volition—in short, the house with 'evil' premeditation: the criminal. As Julia McNair Wright observed in *The Complete Home: An Encyclopaedia of Domestic Life and Affairs* in 1881:

Between the Home set up in Eden, and the Home before us in Eternity, stand the Homes of Earth in a long succession . . . Every home has its influence, for good or evil, upon humanity at large.[77]

Such literature suggested a form of "domestic environmentalism," wherein space had a powerful influence over the development of character.[78] As Arthur Machen noted in *The Three Impostors* (1895):

> It dawned upon me that I would write the history of a street. Every house should form a volume, I fixed upon the street, I saw each house, and read as clearly as in letters, the physiology and psychology of each.[79]

Houses have a "physiology" and a "psychology." Buildings are bodies, susceptible to disease and capable of evil intent. Indeed, by the 1880s and 1890s the equation between 'evil' houses and criminality was being expressed in novel ways. In France in 1893, under the direction of Paul Juillerat, Chief of the Bureau of Sanitation, for example, the Municipal Council of Paris began to create a "sanitary file" of houses similar to the criminal record of a person. Juillerat's method of collating data (house plans, drainage plans, and demographics) "in many ways resembled the one created for the study of criminal types compiled by Cesare Lombroso in *Homo delinquens*"—discussed in the previous chapter by Chiara Beccalossi—as well as the photographic archive increasingly employed by the police to identify crime suspects.[80] At the same time, in London reformers strove to mark out "bad" houses, which were "condemned" for demolition.

CONCLUSION: CONTAGIOUS DELIRIUMS

From the outset, the media reporting of the Whitechapel murders closely associated the identification of crime with disease, an association underscored by publication of the autopsies, which detailed the victims' relative states of health and sickness. For example, Dr. Philips noted in his autopsy report of Annie Chapman: "The deceased was far advanced in disease of the lungs and membranes of the brain."[81] Moreover, the equation of crime detection with the detection and elimination of germs was accentuated by a Hudson's Soap advertisement in December 1888, which played on the media's coverage of the Whitechapel Murderer and their condemnation of the 'filthy' East End (Figure 3.3). Meanwhile, the depiction of the killer as a phantom of "the slum's foul air" by John Tenniel in *Punch* (September 29, 1888) drew on an earlier iconography of cholera as miasmic phantom, in which the disease is featured as a white-sheeted specter or nebulous cloud haunting a "world of slime" (Figure 3.4).[82]

The ghost evokes, here, a particular kind of dematerialized presence, fearful in part because of its insubstantiality. It is this very emptiness and ontological ambivalence ("the indeterminate ontology where things seem slightly human and humans seem slightly thing-like") that allows the ghost to take on multiple meanings: as disease and crime and knife-wielding

Figure 3.3　Advert for Hudson's Soap from *The Graphic*, December 1, 1888. © Museum of London.

Figure 3.4　"The Nemesis of Neglect" by John Tenniel for *Punch*, September 29, 1888.

killer and victim.[83,84] The ghost recalls the phantom figure of 'Jack the Ripper,' a "ghoul-like creature" whose identity appeared to disperse into the city—not unlike a choleric cloud.[85] It also brings to mind the ghostliness of the crime scene the Ripper leaves behind: the dismembered bodies of the women in the slum who are at once anonymized objects in a postmortem inquiry, even as they are bestowed with a new identity by their emplacement in the *scene*.

Advertisements evoked another form of ghostliness or non-presence, which was also associated with crime, and forms of criminal infectivity. Aside from his tour of the murder scene, one of the distinctive features of London that struck Martins during his visit was the preponderance of advertising:

> Advertisement—the bill-frenzy—was among the things that impressed me most. They persecute one everywhere. In the stations they are a delirium. They paint omnibuses with them. They line carriages with them. They put them above the roofs of houses in great letters of gold hanging up for the wind to shake . . . Everything is advertised, absolutely everything.[86]

Even crime. From the 1870s, concerns were increasingly being articulated about the effects that newspapers had on their readership. Cheap, mass publications were helping to produce a criminalized population and, indeed, inducing a "delirium." As *The Illustrated London News* reported, "Seldom is a precocious offender brought into the dock but evidence is given that, on searching him or his dwelling place, a heap of foul fictions is found."[87] Imitation constituted a form of contagion and newspapers were, in part, deemed responsible for the crimes that they reported.[88] Underlying this argument was a belief that scenes of crime could become agents of crime, inciting the violence the press purported to prevent (Figure 3.5).

In the pages of the *Pall Mall Gazette*, W. T. Stead was to quip that the Whitechapel murders should perhaps be seen as the work of a "Scientific Humanitarian" or a "Sociological Pasteur." His editorial "Murder as an Advertisement," published on September 19, 1888, suggested that in their zeal to eradicate crime and disease, modernizing reformers were prepared to sacrifice the few for the many. "What then is more reasonable," Stead concluded facetiously, "than to suppose that these horrors may have been produced in this scientific sensational way to awake the public conscience? If this should after all turn out to be the case, the defence of the scientific Sociologist at the Old Bailey will be a curiosity in the history of criminal trials and may mark the beginning of the scientific era." The suggestion, here, is not only that the murders are part of an 'advertising' campaign aimed at inculcating an awareness of the slums as the "cesspools of brutalized humanity" in the mind of the public, but Stead also intimates that

Figure 3.5   A crowd gathered around an East End newsagents window display, c.1900. © Museum of London.

the 'pasteurizing' agenda of modern science is incriminated in the infectious violence it seeks to 'immunize' against. In so doing, Stead evokes the persistent rumors that the Ripper was someone who possessed "anatomical skill"; a suggestion reinforced in the numerous letters received by the police, which claimed the Ripper's identity as a human vivisectionist, a physiologist, and a demented experimenter.[89]

'Jack the Ripper,' of course, was never apprehended—his disappearance contributing in large part to the enveloping mystery of the Ripper killings. "The fact that the murderer was never caught," Ackroyd has observed, "only seemed to confirm the impression that, somehow or other, the streets themselves had perpetrated the crime. The East End was the 'real' Ripper."[90] In this formulation, place is the killer; the city is both the crime scene and the criminal in one.[91] As Seltzer has suggested, the 'serial killer' represents "a violent literalization of the analogies between bodies . . . persons and landscapes."[92] This chapter has sought to explore this literalization in the case of the Whitechapel murders by setting events within a broader history of how disease and crime came to be discursively co-produced and how they were understood as both place-specific material entities and as "ghostly demarcations," with consequences for the ways in which disease and crime continue to be located in the bodies, persons, and dilapidation of the contemporary city.

NOTES

1. Susan Sontag, *On Photography* (Harmondsworth: Penguin, 1978), 5.
2. Walter Benjamin, *Walter Benjamin: Selected Writings, Vol.2, Part 2, 1931–1934*, ed. Michael W. Jennings, Howard Eiland, and Gary Smith (Cambridge, MA: Harvard University Press, 2005 [1999]), 527.
3. A theory of the 'uncanny' was expounded by the German psychiatrist Ernst Jentsch, author of "On the Psychology of the Uncanny" (1906) and developed by Freud in his influential essay "The Uncanny" of 1919; on the history of the word 'uncanny,' see Nicholas Royle, *The Uncanny* (Manchester: Manchester University Press, 2003), 9–12.
4. Anthony Vidler, *The Architectural Uncanny: Essays in the Modern Unhomely* (Cambridge, MA: MIT Press, 1992), 2–6.
5. Anthony Vidler, *Warped Space: Art, Architecture, and Anxiety in Modern Culture* (Cambridge, MA: MIT Press, 2001), 25.
6. Peter Ackroyd, "Introduction," in *Jack the Ripper and the East End*, ed. Alex Werner (London: Chatto & Windus, 2008), 12.
7. Alexandra Warwick, "The Scene of the Crime: Inventing the Serial Killer," *Social Legal Studies*, vol.15, no.4 (2006): 553.
8. *The Times* quoted in the *Pall Mall Gazette*, Wednesday, September 19, 1888.
9. Vidler, *Warped Space*, 2.
10. Ibid., 1; "murder-inviting nooks" comes from the poem "The Nemesis of Neglect" which appeared in *Punch* in September 29, 1888.
11. The bibliography is too vast to list here, but works include Charles E. Rosenberg, *The Cholera Years: The United States in 1832, 1849 and 1866* (Chicago: University of Chicago Press, 1987); David Arnold, "Cholera and Colonialism in British India," *Past & Present*, vol.113, no.1 (1986): 118–151; Pamela K. Gilbert, *Cholera and Nation: Doctoring the Social Body in Victorian England* (Albany: State University of New York Press, 2003); Christopher Hamlin, *Cholera: The Biography* (Oxford: Oxford University Press, 2009).
12. Lorraine Daston, "Objectivity and the Escape from Perspective," *Social Studies in Science*, vol.22, no.4 (1992): 597–618; Lorraine Daston and Peter Galison, *Objectivity* (New York: Zone Books, 2007).
13. Charles Manby Smith, *The Little World of London, or Pictures in Little of London Life* (London: Arthur Hall, Virtue and Co, 1857), 135.
14. George Gissing, *The Nether World: A Novel* (New York: Harpers and Brothers, 1889), 161.
15. In fact, Atget himself was to describe his photographs as "documents"; see Andreas Krase, "Archives du regard—inventaire des choses: *Le Paris D'Eugène Atget*," in *Paris Eugène Atget: 1897–1927*, ed. Hans Christian Adam (Cologne: Taschen, 2008), 40–42.

16. David P. Jordan, *Transforming Paris: The Life and Labors of Baron Haussmann* (Chicago: University of Chicago Press, 1996), 96.
17. "The sewers of Paris in 1832 were far from being what they are today. Bruneseau had given the impulse, but the cholera was required to bring about the vast reconstruction which took place later on"; see Walter Benjamin, *The Arcades Project* (Cambridge, MA: The Belknap Press, 1999 [1982]), 412.
18. François Delaporte, *Disease and Civilization: The Cholera in Paris, 1832*, trans. Arthur Goldhammer (Cambridge, MA: MIT Press, 1986), 59.
19. Benoiston de Châteauneuf, *Rapport sur la marche et les effets du cholera-morbus dans Paris* (Paris: Imprimerie Royale, 1834), 199–200; quoted in Delaporte, *Disease and Civilization*, 65.
20. Cholera reached Russian in the early 1820s and had spread to Britain by October 1831; the fifth pandemic impacted Europe in the 1880s and 1890s. See Peter Baldwin, *Contagion and the State in Europe, 1830–1930* (Cambridge: Cambridge University Press, 2005), 37–243.
21. Alain Corbin, *The Foul and the Fragrant: Odor and the French Social Imagination* (Cambridge, MA: Harvard University Press, 1986), 151.
22. Ibid., 159.
23. Ibid., 165.
24. Ibid., 157.
25. Ibid., 164.
26. The link between poor living conditions and disease had been noted by many, including Edwin Chadwick in his report on *The Sanitary Conditions of the Labouring Population of Great Britain* (1842).
27. Friedrich Engels, *The Condition of the Working-Class in England: From Personal Observation and Authentic Sources* (London: Lawrence & Wishart, 1973 [1845]), 120–21.
28. Karl Marx, *Capital: A Critique of the Political Economy*, Vol.1, trans. Ben Fowkes (Harmondsworth: Penguin, 1990), 926.
29. On Southwood Smith as a sanitary theorist, see Margaret Pelling, *Cholera, Fever, and English Medicine, 1825–1865* (Oxford: Oxford University Press, 1978), 1–33.
30. C. L. Lewes, *Dr. Southwood Smith: A Retrospect* (Edinburgh: William Blackwood & Sons, 1898), 104.
31. William Booth, *In Darkest England, and the Way Out* (New York: Funk and Wagnalls, 1890), 14.
32. George Godwin, *London Shadows: A Glance at the Homes of the Thousands* (London: George Routledge, 1856), 65.
33. I borrow the term from Mark Seltzer, *Serial Killers: Death and Life in America's Wound Culture* (New York: Routledge, 1998), 33.
34. Ibid., 45.
35. Reported in the *Pall Mall Gazette*, Wednesday, September 12, 1888. On the coverage of the murders in the media, see L. Perry Curtis, Jr., *Jack the Ripper and the London Press* (New Haven: Yale University Press, 2001); and Alexandra Warwick and Martin Willis, eds., *Jack the Ripper: Media, Culture, History* (Manchester: Manchester University Press, 2008).
36. Thomas Beames, *The Rookeries of London: Past, Present, and Prospective* (London: Thomas Bosworth, 1852 [1850]), 149.
37. Henry Mayhew, *London Labour and the London Poor*, vol.1 (London: Griffin, Bohn, and Company, 1861), xii.
38. John Hollingshead, *Ragged London in 1861* (London: Smith, Elder, & Co, 1861), 44.
39. Sarah Wise, *The Blackest Streets: The Life and Death of a Victorian Slum* (London: The Bodley Head, 2008), 140.

40. Charles Booth, *Life and Labour of the London Poor, 3rd Series: Religious Influences* (London: Macmillan, 1902), 67. The 'canonical' list of murdered women includes Mary Ann Nichols, Annie Chapman, Elizabeth Stride, Catherine Eddowes, and Mary Kelly, although the media attributed other killings to the Ripper, including those of Emma Smith in April 1888 and Martha Tabram in August 1888.
41. Reported in the *Pall Mall Gazette*, Wednesday, September 12, 1888.
42. Ibid.
43. Charles Booth, *Labour and Life of the People* (London: Macmillan, 1889), 591–592.
44. Sir Richard A. Cross, *Homes of the Poor in London in the Nineteenth Century* (London: Kegan Paul, 1882), 231.
45. *The Star*, Monday, October 1, 1888; see Curtis, *Jack the Ripper and the London Press*, 263.
46. George Sims, *How the Poor Live* (London: Chatto & Windus, 1883), 6–7.
47. Booth, *Life and Labour*, 153, 101.
48. *The Times*, Thursday, September 27, 1888.
49. Curtis, *Jack the Ripper and the London Press*, 192.
50. See the inquest report in *The Daily Telegraph*, Tuesday, November 13, 1888.
51. Ibid.
52. Photography was being progressively institutionalized within forensic science and crime detection; see Suzanne Bell, *Crime and Circumstance: Investigating the History of Forensic Science* (Westport, CT: Greenwood Press, 2008), 211–213. Photographs of the Ripper's victims Mary Ann Nichols, Annie Chapman, Elizabeth Stride, including two of Mary Janet [sic] Kelly are held in the Public Records Office, National Archives, Kew, MEPO 3/3155.
53. Asa Briggs, borrowing from T. S. Eliot, has written of "things" as "emissaries" of culture and sought to "reconstruct 'the intelligible universe'" of the Victorians; see *Victorian Things* (London: Penguin, 1990 [1988]), 31.
54. Bill Brown, *A Sense of Things: The Object Matter of American Literature* (Chicago: University of Chicago Press, 2003), 13.
55. Ibid., 9, 13.
56. Warwick, "The Scene of the Crime," 566.
57. *The Irish Times*, September 27, 1888. Quoted in Colin Milburn, "Science from Hell: Jack the Ripper and Victorian Vivisection," in *Science Images and Popular Images of the Sciences*, ed. Peter Weingart and Bernd Hüppauf (London: Routledge, 2011), 132. Milburn discusses equations of the 'crime scene' with the physiological laboratory, 143–151.
58. Harold J. Dyos, "The Slums of Victorian London," in *Exploring the Urban Past*, ed. David Cannadine and David Reeder (Cambridge: Cambridge University Press, 1982), 130–131.
59. Anon., *The Bitter Cry of Outcast London: An Inquiry into the Condition of the Abject Poor* (London: James Clarke & Co., 1883), 8–9.
60. Patricia Cornwall uses the painting as evidence that Sickert was, in fact, 'Jack the Ripper'; see *Portrait of a Killer: Jack the Ripper—Case Closed* (New York: Berkeley/Penguin, 2003 [2002]), 56–57.
61. Vidler, *Warped Space*, 1.
62. David Peters Corbett, *The World in Paint: Modern Art and Visuality in England, 1848–1914* (Manchester: Manchester University Press, 2005 [2004]), 206.
63. Sharon Marcus, *Apartment Stories: City and Home in Nineteenth-Century Paris and London* (Berkeley: University of California Press, 1999), 12.
64. See Vidler, *Warped Space*, which explores "the anxious visions of the modern subject caught in spatial systems beyond its control," 1.

65. George Augustus Sala, *Gaslight and Daylight: With Some London Scenes They Shine Upon* (London: Chapman and Hall, 1859), 218–219.
66. Quoted in Judith Flanders, *The Victorian House: Domestic Life from Childbirth to Deathbed* (London: HarperCollins, 2003), 1.
67. Anon., *The Bitter Cry of Outcast London*, 7.
68. George Gissing, *London and the Life of Literature in Late Victorian England: The Diary of George Gissing*, ed. Pierre Coustillas (Hassocks: Harvester Press, 1978), 22–23.
69. Herbert G. (H. G.) Wells, *Tono-Bungay: A Novel* (New York: Duffield & Company, 1909), 48.
70. Oliveira Martins, *The England of Today*, trans. C. J. Willdey (London: George Allen, 1896), 255; reproduced in Rick Allen, *The Moving Pageant: A Literary Sourcebook on London Street Life, 1700–1914* (London: Routledge, 1998), 192–194.
71. Corbin, *The Foul and the Fragrant*, 152.
72. Warwick, "The Scene of the Crime," 553. In the article, Warwick also notes how scholars have sought to elucidate 'serial killing' as a discursive construct that makes apparently random acts intelligible; see, in this context, Alison Young, *Imagining Crime* (London: Sage, 1996); and David Canter, *Criminal Shadows: Inside the Mind of the Serial Killer* (London: HarperCollins, 1994).
73. Arthur Conan Doyle, *Adventures of Sherlock Holmes* (New York: A. L. Burt Company, 1920 [1892]), 56.
74. Quoted in Martin Hewitt, "District Visiting and the Constitution of Domestic Space in the Mid-Nineteenth Century," in *Domestic Space: Reading the Nineteenth-Century Interior*, ed. Inga Bryden and Janet Floyd (Manchester: Manchester University Press, 1999), 127.
75. Florence Nightingale, *Notes on Nursing: What It Is, and What It Is Not* (London: Harrison, 1866), 15.
76. Ibid., 16.
77. Quoted in Mike Hepworth, "Privacy, Security and Respectability: The Ideal Victorian Home," in *Housing and Dwelling: Perspectives on Modern Domestic Architecture*, ed. Barbara Miller Lane (Abingdon: Routledge, 2007), 153.
78. I borrow the phrase from Katherine C. Grier, *Culture and Comfort: Parlor Making and Middle-Class Identity* (Washington, DC: Smithsonian Institution Press, 1988), 6–9.
79. Arthur Machen, *The Three Imposters* (London: John Lane, 1895), 102.
80. George Teyssot, "Norm and Type: Variations on a Theme," in *Architecture and the Sciences: Exchanging Metaphors*, ed. Antoine Picon and Alessandra Ponte (New York: Princeton Architectural Press, 2003), 150–151.
81. Andrew Smith, "The Whitechapel Murders and the Medical Gaze," in *Jack the Ripper: Media, Culture, History*, ed. Alexandra Warwick and Martin Willis (Manchester: Manchester University Press, 2007), 113.
82. On the evolving iconography of infection and ghostliness, see Robert Peckham, "Ghosts in the Body: Infection, Genes, and the Re-Enchantment of Biology," in *The Ashgate Research Companion to Paranormal Culture*, ed. Olu Jenzen and Sally R. Munt (Farnham, UK: Ashgate, in press).
83. Brown, *A Sense of Things*, 13.
84. See the insightful discussion of the "cholera cloud" and "how global cholera pandemics in the nineteenth century produced globalized objects in which a near-universal recognizability and an utterly context-specific set of meanings, visions, and realities could ironically cohabit" in Projit Bihari Mukharji, "The 'Cholera Cloud' in the Nineteenth-Century 'British World': History of an Object-Without-an-Essence," *Bulletin of the History of Medicine*, vol. 86, no. 3 (2012): 303–332.

85. *The Star*, Saturday, September 8, 1888.
86. Martins, *The England of Today*, 34–35.
87. Quoted in Lynda Nead, *Victorian Babylon: People, Streets and Images in Nineteenth-Century London* (New Haven: Yale University Press, 2000), 156.
88. James Greenwood, *The Seven Curses of London* (Boston: Fields, Osgood, & Co, 1869), 52–53.
89. On the motif of 'medical knowledge' in the reporting of the Ripper killings, see Milburn, "Science from Hell."
90. Ackroyd, "Introduction," 29.
91. As campaigners for housing reform argued in the late nineteenth century, however, the real criminals were the slum landlords, many of whom, as it turned out, lived in the West End.
92. Seltzer, *Serial Killers*, 33.

4   Morality Plays
Presentations of Criminality and Disease in Nazi Ghettos and Concentration Camps

Michael Berkowitz

This chapter concerns Nazi efforts to interweave, and exacerbate by selective and cynical manipulation, accusations that Jews embodied and maliciously spread the scourges of disease and crime. While previous chapters have focused on nineteenth-century classifying tendencies and their consequences, here, the aim is to extend the scope of investigation into the twentieth century. In so doing, the chapter develops two key themes explored in this volume: namely, the overlaps and contradictions between biological and social accounts of disease and crime, and the ways in which these explanations formed the basis of coercive state practices. Indeed, the ghetto and the concentration camp mark the radical amplification of the 'crime scene' considered in Chapter 3 by Robert Peckham, where the technologies of modern science were deployed to disclose the hidden causal relations between the pathological and the deviant. Exaggerated tendencies toward criminality and debilitating disease were part of essentialist Nazi constructs of Jews that were a spur to, guide, and justification for actions that culminated in genocide. Suspected of a proclivity to fatal 'contagions,' Jews were treated as criminals.[1] This was related to—but not necessarily synonymous with—the belief that Jews polluted and sought to undermine the so-called 'Aryan' race. Criminality, which was construed as inherent to Jewry, was perceived as a manifestation of disease, as well as a culturally conditioned, learned set of behaviors.

It may be argued that there was a symbiotic relationship between these sorts of antisemitic prejudice, which were given a quasi-scientific caste. Many Nazis were true believers in the myths tying Jews with disease and Jews with criminality. Yet numerous specialists, bureaucrats, and those in the rank and file were aware of these accusations as a sham. Nevertheless, such charges became self-fulfilling prophecies that mutually reinforced each other, especially in the Nazi ghettos and concentration camps. Jews did turn to crime and became dependent on breaking the law for their sustenance—because the Nazis created an environment where this was the only means to survive. And Jews did contract infectious disease—because the Nazis manufactured bizarre conditions that radically fostered ill health, contagion, and mass death. Attention to Jews as perceived principal carriers of disease and crime complements recent interpretations of Nazism by scholars such as Peter Fritzsche and Jeffrey Herf. Fritzsche argues that

the Nazi insistence on understanding their struggle with Jewry as a matter of "life or death" for individual Germans and the Reich was a much
greater force of cohesiveness in National Socialism than scholars have previously assumed.[2] Herf, in surveying a vastly different body of evidence,
convincingly demonstrates that antisemitic propaganda against "the Jewish Enemy" was fundamental to the trajectory of Nazi policy and rational-
ization for their acts that extended well beyond the "Final Solution."[3]

  This discussion begins with a complex fictional work centered on disease in a German cultural context, which was conceived while Nazism
was germinating but before Hitler's takeover of power: Thomas Mann's
The Magic Mountain [*Der Zauberberg*]. Disease is, of course, a recurrent theme in Mann's work: from the suppurating infections in *Buddenbrooks* (1901) to the cholera cloud that hangs portentously over the city
in *Death in Venice* [*Der Tod in Venedig* (1912)], and the neurological illnesses that plague *Doctor Faustus* (1947). Published in 1924, *The Magic
Mountain* is an immense novel, in which coercion and terror, however
subtly deployed, are integral to a quasi-mystical dichotomy of sickness
and health. Although Mann rarely confronts 'criminalization' *per se*,
lapses in morality and resistance to authority have severe consequences
in the minds of patients and doctors in the Davos sanitarium. The book
is by no means anti-Jewish, although antisemitism is predictably interwoven and portrayed as a component of individuals' thoughts and actions.
The most pronounced proto-fascist character, Settembrini, in a chilling
premonition of Nazism, proclaims that those he regards as inferior types
and "sick" should not be deemed human. Settembrini is also fanatical
about obligatory cremation and obsessed with "the latest researches and
experiments." Conversely, his nemesis in the sanitarium, the converted
Jew Naphta, is appalled by such an "idea of discipline and conformity, of
coercion and compliance . . ."[4]

  Unsurprisingly, given the extent to which Mann distanced himself from
Nazism, *The Magic Mountain* allows for an order in which Jews can both
cure and be cured of disease. But non-Jews around them might see any
connection between Jews, blood, and medical matters as ominous. As the
narrator remarks, Elie Naphta, Leo's father

> had been a brooding and refining spirit: student of the Torah, but a
> critic as well, discussing the Scriptures with his rabbi—with whom he
> not infrequently disagreed. In his village, and not only among those
> of his own creed, he had passed for something unusual, for a man of
> more than common knowledge—knowledge for the most part of holy
> things, but possibly also of matters that might not be quite canny, and
> anyhow were not in the ordinary run. There was something irregular,
> schismatic, about him, something of the familiar of God, a Baal-Shem
> or Zaddik, a miracle man. Once he had actually cured a woman of a
> malignant sore, and another time a boy of spasms, simply by means of
> blood and invocations. But it was precisely this aura of uncanny piety,

in which the odour of his blood-bolstered calling played a part, that proved his destruction. There had been the unexplained death of two gentile boys, a popular uprising, a panic of rage—and Elie had died horribly, nailed crucifix-wise on the door of his burning home. His tuberculous, bedridden wife, the boy Leo, and four brothers and sisters, all wailing and lamenting with upflung arms, had fled the country.[5]

Although Leo had inherited his father's "slenderness of build" and "the seeds of his lung disease from his mother," these were not fixed Jewish characteristics as purported in nineteenth-century and Nazi racism.[6,7] In his work as a ritual slaughterer, Elie had been assisted by "a powerful youth of the athletic Jewish type."[8] *The Magic Mountain* certainly is not free of antisemitic stereotypes, but overall Jews are depicted sympathetically and humanely in Mann's work.

But how German is this? Failing to locate an English or American analog to *The Magic Mountain*, we can turn to *Buddenbrooks*, Mann's hefty, generational family tale.[9] *Buddenbrooks* also engages with sickness and health and its connection to the moral fiber, vitality, and longevity of an upper-class Lübeck family. This is memorably realized in the book's penultimate chapter, which begins: "Cases of typhoid fever take the following course."[10] As Todd Kontje has recently noted, Thomas Buddenbrooks borrows the language of a prevalent antisemitic discourse when he likens his 'degenerate' brother to a parasitic infection: "You're an abscess, an unhealthy growth on the body of our family."[11] What might be termed an English counterpart to *Buddenbrooks* is the voluminous *The Forsyte Saga* (1906–1934) by John Galsworthy.[12] (Here, too, there is not a great deal about Jews, but what exists is rife with implications.) The state of a person's physical well-being in *The Forsyte Saga* is widely understood to be a consequence of one's personal finances—especially the possession, or not, of substantial real estate. While eschewing stereotypes, we are reminded why some works are indeed classics—they do capture profound structures of social worlds. The British remain obsessed, as a nation, by 'house prices' and real estate practices. In Galsworthy's England, one's private property and the body are nearly one. Compared to *The Forsyte Saga*, in terms of the relationship between authority, control, health, and morality, *The Magic Mountain* is almost more Foucauldian than Foucault and possibly more insightful about Nazi ghettos and concentrations camps than one would ever imagine for a novel of 1924. A similar argument might be made about Robert Musil's *Young Törless* (1906). Published more than a decade before the first stirrings of Nazism, it too might be read as prefiguring a fascist mind-set.

PUNISHMENT AND TREATMENT, PRISONER AND PATIENT

Since the publication of Hannah Arendt's *The Origins of Totalitarianism* (1951; published in Britain as *The Three Pillars of Hell*), scholars have been challenged to confront the fact that Hitler and Nazism were the people's choice. In retrospect, we know that the Nazis brought chaos and war. However, they were supported, initially, because it was assumed they would engender law and order. National Socialism also professed to know both the science and secrets behind diseases that were threatening the nation's health, especially in times of war. Robert Proctor has shown that regarding the prevention of cancer and treatment of the disease, Nazi medicine was, in fact, effective.[13] In the beginning of his history of Theresienstadt, H. G. Adler includes a glossary (*Wörterverzeichnis*) with entries on Nazi organizations, abbreviations, and terms, as well as plays on language as conceived by Holocaust victims and perpetrators. Scores of these are related to crime, disease, and sanitation.[14]

Elsewhere, I have argued that although the Nazis used a number of euphemisms to malign Jews and to cloak atrocities and mass murder—which have now been examined by scholars—the axiomatic identification of Jews as 'prisoners' also deserves further scrutiny. While Jews were assumed by the Nazis and their accomplices to be 'prisoners,' it was also taken for granted that they represented 'patients' or inmates in a hospital or clinic—that is, they were sick with some kind of disease. Labeling all Jews in their domain as prisoners and bearers of disease, and those outside as potential prisoners and prone to disease, was not an abstraction but a mechanism devised by the Nazis to separate, and after Operation Barbarossa (June 1941), to annihilate European Jewry.

The historian Martin Broszat has explained how the concept of *Schutzhaft* (protective custody) stemmed from the emergency decree of February 28, 1933. It was not devised "as an instrument for dealing with punishable offences but as a 'preventive' police measure aimed at eliminating 'threats from subversive elements.'" As bizarre as it sounds, after 1945 those who helped devise concentration camps argued for leniency because they claimed to have "suppressed illegal concentration camps and other abuses."[15] The underlying notion, here, is that the 'legal' concentration camps were more rational and humane than those that emerged more spontaneously. Similarly, medicalized 'euthanasia,' first focused on the handicapped, and later applied to extermination camps, was justified as a humane and sensible option, compared to killing by bullets.[16] The most brutal of the Nazis, Heinrich Himmler, repeatedly stressed the development of the "Final Solution" as the healthiest means of solving the Jewish problem, which also took into account the total well-being of the Nazi perpetrators.

Although Jews were routinely and unquestionably called "prisoners," the vast majority of Jews under National Socialist control were neither prisoners of war, as defined by the Geneva Convention, nor prisoners as envisaged in modern criminological discourse.[17] The notion of a pre-emptive, preventative state action was another purported rationale for health-related interventions. A typical sequence of events, in which people are quarantined after the outbreak of disease, was inverted as the institutionalization of the supposedly diseased into ghettos and camps occurred prior to reported epidemics.

GHETTOS, CAMPS, AND QUARANTINES

An immense body of historiography has revealed that local conditions and officials influenced the Nazi erection of ghettos, concentration camps, and installations solely for the purpose of mass-murder. Above all, however, a chief aim of Hitler and Himmler in particular was to create an absolute Aryan realm that would dominate the rest of the world. Jews were the chief objects of a vast racial undertaking, the culmination of which would even re-order the cosmos, through what Saul Friedlander has termed "redemptive antisemitism."[18] In a similar way to seeing the potential criminality of Jewry as a rationale for their incarceration, it is also possible to conceive their treatment in ghettos and concentration camps as a sort of 'preventive' measure in light of the supposed relationship between Jews and contagious diseases—especially the dreaded typhus, as exemplified in film, poster, and press campaigns. When the "self-fulfilling prophecy" emerged, as "the Warsaw Ghetto was stricken by epidemics of typhoid, the slogan 'Jews-Lice-Typhoid' was spread by the Germans among a not unreceptive Polish population."[19] The Nazis incessantly portrayed "disease-ridden" Jews as swarming in a morass of "filth." As Christopher Browning has explained, the Nazis were unsettled upon seeing that some Jews "remained fit and alive" and when there "was a significant decline in the incidence of disease."[20] In his discussion of "Eichmann's Men," Hans Safrian has even considered climatic-related conditions, such as frostbite, as an element of genocide.[21]

Jews needed to be contained and closely watched, the Nazis contended, because of their propensity for criminality, and they had to be dealt with aggressively, because Jewish communal existence was said to be an incubator for vice, and their habits, a crucible for disease. A great amount of thought, energy, and effort was directed, then, to substantiating the stereotype that Jews were always and preeminently a community of sick crooks and that the key to managing and controlling Jews en masse was dealing with the phenomenon of Jewish criminality and sickness. It was a matter that spanned routine policing, public health, and ostensibly national security.

In his pioneering study of the Lodz ghetto, Isaiah Trunk asserted, "the entire legal-administrative system that the Germans introduced into the ghettos was a mockery of the most elementary principles of legality, even in times of war. Therefore, the concepts of 'crime' and 'punishment' were very elastic in the ghetto," if not meaningless, given the "absence of rights" and "arbitrary" nature of the penalties imposed—including countless deaths by shooting, hanging, and beating.[22] Similarly, the Nazi medical structures pertaining to 'health' did not in fact promote health, or aim to overcome sickness, but sought to stigmatize disease as a preeminent and 'natural' component of Jewish existence. Charles Roland argues in *Courage Under Siege: Starvation, Disease, and Death in the Warsaw Ghetto* that one of the most remarkable aspects of Jewish resistance to the Nazis was the extent to which they were able to confront the assault on their people's health.[23] The author's understanding of pathology, epidemiology, and medical institutional history provides a context that differentiates his study from most Holocaust historiography. Particularly impressive is his elaboration on the difference between typhus and typhoid fever and the fatal spread of tuberculosis. He also offers an insightful critique and summary of a study from 1979, based on the ghetto doctors' contemporary research, on systematic starvation in the ghetto.[24] Roland does not sufficiently explain, however, that much of what he found inventive and heroic derived from the interwar period, as physicians and administrators were building on a well-established tradition of medical self-help and even research stemming from organizations such as CENTOS (Organization for the Care of Orphans), TOZ (Society to Protect the Health of the Jewish Population), and ORT (Institute for Vocational Guidance and Training).[25]

In the process of ghettoization and the murderous sweeps of the *Einsatzgruppen,* the charge of "Jewish criminality" played at least as significant a role as the purported threat of Jews as a biological menace to the Nazi racial project. This is implicit in one of the more transparent Nazi reports on the annihilation of Eastern European Jewry, the *Jaeger Report.* The "Jewish criminality" canard was ubiquitous and provided an ideological support for Jaeger and other *Einsatzgruppe* operatives. It is intriguing that in the *Jaeger Report,* which was not intended for the press or otherwise for public consumption—"a secret Reich matter" (*Geheime Reichssache*)—an SS man describes his unit's work as a "police task." Why did Jaeger, the equivalent of a colonel in the SS, not describe these deeds as a project of racial cleansing or a state service in the name of eugenics? After all, he and his men expended great effort to annihilate all of those who were "undeserving of life" according to Nazi racial ideology. Were the Nazis and SS not, above all, concerned with race? Jaeger's only recourse to the term 'hygiene' was bemoaning the sanitary conditions in an overcrowded Lithuanian jail. This is a reminder that the discourses of race, criminality, and disease did not, necessarily, have to be joined—they could exist and even thrive independently.[26]

In selecting the Batut district of the city for the Lodz ghetto, the Nazis were acting on notions of both crime and disease. This area, which had been the poorest, most run-down part of this large industrial city, now 'accommodated' Jews who were essentially captives. "Before the war, thieves, black marketeers, and other unsavory characters lived among hard-working, honest Jews and Christians, but once the war began, the Christians were made to leave." That Jews should be herded into areas already associated with the "underworld," "pick-pockets," "gangsters," jails, and poor hygiene was made to appear a natural process.[27]

Similar to other aspects of the Nazi treatment of Jews that can be described as a self-fulfilling prophecy, National Socialism contrived and nurtured Jewish enclaves to accentuate the stereotype that Jews were prone to criminality, and that criminality, especially smuggling, "black marketeering and theft," was endemic in any Jewish milieu. Criminality, in this sense, is analogous to the Nazi interweaving of myths and realities concerning contagious diseases, especially typhus, to bolster the anti-Jewish policy. "In a bitter twist of fate," one historian writes of the Warsaw ghetto, "German policy thus unleashed the very epidemic that had been invoked as the rationale for sealing off the Jewish district in the first place. Famine led to typhus, typhus was followed by tuberculosis, and after that came the deportations."[28]

In the Bialystok ghetto, holding some 41,000 Jews, Nazi plans did not envision a hospital or even a clinic. In this case, however, the Judenrat (Jewish council) was able to turn the stereotype of the diseased Jew to its advantage. As "rumor spread of epidemics on the Aryan side" of Bialystok, "the Judenrat, on August 11, 1941, put up a notice warning of the danger of an epidemic inside the ghetto, too"—which was a deliberate exaggeration. At that point the Nazis wished to mainly exploit the ghetto for forced labor. Late in November the leader of the Jewish Council "announced nineteen cases of typhus and warned that 'if God forbid the epidemic spreads to the ghetto, not only will people's lives be at stake, but the ghetto will be sealed, and people will be barred from entering or leaving.'" The Judenrat was remarkably successful in establishing "a hospital for infectious diseases and a pharmacy" within the first month of its administration, during what historian Sara Bender calls its "Period of Calm, November 1941–November 1942." The building of the TOZ "was converted into a general hospital, directed by Dr. Ovadiah Kaplan, with four departments, including a surgery and x-ray department. In time, the hospital expanded and took over the building opposite it."[29] For the most part, however, associations between Jews and disease during the Second World War worked to their detriment.

In a diary entry of April 2, 1941, Chaim Hasenfus provides a stark illustration of what Herf has termed "the translation of Nazi ideology into narrative," as he wrote of Warsaw:

> Tens of thousands of Jews have been relocated from the provinces and crammed into a closed district inside Warsaw, which was already packed with half a million. The move has meant the ruin of many families. Add to that the range of economic prohibitions and it's no wonder that people are turning to begging and thieving.[30,31]

In ghettos, the supposed criminality of Jews was cited as a reason for their confinement, as well as their continued harassment with a barrage of legislation that further circumscribed their ability to move about and procure basic sustenance. Stanislaw Sznapman, who escaped the Warsaw ghetto in July 1943, recalled that after the Nazi invasion "a huge propaganda campaign designed to vilify Jews in the eyes of Poles" was instigated "to drive a wedge between Poles and Jews and to thwart possible joint action against their common enemy . . . Walls were covered with posters depicting Jews as repulsive and dangerous criminals or as vampires sucking Polish blood."[32] Thomas Mann wove a popular belief in connections between Jews and the magical properties of blood in *The Magic Mountain* as a literary device, but in Nazi hands it became grounds for a brutal policy.

As the Criminal Police and the Gestapo competed over who was to get greater control of the Lodz ghetto, Kriminal Inspektor Bracken supported the extension of his jurisdiction by announcing that "in the ghetto live, at any rate, about 250,000 Jews, all of whom have more or less criminal tendencies." This was considered convincing, and his "detachment moved in." In February 1941, the three factors mentioned as necessitating the creation of the Warsaw ghetto were "first, epidemics; second, Jewish black market activity and price gouging; and third, 'political and moral reasons.'"[33] The Nazis were always anxious to show that crime and disease were prevalent in the ghettos.

Historians of the Nazi ghettos such as Samuel Kassow, Sara Bender, and Isaiah Trunk assert that it was above all hunger and the incessant quest for food and warmth that "weakened concepts of morality and ethics among a portion of the population" and led to widespread activity which might appear as "criminal." In the Lodz ghetto, because "people could not survive for long on the meager food and heating fuel allotments and wages," they "sought out all sorts of ways to bring home in an illegal fashion a little food, heating fuel or money, so as to be able to buy something additional on the black market." Bloodshed and killing "motivated by hunger" did occur, but such cases were sparse, compared to the countless "crimes" of the "organizing" variety.[34] Out-and-out murder, Jews killing other Jews, was not notable until the attempted assassinations of those deemed collaborators, beginning August 1942, and then again as the Warsaw ghetto uprising was underway in 1943.

In 1944, Calel Perechodnik described his experience employed as a Jewish policeman in the Otwock ghetto, contrasting his own position to that of the German and Polish police. "Let us not forget," he noted, "that all of Jewish life during the war was illegal."[35] Here, Perechodnik, like other Jewish commentators, suggests that to ensure their very existence, all Jews were forced to act illegally. With ingenious staging, the Nazis created the impression of rampant criminality in the ghettos. "This was a real theater of marionettes," Perechodnik observed, "but what a tragic theater! Nevertheless, the manner in which the Germans implied to all the Jews, without exception, that they were doing all this for themselves, for their own good, for securing their material well-being for the future, this will remain forever Satan's secret."[36] Emmanuel Ringelblum's journal begins on January 1, 1940, with the assertion that a photograph featured in the Berlin *Illustrated Daily* was evidently staged: "They imported five Jews who had been picked up elsewhere and photographed them being caught in a raid . . . *The intent is clear.*" The following year, Ringelblum described the "trickery" employed by the Nazis in making a film about the life of the Jews in the ghetto: "A German guard stands in the middle of Zgierza Street in the Lodz ghetto; he is flanked on either side by Jewish guards. The German guard detains a German police officer for jaywalking; he orders the Jewish guards to hold the German police officer. And they film that." One of the Nazis' overarching concerns, for the sake of propaganda and perhaps also to convince themselves of the rightness of their case, was to prove that they were allowing the Jews a great deal of autonomy—in administering justice and health—and the result was self-destruction.[37]

A fundamental connection between ghettos, concentration camps, and labor camps in the Third Reich was the Nazi effort to cast all Jews as convicted criminals. In earlier work, I have focused on three categories of Nazi control in the camps that sought to concretize the preconception that all Jews deserved incarceration (without possibility of parole or release), harsh treatment, slave labor, and, ultimately, execution. The first category of control was through the development of specific criminal-bureaucratic procedures within the camps that aimed to reinforce the notion that the terms 'Jews' and 'criminals' were interchangeable. In so doing, the aim was also to reframe the concentration camps as penal institutions, where Jews were incarcerated to be punished for their 'crimes.' The second category was the deployment of 'criminal photography,' which played a distinct role in Nazi administration and self-perception. The third tool of control was the use of 'ceremonial' devices to give a symbolic credence to the Jew-crime equation. Thus, in many camps, scenes featuring Jews were staged for the benefit of both staff and inmates. The Nazis imbued these performances with a quasi-religious significance. They functioned, on the one hand, as a way of reinforcing a hierarchy and value system within the camps. On the other hand, they underscored the 'Otherness' of the Jew, perpetuating and dramatizing the conflation of Jews with criminality. Of all the ritualized performances orchestrated by the Nazis, two were particularly common as ways of reaffirming Jewish criminality: public hangings as retribution for "Jewish crimes" and public assemblies, which were instituted after prisoners had been killed—so it was claimed—for "attempting to escape."

While the Jews' status as criminals added to the Nazi license to use them in medical experiments, the architectural and spatial configurations of the concentration and labor camps emphasized the criminal identity of the inmates.[38] Gallows were positioned conspicuously and in ways that framed the camps as 'laboratories'; that is, as ensembles of discrete but interconnected spaces furnished with precision instruments designed for mass experiments—in this case, experiments on punitive methods. The 'laboratory' extended from the gallows to the gas chambers and the medical experiment rooms in the Nazi racial *Weltanschauung*. From this perspective, the gibbets and prisons within the camps served metonymically for the 'penal' rationale of the camp system as a whole. Because they were sequestered or, in the case of the Operation Reinhard camps (Belzec, Sobibor, and Trebilinka), deliberately concealed, there was not as much of an effort to promote the illusion of the camps as incubators of disease, as was the case with ghettos. But in the attempts by antisemitic deniers of the Holocaust to obliterate or minimize the Nazi genocide, an argument has been made that the gas chambers were mainly used to disinfect clothing and people and that the deaths that did occur were a result of collateral disease, as opposed to systematic mass killing. In such malicious idiocy, Nazi ideas of Jews and disease have, pathetically, infiltrated discourse about the Third Reich.[39]

An "amphitheater of torture," was how one survivor poignantly described the concentration camp of Natzweiler-Struthof, which occupied a mountaintop, with a high plateau serving as the parade ground, where the gallows were placed. The gas chamber, converted from an existing hotel building, was a few hundred meters down the road from the camp entrance—present, but not nearly as conspicuous, as the formidable gibbet and the prison building, occupying opposite ends of the camp. Overall, it is clear that punishment was largely random, but superficially it was meant to show that the Nazi rulers were pursuing their grand schemes in the realms of both law and order—Struthof was notorious as a final destination for apprehended members of the French resistance—and "racial hygiene."[40] "In August 1943, a gas chamber was constructed in Natzweiler-Struthof" and the bodies of some Jewish prisoners murdered there were shipped "to the Strasbourg University Institute of Anatomy. There, anatomist Dr. August Hirt amassed a large collection of Jewish skeletons in order to establish Jewish 'racial inferiority' by means of anthropological study. The gas chamber was also used in pseudo-scientific medical experiments involving poison gas. The victims of these experiments were primarily Roma (Gypsies) who had been transferred from Auschwitz. Prisoners were also subjected to experiments involving treatment for typhus and yellow fever."[41]

Memoirs and diaries also help to reconstruct the conflation of criminality with disease. Malnutrition, a direct result of Nazi policy, was regarded as a state that had been caused by Jews themselves as an irritant to Nazi rulers. A doctor for concentration camps in the Posen region, Elise Kramer, apprised an apparently reasonable Nazi supervisor of the horrific conditions of prisoners and "he tried to bring about some improvement." He advised Kramer to submit a report on matters of hygiene and nutrition. He offered his support and specified that she state "malnutrition" as the cause in reporting deaths. To Kramer's surprise, malnutrition was somewhat relieved, and forced labor details made less lethal. "The prisoners," she wrote, "thanked me for my help." But some weeks later Kramer herself was arrested. Charged with "sabotage of German work" she was physically threatened and was incarcerated in "wretched conditions."[42]

CONCLUSION

I conclude this chapter with some snapshots from the immediate postwar period to show how Jewish displaced persons (DPs) themselves dealt with matters relating to their physical well-being, law, and order. Historian Atina Grossmann has analyzed the social life of the DPs with particular attention to gender roles and the relations between Jews and Germans. Among the signal images in Grossman's interpretation are Jewish women pushing baby carriages, beaming with pride and satisfaction at having brought a new generation into the world. A great deal of thought and activity was dedicated to making the surviving remnant of Jews healthy and then showing off their hale and hearty state.[43] After 1945 the Jewish DPs—although they were obviously compelled to confront continued physiological and psychological problems—strove to present themselves as preeminently healthful and law-abiding, with their bodily and moral lives largely in harmony. This was realized in numerous depictions of the police forces among the Jewish DPs.

The archive of Jewish persons serving in professional capacities is extensive, and the documentation includes hundreds of images of clinics, hospitals, medical units, and personnel, as well as photographs of Jewish police. There is little to distinguish these portraits from the pictures of any other police force around the world, save perhaps for the Hebrew text and the presence of Jewish symbols in the composition. Yet, they do differ in one important respect: there is an explicit camaraderie between the men, suggested by the way they touch each other. Thus, in a portrait of the Feldafing (DP camp) police, ostensibly from Dachau, where they "had gone to identify SS men for a later war crimes trial," their chief, Erwin Tichauer, has his arms draped around three colleagues, while his hand rests on the shoulder of another. That man has his hand on the shoulder of the man kneeling in front of him. The men include former soldiers in the Greek Army, as well as Jews from Romania and Poland. While the photograph may, of course, simply reflect photographic conventions, the men's pose conveys amity, a mutual pleasure in each other's company, and a gratification with their job. The subjects are sturdy, healthy, and manly.[44]

Most of Nazi officialdom, and German non-Jews in postwar Germany, were aware that Jews were neither 'criminals' nor inherently 'sick.' Even as the Holocaust unfolded, Jews themselves recognized that their patho-criminalization in the ghettos and concentration camps was an act of mass-deception. In the postwar period, with their freedom restored, they published newspapers, played chess and soccer, boxed, and protested what they judged to be both large and small injustices. Some Germans persisted, however, in imagining Jews as "the kind of people they should be rid of."[45] The stigma of Jews as bearers of disease gradually faded, but the criminality canard lingered on—fueled not only by the long history of the association between Jews and criminality, but the fact there were some highly visible black-market 'operators' among the Jews.[46] Grossmann shows, in contrast, that among the areas where Jews and Germans interacted on an especially intimate basis were matters of childcare and health. This may have played some part in the erosion of belief in, or willingness to accept, the axiom of the diseased, criminal Jew.

NOTES

1. For a full context, see Michael Berkowitz, *The Crime of My Very Existence: Nazism and the Myth of Jewish Criminality* (Berkeley: University of California Press, 2007).
2. Peter Fritzsche, *Life and Death in the Third Reich* (Cambridge, MA: Belknap Press of Harvard University Press, 2008).
3. Jeffrey Herf, *The Jewish Enemy: Nazi Propaganda During World War II and the Holocaust* (Cambridge, MA: Belknap Press of Harvard University Press, 2006).
4. Thomas Mann, *The Magic Mountain* [*Der Zauberberg*], trans. Helen T. Lowe-Porter (New York: Vintage, 1969), 454–457.
5. Ibid., 441.
6. Ibid.
7. Marc Weiner, *Richard Wagner and the Anti-Semitic Imagination* (Lincoln: University of Nebraska Press, 1995); Sander Gilman, *The Jew's Body* (New York: Routledge, 1991).
8. Mann, *Magic Mountain*, 440.
9. Thomas Mann, *Buddenbrooks*, trans. Helen T. Lowe-Porter (New York: Vintage, 1984).
10. Ibid., 598.
11. Quoted in Todd Curtis Kontje, *Thomas Mann's World: Empire, Race, and the Jewish Question* (Ann Arbor: University of Michigan Press, 2011), 42.
12. John Galsworthy, *The Forsyte Sage*, vols.1 to 3 (London: Penguin, 2001).
13. Robert Proctor, *The Nazi War on Cancer* (Princeton: Princeton University Press, 2009).
14. Hans G. Adler, *Theresienstadt, 1941–1945. Das Antlitz einter Zwangsgemeinschaft*, 2nd ed. (Tübingen: J. C. B. Mohr (Paul Siebeck), 1960), xxix–lix.
15. Martin Broszat, Helmut Krausnick, and Hans-Adolf Jacobsen, *Anatomy of the SS-State*, trans. Dorothy Long and Marian Jackson (Frogmore, United Kingdom: Palladin, 1968), 146; Colonel Neave Report: Final Report on the Evidence of Witnesses for the Defense of Organizations Alleged to Be Criminal, Heard before a Commission Appointed by the Tribunal Pursuant to Paragraph 4 of the Order of the 13th of Mark, 1946, in *Nuremberg Trial Proceedings*, vol.42, Avalon Project at Yale Law School: http://avalon.law. yale.edu/imt/naeve.asp, 40 (accessed January 28, 2013).
16. This emerged in the pioneering work of Henry Friedlander, *The Origins of the Nazi Genocide: From Euthanasia to the Final Solution* (Chapel Hill: University of North Carolina Press, 1995).
17. Broszat, et al., *Anatomy of the SS-State*, 146; Colonel Neave Report: Final Report on the Evidence of Witnesses for the Defense of Organizations Alleged to Be Criminal, Heard before a Commission Appointed by the Tribunal Pursuant to Paragraph 4 of the Order of the 13th of Mark, 1946, in *Nuremberg Trial Proceedings*, vol.42, Avalon Project at Yale Law School: http://avalon. law.yale.edu/imt/naeve.asp, 40 (accessed January 28, 2013).
18. Saul Friedlander, *Nazi Germany and the Jews: Volume One: The Years of Persecution* (New York: HarperCollins, 1997).

19. George L. Mosse, *Toward the Final Solution: A History of European Racism* (New York: Harper & Row, 1980 [1978]), 225.
20. Christopher Browning, *The Origins of the Final Solution: The Evolution of Nazi Jewish Policy, September 1939–March 1942 (Comprehensive History of the Holocaust)* (Lincoln: University of Nebraska Press, 2004), 431, 461, 151, 162.
21. Hans Safrian, *Eichmann's Men*, trans. Ute Stargardt (Cambridge: Cambridge University Press, 2009), 48, 193.
22. Berkowitz, *The Crime of My Very Existence*, 254, n. 10.
23. See also Dalia Ofer, "Another Glance through the Historian's Lens: Testimonies in the Study of Health and Medicine in the Ghetto," *Poetics Today*, vol.27, no.2 (2006): 331–351.
24. Myron Winick, ed., *Hunger Disease: Studies by the Jewish Physicians in the Warsaw Ghetto*, trans. Martha Osnos (New York: Wiley, 1979).
25. Charles Roland, *Courage Under Siege: Starvation, Disease, and Death in the Warsaw Ghetto* (New York: Oxford University Press, 1992), 38–39, 56.
26. Berkowitz, *The Crime of My Very Existence*, 50–51.
27. Ibid., 53.
28. Boehm, "Introduction," 11; see, also, Grynberg, *Words to Outlive Us*, 43; Berkowitz, *The Crime of My Very Existence*, 54.
29. Sara Bender, *The Jews of Bialystok During World War II and the Holocaust*, trans. Yaffa Murciano (Waltham, MA: Brandeis University Press, 2008), 143.
30. Herf, *The Jewish Enemy*, 17.
31. Quoted in Berkowitz, *The Crime of My Very Existence*, 54.
32. Ibid.
33. Ibid., 55.
34. Ibid., 63–64; Samuel Kassow, *Who Will Write Our History? Emanuel Ringelblum, the Warsaw Ghetto, and the Oyneg Shabes Archive* (Bloomington: Indiana University Press, 2007); Bender, *The Jews of Bialystok*.
35. Ibid., 64.
36. Calel Perechodnik, *Am I a Murderer? Testament of a Jewish Ghetto Policeman*, ed. and trans., Frank Fox (Boulder, CO: Westview, 1996), 29.
37. Ibid., 64–65.
38. Ibid., 74–77.
39. Robert Jan Van Pelt, *The Case for Auschwitz: Evidence from the Irving Trial* (Bloomington: Indiana University Press, 2002), 312, 354, 421.
40. See, Jean Simon, ed., *Le camp de concentration du Struthof. Konzentrationslager Natzweiler. Collection documents-tome III* (Schirmeck, France: Essor, 1998), map opposite 336; Klaus F. Schmidt-Macon, *Aschenspur. Gedichte. Trace de Cendres. Poems* (Wörthsee bei München: Groh, 1988), v; Berkowitz, *The Crime of My Very Existence*, 77–78.
41. Entry for "Natzweiler-Struthof" in *Holocaust Encyclopedia* of the United States Holocaust Memorial Museum: http://www.ushmm.org/wlc/en/article. php?ModuleId=10007260 (accessed February 2, 2013).
42. Elise Kramer, "Hell and Rebirth: My Experiences during the Time of Persecution," RG-02–037, 7, 14–15, United States Holocaust Memorial Museum; Berkowitz, *The Crime of My Very Existence*, 93.
43. Atina Grossmann, *Jews, Germans and Allies: Close Encounters in Occupied Germany* (Princeton: Princeton University Press, 2007).
44. The Feldafing DP Police Force. [photograph]. Reproduced courtesy of Jack Kugleman, pictured at the front right. Desig. No. 322.38305, W/S no. 97112, CD no. 0263, United States Holocaust Memorial Museum; Berkowitz, *The Crime of My Very Existence*, 218.

45. Shmuel Gringauz, "Di psikhologishe wurtseln fun neo-antismitizm: naye vintn alte mitln" ["The Psychological Roots of Neo-Antisemitism: New Winds, Old Means], *Yiddishe Tsaytung*, vol.106, no.38 (May 23, 1947): 5, quoted in Zeev Mankowitz, *Life Between Memory and Hope: Survivors of the Holocaust in Occupied Germany* (Cambridge: Cambridge University Press, 2003), 184; Berkowitz, *The Crime of My Very Existence*, 219.
46. Philip S. Bernstein, "Displaced Persons," in *The American Jewish Year Book, vol. 49, 1947–1948* (New York: American Jewish Committee, 1947), 7.

Part II

5   The "Bad" and the "Sick"
Medicalizing Deviance in China

Børge Bakken

INTRODUCTION: MEDICALIZATION IN CHINA

In China, a wide range of anti-social behaviors are increasingly being reframed as clinical 'disorders' that require specific medical interventions to cure. Stories of 'insatiable desire,' 'addiction,' and 'contagion'—particularly in relation to juvenile behavior—pervade the media. This 'medicalization' may be understood as a form of control: social boundaries are redrawn and policed in the face of 'unwholesome' and destabilizing global influences. The pathologizing of 'deviant' behavior in China, then, has little to do with the technical repair of the body but a lot to do with social, cultural, and political processes.

In this chapter, I explore these processes by investigating the pathologization of Chinese youth behavior in three specific settings. First, I consider the alleged 'disorders' and deviant manners associated with the only child. Second, I examine moral panics in relation to juvenile delinquency, and in particular anxieties linked to the 'wayward girl' in a phenomenon known popularly as 'premature love' (*zaolian*). Third, I outline the emergence of a new deviance in the form of Internet 'addiction.' Indeed, 'Internet Addiction Disorder' (IAD) has become the most significant and concerted recent attempt to medicalize deviance in China. By the late 1990s, a discernible shift had taken place in alarmist stories about youth deviance. While the 'disco' and the 'dance hall' had formerly taken center stage in these stories, increasingly the emphasis in contemporary narratives has shifted to the 'Internet bar' (*wangba*) as a threatening site of contagious criminality.

Although psychiatry continues to be mobilized in China as a tool against dissident views, with political opposition frequently branded as mentally ill, I have chosen not to discuss this issue here, since it belongs to another—albeit related—argument.[1] Recently, a Beijing professor claimed that members of the public who petitioned the state for redress on social issues were, in fact, most likely to be suffering from psychological problems than harboring genuine social grievances. His comments elicited widespread condemnation. Although the professor quickly retracted his statement and apologized for any offense he might have caused, his remarks underscored the extent to which dissent continues to be framed in China primarily as a mental health problem. Politics lurks behind most narratives of deviance in the People's Republic, recalling Howard Becker's remark in *Outsiders: Studies in the Sociology of Deviance* that the labeling of any behavior or action as 'deviant' is necessarily a political matter.[2]

One classic study in the sociology of deviance is Peter Conrad and Joseph W. Schneider's work on the historical transformation of definitions of deviance from 'badness' to 'sickness.'[3] Their insights remain highly relevant to the situation in China, although with certain key modifications when applied to a Chinese context. There, the institutionally weak medical/psychiatric profession and the strong political/ideological discourse has led to a troubling conflation of the 'medical' with the '(im)moral' and the 'criminal.' The 'sick' are conflated with the 'bad,' and 'sickness' is invariably understood as a secondary sign of 'badness.' In this context, Stanley Cohen's concept of 'moral panic' is also suggestive, particularly as it has been developed by Erich Goode and Nachman Ben-Yahuda.[4] Drawing on this body of theoretical work, as well as on my previous research in China, my aim in this chapter is to consider the continuities and discontinuities in attitudes to deviance.[5] On the one hand, novel panics are being understood within a new medico-moralistic discourse, while the Communist era's strong belief in political-ideological correctness and 'exemplary behavior' is being reconfigured and grafted in new ways onto the pan-moralist tradition of ancient China.[6] On the other hand, however, what I have previously termed "super-social norms" or "exemplary norms" continue to shape the discourse of deviance.[7] The central claims-maker and provider of such "exemplary norms" remains the strong Party State and its formidable propaganda machinery.

Becker long ago noted that deviance is the product of what he termed "moral enterprise": that is, the overlapping processes involved in bringing a social issue to the fore, in its labeling as an 'issue,' its formalization in statute, and the subsequent enforcement of the law. 'Deviance' is the product of a complex political negotiation.[8] However, where Becker uses 'political' in the broadest sense of the term to denote government and the social relations that underpin authority, in China the 'political' is directly linked to the policies and apparatuses of the Party State. In other words, 'politics' can be understood in a much narrower, operational sense than in Becker's account. The Propaganda Ministry and its networks together with the Public Security forces actively define deviance as part of a state-sponsored orchestration of moral/political order. Just as the Church had a monopoly in defining morality and immorality in the Western world in the past, in contemporary China deviance is defined by the Party State in a more direct fashion than Becker could have thought possible working in another political and cultural context.

Party-driven moralist discourse thus remains strong in China, as opposed to the 'medicalization' propagated by medical institutions, which has only been moderately successful. While medicalization is predicated on the development (and power) of medical institutions, the medical profession itself does not have an independent role in China, thereby restricting any capacity health professionals might have to function as moral advocates. To be sure, the medical profession is sometimes at odds with the Party State and its definitions of deviance as illness. Some years ago, I interviewed a petitioner in Beijing who had been an activist lobbying against the widespread practice of tearing down houses in the *hutong* (alleys comprised of traditional courtyard residences) in Beijing. She had been arrested by the police on several occasions as a consequence of her protests. The police regularly sent her to a psychiatric hospital and asked the doctors there to 'cure' her of her 'delusions.' Although the doctors disapproved of this practice, they were compelled to admit her and prescribe her 'medicine' since the police had brought her in, even though they were unable to find anything wrong with her. Thus, while the medical profession may not have the same status as 'moral entrepreneur' in China today as it has had in the Western world over the last decades, it does not always play on the same side as power, even if there are numerous counter-examples of cooperation.

The 'medicalizing' drive in China is being led by forces outside the medical establishment. The leading protagonist crusading against IAD, for example, Dr. Tao Ran, wears a military uniform. Boot camps (or 'reboot' camps as they have been termed abroad) are often leased out by the People's Liberation Army, eager to cash in on the big sums paid by anxious parents to have their offspring 'cured' of Internet addiction. While the Party State lurks behind the scene and still dominates the role of the crusading reformer, commercial interests are increasingly exploiting these anxieties for their own benefits. The treatment of deviance and addiction is now big business in China through the boot camp regime. In short, the nature of socially constructed deviance designations in China follows a pattern related to the increased official propaganda of social order and 'harmonious society' (*hexie shehui*).

Social stability and order have been closely linked to illness metaphors in the sociological literature. In *The Social System*, for example, Talcott Parsons points out that both 'crime' and 'illness' function as different forms of deviance, which threatens the social system.[9] According to Parsons, different mechanisms of social control should be implemented to deal with these two different forms of deviance: one *willful*, the other *unwillful*. In China, however, illness and crime are conflated so that any distinction between the 'willful' and 'unwillful' has been lost in the climate of moral crusade. In the pages that follow, my aim is to show how 'badness' has become inseparable from 'sickness,' with the consequence that moralized and medicalized narratives go very much hand in hand. 'Medicine,' even when administered as electroshocks, has become an 'appropriate' method of social control for the 'bad,' as well as the 'sick.' It may be appropriate, in this context, to speak of a 'medical socialization' or perhaps even of a 'social engineering' linked to moral notions of what I have elsewhere termed "exemplarity."[10]

THE DEVIANT ONLY CHILD OR DEVIANCE BY MAJORITY

The cohorts of 'only' children have come to dominate China today. In the cities, children seldom have siblings. Economic modernization and the one-child policy followed each other closely from the start. Only children, however, even if this policy was prescribed by the Communist Party itself, were frequently referred to as 'problem children' (*wenti ertong*).[11] China suddenly found itself experiencing the deviance of a majority. And the majority became the object of a paradoxical moral panic about the only child—paradoxical, because the one-child policy has been official state and party policy.

The moralizing and medicalizing agenda was conspicuous from the start of the one-child policy. The policy created a form of modern moral panic since the prevailing traditional code in China was to have male descendants. With a one-child policy, the chances of achieving this aim were drastically reduced. The start of the reforms triggered a social prejudice against the only child, and early Western medical panics about the only child soon became the vocabulary of medicalized deviance in China. American psychologist Granville Stanley Hall (1844–1924) became a favorite for quotations on the only child in China. Particularly popular was his notion that "being an only child is a disease in itself."[12] Psychiatrist Abraham Arden Brill (1874–1948) became another unlikely crusader against only children in China a century later. His most frequently quoted punch line was: "It would be best for the individual as well as the race that there should be no only children."[13]

A history of only-child prejudice originating in Europe and the US re-emerged in China in the 1980s and 1990s. The reason for such prejudice stemmed from the only child's symbolic representation as a 'modern danger' rather than from the child's actual behavior. The only child became representative of the threats posed by modern deviance in China as it had in Western countries in the past where such children became linked to panic induced by the perceived 'dangers of modernity.' The only child was also an upper-class novelty, and class thus played a part in the process of only-child prejudice and scapegoating, creating myths that we still struggle with today.[14]

Western stereotypes stemming from the nineteenth and early twentieth centuries were formed in a period of strong tension between the traditional and the modern within society. The long list of alleged only-child defects was repeated with the zeal of a true moral entrepreneur. As one Western commentator noted in 1928:

> Because of the undue attention he demands and usually receives, we commonly find the only child jealous, selfish, egotistical, dependent, aggressive, domineering and quarrelsome.[15]

The Chinese equivalent was to brand the only children 'little emperors' (*xiao huangdi*) and 'little princesses' (*xiao gongzhu*) because of their alleged selfish and demanding behavior. A whole literature of prejudice developed in China during the 1980s in the wake of the only-child policy. An extreme emphasis on moral and social order defined tales of disorderly only children. Some of the 'findings' detailed in a series of biased 'research reports' purported to demonstrate that the onlies were "selfish, individualist, hyper-critical, self-centered, and dependent"; that they "lacked cooperative character"; and that they evinced "laziness, willfulness and carelessness." They were deemed to be "without scruples" (*wusuo guji*), suffered from "insatiable desires," and were "unsociable and eccentric" just to mention a few of their failings.[16] Even the party's own theoretical journal added to the moral panic by insisting that the onlies were "pampered, arrogant, and selfish."[17] A report from the early 1990s contended that the only child showed far more undesirable behavior than the non-onlies. More than 70 percent of the only children were "picky about food" compared to less than 30 percent of non-onlies. Sixty-five percent of the onlies were "wilful" compared to only 20 percent of the non-onlies, and the onlies were much more likely to "not show respect for parents and to tell lies." The survey conceded, however, that all groups—only children as well as non-only children—had shown a marked deterioration in their behavior between 1980 and 1991.[18]

Yang Chengpu, in an article published in 1988, exemplified the moral argument when he summed up the perceived "dangers" posed by the only child. His list of "evils" among onlies resembles Hall and Brill's "early warning signals" from the turn of the century: "All the weaknesses in psychology and behavior among only children can already basically be described as an 'epidemic disease' (*liuxing bing*)."[19] Such surveys lay claim to an irrefutable scientific authority, framing behavior in terms of an 'epidemic disease,' and thereby rendering the social in terms of biology and pathology. Although the old psychoanalytic attacks on only children and their denigration in popular Chinese stereotypes have time and again been refuted, it is one of the characteristics of stereotypes to resist counter-evidence by tapping into deep-rooted prejudices and fears.[20] On popular beliefs and stereotypes about only children, Judith Blake has noted:

> [T]he fact that only children have been found, in study after study, to be intellectually advantaged, does not bear on the popular belief that singletons are 'spoiled,' maladjusted, asocial, lonely, and self-centred ... No evidence supports such popular stereotypes.[21]

Toni Falbo and Denise Polit, in their analysis of the research literature on the only child systematized results about achievement, adjustment, character, intelligence, parent-child relationships, and sociability. From their analysis of the literature spanning several decades, they concluded:

> [T]he results ... contradict the theoretical notions that only children are deprived or unique. In achievement, intelligence, and character, only borns excelled beyond their peers with siblings ... Furthermore,

across five developmental outcomes, only children never differed significantly from firstborns or people from two-child families.[22]

Fieldwork in China some years later confirmed the findings from the meta-analysis.[23] Only children did not differ significantly from families with multiple siblings. Comparative representative samples from Changchun and Beijing

> indicated that the only-child advantages in achievement were found among children from urban families, not rural peasant families. While significant differences . . . were found in all three samples . . . [n]one of the analyses indicated that only children had undesirable personalities, as judged by teachers and mothers.[24]

Chinese research reports soon came up with similar findings, while the leading universities had been telling the true story as early as the 1980s to more or less no avail. As the Sociology Department of Beijing University, for example, reported in a survey of Hubei in 1984: "The ingrained belief that the offspring of one-child families are pampered and behave like little emperors is naïve, if not prejudiced."[25] In another study, Mao Yuyan, comparing onlies and non-onlies, concluded: "[T]here were no significant differences in adaptive behaviour between these two groups of children."[26]

The 'spoiled only child' is a cultural truism found in the West, as well as in China. The moral crusaders against this novel 'danger of modernity' claimed 'sickness' all over the line when they described the only child. It could be argued that these truisms stem from a 'solidarity of prejudice' since in China there is no welfare system to support the elderly, other than having (male) offspring. The preferences for multiple children was particularly strong in China during the 1980s, but has prevailed throughout the era of modernization.[27]

In short, we need to see such 'cultural truisms' in their historical and socio-cultural contexts to understand norms of prejudice and stereotyping processes. Today, repeated reproduction is still considered a 'moral imperative,' even in countries such as the US, although less so in Europe. In the US, the ideal family size remained two to four children as late as the 1970s. In China, non-reproduction persists in being regarded as a social sin.[28] The regime may have succeeded to some degree in reducing family size preferences, but this trend is considerably more developed in modern cities than in the traditional countryside, where the one-child policy was never implemented in the same manner as in the cities. The countryside has often had a two-child policy, and for some groups like national minorities, even a multiple-child policy.

In the perception of danger and the moral panics that they generated, then, there is a rational core. The only child poses a social threat and upsets the certainties of the past. Onlies prompt a range of different but entangled

moral panics which reflect anxieties about the loss of parental authority, departure from collective solidarity, blatant individualism, new and
excessive consumer patterns, and generally bodily and social imbalance.
The only child threatens to rupture social bonds and thus calls for the re-
imposition of order and for the prescription of a 'treatment' to deal with the
'dis-order.' In China, the answer to the dilemma of the only child has been
an official moral crusade that seeks to enforce the (re)education of parents
and only children alike, with a view to strengthening their personal 'quality' (*suzhi*). The only child has become part of a policy of 'parading evil'
in order to counter the unintended consequences of modernity. A whole
campaign against 'spiritual pollution' (*jingshen wuran*) was launched in
the 1980s, even though the 'pollution' embodied in the only child was itself
a product of party policy. The 'majority deviance' of the only child still
prevails in China today.

'BOUNDARY CRISIS': THE DEVIANCE OF
'PREMATURE LOVE' (*ZAOLIAN*)

The term 'premature love,' or *zaolian* in Chinese, designates what Western
scholars have termed the '"kicking in' of the biologically romantic based
attachment systems" during puberty with the onset of female menarche
and the production of sex hormones among boys, something that generally
starts earlier in modernizing societies.[29] This has often led to moral panic
among Chinese parents. I have formerly ascribed such phenomena, and the
moral panics they trigger, to the perceived 'dangers of modernity' on the
part the older generations. In China, recent decades have seen increasing
medicalized moral panics surrounding such phenomena. The differences I
can discern from the former moral panics in this regard are relatively small.
The alarmist language from the 1980s and 1990s continues to be used in
the literature.

I have previously noted how, during the 1980s and 1990s, there was
a marked tendency to medicalize 'premature love.'[30] In many ways, these
medico-moral descriptions coincided with similar descriptions of the only
child, but here the moral crusaders' attack was in particular directed against
the 'wayward girl.' This moral crusade stressed the connection between
the 'first love' (*chulian*) and a series of progressive 'dis-orders' that ended
with complete social breakdown. The 'first time' thus became a symbol
of the initial transgression of social borders. The medico-moral discourse
which identified the 'sexual disorder' of 'premature love' or puppy love as
a quasi-clinical condition, concentrated on 'purity and chastity,' defending
traditional morality in a rapidly changing and modernizing society. The
physical body was seen as threatened by uncontrollable forces, thus putting
society at large in peril. Kai Theodor Erikson in his analysis of deviance in
seventeenth-century Puritan America, stressed the 'boundary crisis' which

'wayward puritans' precipitated in seventeenth-century America.[31] In a similar way, the 'premature love' of the so-called 'wayward girl' reflects a similar 'boundary crisis.' Defending the primary social boundaries against the rapid erosion caused by modernization, 'exemplary' norms and categories ('normality' and 'abnormality') are articulated as a means of defending society from the corrosive practices of youthful romantic love. 'Disorderly sexuality' becomes a symbol of the threat to collective identity in China in the wake of the shock effect of the modernization program started in the late 1970s and early 1980s. Sexuality is increasingly subsumed within a scientific (and often pseudo-scientific) discourse of medicine and psychology, and criminology as a discourse of power, human improvement, and purification. 'Premature love' is viewed as debasing humanity and obstructing the creation of a new 'spiritual and material civilization'—at least, according to the official propaganda.

While traditionally having a boyfriend was seen as shameful and embarrassing, even illegal, 14-year-old girls and boys now regarded it as something to boast about. "The more it was prohibited, the more it spread," declared the anti-premature love manuals of the 1980s.[32] The term 'sexual disorder' (*xingluan*) was used to describe a wide range of activities, from the innocent 'talk of love' (*tan lianai*) among juveniles to sexual deviance and sexual crime. As late as October 1991, when I was working as a research fellow in Beijing, Beijing Normal University decided to ban hugging and kissing on campus. A system of warnings and fines was introduced to make the regulation effective.

Medical reports of the 'premature lover' became common. In particular, the 'truth' that premature lovers were particularly weak students became one of the truisms of the times. There was a close connection between 'early love affairs,' school results, and 'moral quality' according to such reports.[33] According to the Chinese police authorities, there was even a "clear indication" that young love was a direct *cause* of crime. One central police document claimed that "premature love is a very important factor in bringing about criminal activities in secondary school children." These allegations were based on a (not so representative) survey showing that among 33 students involved in premature love, 31 were also involved in criminal activities. In contrast, a control group of 300 students not involved in early love affairs had only two offenders among their ranks.[34] That the 'wayward girl' became the focus of the attacks on premature love is illustrated by the inmate numbers of one detention center. While only 10 percent of the boys had been arrested for 'sexual crime' (*xing fanzui*), as many as 95 percent of the girls were there because of 'sexual crime.'[35] Statistical material from the whole country in 1988 showed that as much as 90 percent of all crime among young girls was defined as 'sexual criminal offences' (*xing zuicuo*).[36] There is less tolerance for girls transgressing social and moral boundaries. This is the case in China as it is in the West. A Swedish researcher, Gustav Jonsson, basing his conclusions on a survey of Swedish juvenile correction institutions, reminds us that there are 'sex-girls' but no 'sex-boys' in this regard.[37]

In one description of the girls who were incarcerated for 'sexual crimes,' we read that 72 percent are prone to 'insatiable desires' (*tanyu*) for food, clothes, luxury items, and sex. 'Unrestrained individualism' was displayed by a strong tendency to 'become visible' or 'manifest oneself' (*xianlu ziji*). Such 'self parading' and extrovert activity was unfitting for a girl.[38] The report further noted that "extreme egoism, unrestrained squandering, pleasure seeking, and sexual freedom [are the catalysts of] hooligan crime." The standard expression *chi-he-wan-le* [to eat, drink, and have fun] became almost obligatory in descriptions of sexual crime.[39]

The medical crusaders diagnosed medical disorders in the early and too frequent lovers. For persons who suffer from 'sexual hyper-function' (*xingkangjin de ren*) and 'sexual addiction' (*xingpi de ren*), psychological and medical treatment should be applied. Medical treatment is needed to regulate sex hormones in order to transform the deviants' "defective mental structure" and rectify their "evil individuality."[40] 'Sickness' and 'badness' go hand in hand, being invariably discussed in the same fashion —with the same remedies required—the message here being that medicine is a tool in the fight against evil. By the same token, criminology reiterated the pathological precondition of crime. "An unhealthy sexual psychology" is listed as one of the "major, objective factors leading to crime." One researcher claims that premature love causes crime and that early love affairs cause endocrinopathy, or 'internal secretion disorder' (*neifenmi shitiao*) that again leads to "violent physical impulses in the form of sexual hyperfunction" which in turn leads to social disorder.[41] It all sounds like a take on Confucius's *Analects* with a medicalized twist.

The dance hall and the disco are seen as the major sites of this pathological 'vice.' The independent and sexually active girl is portrayed as a dangerous criminal, and the dance halls are depicted as 'temples of evil.' A genre of moralizing, cautionary tale in youth magazines and educational publications of the 1980s and 1990s centered on 'fallen' teenage girls and invariably begins at the dance halls, concluding with the girl's loss of virginity and self-respect, crime, and prostitution. The moral double standard was evident in the fact that young girls became the primary target of attack. Tales of the 'early lover' extolled passivity, dependence, and submission as appropriate behavior for girls more than for boys. Early love is, in addition, associated with a 'psychology of defiance' found in children. According to one comment, "[I]f this psychology of defiance among the young is allowed to spread, it can even lead to setbacks in the national economy and social civilization."[42] In traditional Chinese literature and folk beliefs, the independent girl was often portrayed as an evil 'fox spirit' or *huli jing*. She now appears in the guise of a new 'folk devil' and the target of a moral panic.[43]

Today, the basic 'problem' of premature love is still very much evident in China, although the medical narrative has seen some recent modifications. One change in focus has been the warnings in the medico-moral literature against the danger posed by food hormones. Such hormones can cause early puberty according to some researchers, leading even primary school children to show interests in the opposite sex prematurely.[44] Thus, the debate on premature love has gone hand in hand with food scares recently occurring in China. Such scares include the tainted milk scandal which received global coverage. Baby milk powder produced by the Chinese milk giant Sanlu was found to be contaminated with the chemical tripolycyanamide, leading to infant deaths all over China. The case led to the subsequent conviction and execution of the person found ultimately responsible for the matter. The Sanlu milk scandal was preceded by similar incidents. In 2004, 13 babies in Eastern China died after they were fed milk made with powder that contained little of nutritional value. That incident was known as the "big headed babies" scandal because the malnourished children developed swollen heads.[45] It is interesting to see how one scare has triggered a further scare and how premature love has become entangled with medical concerns about contaminated food. Fear is still part of the rationale and the basis of moral panics.

The age issue has also become increasingly emphasized by recent research in China. Clearly, the age of *zaolian* or premature love has now extended, and there is currently as much talk of primary school students (6–12 year olds) as there is of juvenile 'bad' or 'sick' romantic and sexual practices.[46] Some of the explanations are not directly medicalized but lead us to other moral panic sites like the Internet. Primary school teacher Liu Juan, for example, notes that Internet horoscope love matching has become enormously popular among her students.[47]

Cautionary tales about premature love that I noted in the literature in the 1980s and 1990s still prevail. There is an abundance of stories about innocent girls who begin by falling in love but who then suffer the horrible consequences of "losing their bod[ies]" and falling into a life of misery and crime because of this.[48] However, although exaggerated medical concerns about the practices of *zaolian* are still being articulated, these concerns are now being contradicted and dismissed in public by the voices of other researchers and teachers. Such critics have drawn attention to the labeling processes, assumptions, and prejudices that shaped the premature love panics in the 1980s and 1990s. Some Chinese observers point out that alarmist teachers and parents may mistake normal friendship relations for premature love affairs. They simply misinterpret normal behavior in the light of alarmist stories about premature love.[49]

Another new trend among psychologists is to point out that premature love may be a symptom of dysfunctional families rather than deploying the 'badness' or 'sickness' labels attached to the young in the past. It has been found that adolescents experiencing poor parent-child relationships are more likely to engage in premature love.[50] This finding is in line with Trent Bax's research concerning the causes of so-called 'Internet addiction.'[51] Bax argues that the medicalization of Internet use as IAD is a result of failed family relations and an escape from authoritarian family structures. Bax's notion of the 'family war-machine' find its 'premature love' equivalent in the interviews of parents about premature love conducted by Zou Daipeng in 2004. One of the parents interviewed by Zou employs exactly the same expressions of 'spiritual opium' about premature love as the boot camp protagonists of Internet addiction use to describe that alleged 'disorder.' Mr. Gao, one of the interviewees and a father of a girl practicing 'premature love,' declares:

> Premature love is spiritual opium (*jingshen yapian*). I'd rather prefer my child to hate me for a short period of time than her regretting (her deeds of premature love) for the rest of her life.[52]

At the same time, there are novel voices emphasizing the positive side of premature love. Some claim that a relationship between boys and girls can improve their motivation and study results.[53] Some students even report that their teachers encourage couples to work together to improve study results, underlining the positive effects of youth relationships.[54] Other commentators attack the school authorities for imposing fines on students who have love affairs and for using the secondary school code of conduct to ban such relationships, advising teachers to gain students' trust instead of punishing them.[55,56] Finally, a professor at Zhongshan University in Guangzhou, Qiao Xinsheng, has criticized schools and parents for their overprotection, control, and surveillance of youths and children, suggesting such 'slave mentality' (*nüxing*) should be abolished completely.[57] Instead of the moral crusade against premature love, he suggests that the re-education of parents and teachers should be the first step to handling premature love. As Qiao concludes, depriving children of the right to love and the freedom to make friendships with the opposite sex bodes ill for the future of China.

'INTERNET ADDICTION' AND IAD

One entirely new development in the field of deviance compared with the 1980s and 1990s is the introduction of the Internet in China and the perceived disorders that it has brought to the country. The moral crusaders have rallied to this field, and it has become the center of the debate on deviance and modern dangers in contemporary China. Internet use is a part of the modern society of consumption and communication technology, and China is now rapidly moving into the number one spot in the world in terms of numbers of Internet users, surpassing the US. The latest figures suggest a Chinese Internet population of around 380 million people. It is still a fairly urban and youthful phenomenon, although this is also about to change. Around 60 percent of the 380 million Internet users in China at the end of 2009 were aged between 10 and 29, which means that about 228 million of the altogether 375 million or so aged between 10 and 29 years in China are getting online. In 2009, 175 million, or 51.8 percent of all Internet users, were teenagers, while 28.8 percent of this 380 million were students.[58] Mobile Internet users increased from 117 million in December 2008 to 233 million in December of 2009.[59] CNNIC's 24th report points out that mobile Internet use is not merely a useful portable electronic tool but has now become a symbol of fashion and an integral part of popular culture.

This part of popular culture, however, has become the breeding ground for another moral panic and another field of medicalized moral crusade against social disorder. The same alarmist medical metaphors apply to Internet addiction as we have seen applied to the only child and the 'premature lover.' Bax has shown that the Internet addict is now described as being "poisoned by" or "intoxicated with" Internet games. Or the youngsters simply possess an "insatiable desire for" play. Metaphors of pollution also show up in this new narrative of Internet addiction. According to Wu and Zhang, having weak self-control over this new modern technology causes youths to suffer from "information pollution," and therefore they waste "their 'golden time' and 'precious youth.'"[60]

In contrast to the medicalized tales of the only child, the issue of crime is more closely linked to the new disorder of IAD. A recent unverified report from the Public Security Police claimed that as much as 76 percent of juvenile criminals in the People's Republic of China have Internet addiction or *some kind of relation* with the Internet.[61] The underlying assumption is that the content and structure of so-called violent video games 'teaches' the gamer to fight, steal, and kill, and as a result the gamers' moral system and moral judgment dissolves under the constant exposure to, and proficiency toward, virtual violence.[62] In the fight against such deviance, there are now medical professionals prescribing drugs as well as electroshocks against the new deviant, the 'Internet addict.'

There is, however, clear opposition to the pseudo-scientific medicalized moral crusade aimed at the deviant 'Internet addict.' In his thorough discussion of the battle around IAD, Bax distinguishes between the moral crusader Tao Ran, contrasting this camp to the much more humanistic and sociologically informed camp around Tao Yongkai. The medical and moral crusader Tao Ran bases some of his ideas on the American IAD activist Kimberly Young, and Bax terms this camp the Young-Tao model of claims-making. While Tao Ran has been advocating—using the Internet addiction concept—a psychiatric-based medicalized discourse for framing the problem, Tao Hongkai has been arguing that what China is facing is a set of societal problems, in particular a problematic education system and counter-productive parenting.[63] In China, the moral crusaders against alleged Internet addiction are contradicted by a well-articulated opposition. This is a new and hopeful development in the People's Republic, although the picture is still one of constant pressure exerted by a moral-political crusading.

International viewpoints, however, make the argument of the moral cru-saders somewhat more complicated. According to the American Psychiatric Association's latest *Diagnostic and Statistical Manual* (DSM-IV), neither deviant behavior nor conflicts that are primarily between the individual and society are mental disorders, such as 'Internet addiction' or 'sexual addiction' unless the deviance or conflict is a symptom of a dysfunction in the individual.[64] Many of the moral panics launched in China over the last 30 years, however, have done just that: interpreted conflicts between the individual and society as mental and individual disorders. Perhaps the new moral crusade against IAD has been the clearest distortion of such interna-tional definitions of medical disorders.

CONCLUSION

Today, as in the 1980s and 1990s, the Party State in China still massively dominates the moral crusade against a range of social behaviors. The pseu-do-medical claims are still there as they were at the outset of the reforms, framing such behavior as pathological and criminal. To be sure, there are more liberal voices present today, and there is an intellectual opposition against the old order, particularly in the case of premature love and Inter-net addiction. And while the truisms of deviance and prejudice held against the only child persist, changes seem to be coming in that area as well, pos-sibly altering the strict policy of only-child families in the cities. Despite this, however, the culture of prejudice against onlies is set to remain. As for the Internet addict, there is vocal opposition to the practices of the military style Tao Rong approach of boot camps and pseudo-medical procedures.

As I have sought to argue in this chapter, in many ways the moral panic in China reflects a more general panic about youth in a modernizing society. The 'anti-crime campaigns' (*yanda*) against alleged juvenile gangs in 1983 were probably among the biggest moral panics about youth experienced anywhere during the last century. China's shifting demography explains part of this phenomenon, another explanation resides in latent fears of 'Western pollution' and in the concomitant need to preserve and police China's moral and cultural boundaries in a period of rapid liberalization and globalization. In the decade or so between 1975 and 1987, the number of young people between 14 and 24 years of age increased from about 170 millions to over 270 millions. This young population is set to decrease to about 150 millions by 2020, and it will be interesting to see if this demo-graphical reversal will ease the moral panics against young people (in com-bination with a more modern and less crusading regime of politics) and whether there will be a moral panic and discrimination directed against a more visible and expanding category: namely, the elderly.[65]

The pseudo-scientific tools of the Chinese moral crusaders against devi-ance have been highly politicized, and turned much more directly political than ever anticipated by Becker's observations in the early 1960s. The medical profession, however, has been less independent and less powerful than in the Western examples, and the state and the party has a virtual monopoly when it comes to claims-making, leading the moral crusades with a tight hand through its organizations of propaganda.

The distinctions between Conrad and Schneider's 'badness' versus 'sickness' and Parson's distinction between 'willful' and the 'unwillful' deviance seem to be muddled in the often centralized quest for order. The reactions against the 'dangers of modernity' can undoubtedly be described in Cohen's language of moral panic, and such panics do come from below as well as from the elite. To borrow an expression coined by Goode and Ben-Yahuda, the moral panics we have seen in China during the period of modernization have been *elite engendered moral panics* with a resonance in the *laobaixing*—the so-called 100 names—or the common man and woman in China.[66]

The moral crusaders might have popular backing, but in the last instance, these are state and party engendered elite crusades aimed at achieving social and political order, or in the present language of party propaganda, to maintain the 'harmonious society' (*hexie shehui*). The moral crusades are about the same type of boundary crisis described by Erikson in his account of Puritan America and concern the redrawing of social boundaries in an era of rapid modernization. One might here employ Mary Douglas's distinction between 'purity' and 'danger.'[67] In particular, the metaphor of 'pollution' is pervasive in the ideological-political construction of deviance in contemporary China. There was even a centrally led political campaign—or *yundong*—against 'spiritual pollution,' introducing the topic on a nationwide political level in the 1980s.[68] A lot of that campaign was directed against perceived threats of modern deviance. The party is rallying support against the 'moral dangers' brought about by the forces of modernity threatening the stability of their power. Thus, following Erikson, we might say that the powerful crusaders are rallying to safeguard their boundaries of power, managing China's ongoing 'boundary crisis.' These pictures of deviance and deviance control are strictly political in character. They are ultimately addressing the issue Marx and Engels described in the *Communist Manifesto* when they remarked that "Modern bourgeois society . . . is like the sorcerer, who is no longer able to control the powers of the nether world whom he has called up by his spells."[69]

Paradoxically, the Communist Party is now in the same situation as the modern bourgeois society was when Marx and Engels wrote the *Manifesto*. The Chinese program of modernization can be described as an attempt to manage the direction and pace of modernity. Yet, the regime is torn between two contrary impulses: to put brakes on the runaway engine and to let it run and exploit the benefits of global capital. The moral crusades and moral panics that characterize China's reform era are ultimately about another sociological issue than deviance as such—social control and power.

NOTES

1. Robin Munro, *China's Psychiatric Inquisition: Dissent, Psychiatry and the Law in Post-1949 China* (Hong Kong: Simmonds & Hill Publishing, 2007).
2. Howard S. Becker, *Outsiders: Studies in the Sociology of Deviance* (New York: The Free Press of Glencoe, 1963), 7.
3. Peter Conrad and Joseph W. Schneider, *Deviance and Medicalization: From Badness to Sickness* (Philadelphia: Temple University Press, 1992).
4. See Stanley Cohen, *Folk Devils and Moral Panics* (Oxford: Martin Robertson, 1980); and Erich Goode and Nachman Ben-Yahuda, *Moral Panics: The Social Construction of Deviance*, 2nd ed. (Chichester, UK: Wiley-Blackwell, 2009).
5. Børge Bakken, "Prejudice and Danger: The Only Child in China," *Childhood*, vol.1, no.1 (1993): 46–61; and Børge Bakken, *The Exemplary Society: Human Improvement, Social Control, and the Dangers of Modernity in China* (Oxford: Oxford University Press, 2000).
6. Bakken, *The Exemplary Society*.
7. Ibid., 26–27.
8. Becker, *Outsiders*, 162.
9. Talcott Parsons, *The Social System* (New York: The Free Press, 1951), 428–479.
10. Bakken, *The Exemplary Society*.
11. Xin Yang, ed., *Zhongguo banzhurenxue* [*Chinese Class Teacher Studies*] (Changchun: Jilin jiaoyu chubanshe, 1990), 256.
12. Norman Fenton, "The Only Child," *The Pedagogical Seminary and Journal of Genetic Psychology*, vol. 35 (1928): 546–556; *Jiaoyu da cidian* [*Encyclopedia of Education*] (Shanghai: Shanghai jiaoyu chubanshe, 1990), 172; and Xin, *Zhongguo banzhurenxue*, 255–256.
13. Abraham A. Brill, *Psychoanalysis: Its Theories and Practical Applications* (Philadelphia: Saunders, 1917 [1912]), 288.
14. Bakken, "Prejudice and Danger."
15. Fenton, "The Only Child," 547.
16. Zhou Lishun, "Dusheng zinü jiaoyu zhong jiedai jiejue de wenti" ["Pressing Problems in the Education of Only-Children"], *Shanghai jiaoyu keyan*, no.4 (1988): 55–56; and Yang Chengpu, "Dusheng zinü de xianzhuang ji jiaoyu duice" ["The Present Situation among Only-Children and Its Educational Countermeasures"], *Rensheng*, no.7 (1988): 3–5.
17. Deng Hongxun, "You'er jiaoyu shi peiyang yi ge xinren de diaoni gongcheng" ["Infant Education Is the Important Project of Fostering a New Person"], *Hongqi* (1987): 30–33.
18. Shanghai shi ertong jiaoyu yanjiu shi [Shanghai Municipality Office for Child Education Research], "Tantan dusheng zinü de jiating jiaoyu" ["Discussing the Family Education of Only-Children"], *Zhongguo funü* [*Chinese Women*], no. 5 (1980): 16–17; and Wang Caiping et al., "Jiu dusheng ertong xingwei wenti tan yousheng youyu" ["Discussing Good Pre-Natal Education with Regard to Behavioural Problems among Only-Children"], *Renkou yanjiu* [*Population Research*], no.2 (1991): 47–50.
19. Yang, "Dusheng zinü de xuanzhuang ji jiaoyu duice."
20. Judith Blake, *Family Size and Achievement* (Berkeley: University of California Press, 1989).
21. Ibid., 46.
22. Toni Falbo and Denise F. Polit, "Quantitative Review of the Only Child Literature: Research Evidence and Theory Development," *Psychological Bulletin*, vol.100, no.2 (1986): 176–89.

23. Toni Falbo, Dudley L. Poston, G. Ji, S. Jiao, Q. Jing, S. Wang, et al., "Physical Achievement and Personality Characteristics of Chinese Children," *Journal of Biosocial Science*, vol.21, no.4 (1989): 483–496; and Dudley L. Jr. Poston and Tony Falbo, "Academic Performance and Personality Traits of Chinese Children: 'Onlies' versus Others," *American Journal of Sociology*, vol.96, no.2 (1990): 433–451.

24. Falbo, et al., "Physical Achievement," 483.

25. Wan Chuanwen, Fan Cunren, and Lin Guobin, "Wu sui dao qi sui dusheng he fan dusheng zinü moxie gexing tezheng de bijiao ji xingbie chadao de yanjiu" ["A Comparative Study on Certain Differences between Five to Seven Year Old Onlies and Non-Onlies"], *Xinli xuebao*, no.4 (1984): 383–391.

26. Mao Yuyan, "Dushengzi yu fan dushengzi zai ruyuan shiying fangmian de bijiao yanjiu" ["A Comparative Study of the Adaptive Behaviour Between the Only-Child and the Non-Only Child"], *Xinli xuebao*, no.3 (1984): 240–249.

27. Martin King Whyte and S. Z. Gu, "Popular Response to China's Fertility Transition," *Population and Development Review*, vol.13, no.3 (1987): 569–571.

28. Li Yanfeng, "Dusheng zinü de 'du'" ["'Only' as in Only-Child"], *Shidai*, no.6 (1988): 21.

29. Reed W. Larson, Gerald L. Clore, and Gretchen A. Wood, "The Emotions of Romantic Relationships: Do They Wreak Havoc on Adolescents?" in *The Development of Romantic Relationships in Adolescence*, ed. Wyndol Furman, Bradford Brown, and Candice Feiring (Cambridge: Cambridge University Press, 1999), 24.

30. Bakken, *The Exemplary Society*, 354–376.

31. Kai T. Erikson, *Wayward Puritans: A Study in the Sociology of Deviance* (New York: John Wiley, 1966).

32. Xin, *Zhongguo banzhuren xue*; Ding Yu, "Tantan ruhe zhengque chuli zhongxuesheng 'zaolian' de wenti" ["On How to Handle Correctly the Problem of 'Premature Love' among Secondary School Pupils"], *Renmin jiaoyu*, no.3 (1988): 21.

33. Wang Xiaoling, "Zhongxuesheng lianai qingkuang de diaocha" ["An Investigation of the Situation of Love Affairs among Secondary School Pupils"], *Shanghai jiaoyu*, no.2 (1986): 12.

34. Li Guofang, "Guanyu zaolian yu zhongxuesheng weifa fanzui de diaocha" ["An Investigation of Premature Love and Crime among Secondary School Students"], in *Zhongguo qingshaonian fanzui yanjiu* [*Yearbook of Chinese Juvenile Delinquency Studies*] (Beijing: Chunqiu chubanshe, 1988), 212.

35. Yuan Jinhua, "Qingshaonian fanzui yu xuexiao jiaoyu de guanxi de diaocha" ["Survey on the Connection between Juvenile Crime and School Education"], *Jiaoyu yanjiu*, no.11 (1986): 4.

36. Cao Manzhi, ed., *Zhongguo qingshaonian fanzuixue* [*The Criminology of Chinese Juvenile Delinquency*] (Beijing: Qunzhong chubanshe, 1988), 261.

37. Gustav Jonsson, *Flickor på glid: en studie i kvinnoförtryck* [*Slipping Girls: A Study in the Oppression of Women*] (Borås: Tiden Folksam, 1977), 39.

38. Zhang Jian and Zhang Wenbang, "Dui Zhejiang sheng nü fanzui fuxing qijian de tuanhuo huodong fenxi" ["Analysis of the Gang Activities of Female Prisoners in Zhejiang Province during the Period of Incarceration"], in *Zhongguo qingshaonian fanzui yanjiu nainajian 1987* (Beijing: Chunqiu chubansje, 1988), 414.

39. Shao Daosheng, *Dangdai shehui de bingtai xinli* [*The Morbid Psychology of Today's Society*] (Beijing: Shehui kexue wenxian chubanshe, 1990), 238.

40. Zheng Yunzhen, "Xing fanzui nü qingshaonian de gexing pianqing he tiaozheng" ["Individual Character Deviation and the Correction of Young Sexual Criminal Girls"], *Jiaoyu lilun yu shijian*, no.1 (1986): 61–63.

41. Zhonghua renmin gongheguo gonganb [The PRC Ministry of Public Security], "Zhongguo qingshaonian fanzui de qushi he yufang" ["Trends of Chinese Juvenile Crime in China and Their Prevention"], in *Zhongguo qingshaonian fanzui yanjiu nianjian 1987* [*Yearbook of Chinese Juvenile Crime Research 1987*] (Beijing: Chunqiu chubanshe, 1988), 41–47.
42. Ming Xu, Chu Xian, Song Defu and Qiang Wei, eds., *Sixiang zhengzhi gongzuo daoxiang* [*Guidance in Ideological-Political Work*] (Beijing: Kexue chubanshe, 1990), 193.
43. Cohen, *Folk Devils and Moral Panics*.
44. Hu Hong, "De budao ai de haizi cai zaolian" ["Premature Love Children Are Those Who Cannot Get Love"], *Shuo ni xingfu (zhixin)*, no.1 (2009): 9.
45. Austin Ramzy and Lin Yang, "Tainted Baby Milk Scandal in China," *Time Magazine*, September 16, 2008: http://www.time.com/time/world/article/0,8599,1841535,00.html (accessed January 28, 2013).
46. Hu Rong, "Yi mei suan de guo: tan tan zhongxiao xuesheng zaolian" ["A Sour End: Premature Love among Primary and Secondary School Children"], in *Jiangxi jiao bian jibu youxiang*, no.8 (2008): 11–13; Jin Shicheng, "Jiajiang xiaoxuesheng zhengzhi sai xiangdao de jiaoyu yufang zhongxiao xuesheng zaolian" ["Strengthening Political and Moral Education for Primary and Secondary School Students and the Prevention of Premature Love"], *Keji xinxi (xueshu zhujiu) bianji bu you xiang*, no.12 (2008): 537–575; and Liu Juan, "Xiaoxuesheng 'zaolian' xianxiang de fenxi yu duice" ["An Analysis of How to Handle the Phenomenon of 'Premature Love' among Primary School Students"], *Xiandai jiaoyu kexue*, no.4 (2008): 57–58.
47. Liu, "Xiaoxuesheng 'zaolian' xianxiang de fenxi yu duice."
48. Jiang Xin, "Jishi women shi jimo" ["Because We Are Lonely"], *Hao fumu*, no.11 (2003): 10–11; Lin Xi "Zaolian de houguo" ["The Consequences of Premature Love"], *Kewai yuedou*, no.3 (2008): 28.
49. Shen Weiping, "Zhongxuesheng zaolian diaocha jifenxi" ["Investigation and Analysis of Premature Love among Secondary School Students"], *Quan guo jiaoyu keyan "shiwu" cheng guo lunwen ji*, no.5 (2005).
50. Hu, "De budao ai de haizi cai zaolian."
51. Trent Bax, *Youth and Internet Addiction in China* (New York: Routledge, in press).
52. Zou Daipeng, "Ju jiao zaolian: esha haishi kuanrong haizi 'qingan wenti'?" ["Focus on the Phenomenon of Premature Love: Killing or Showing Mercy towards the 'Problem of Juvenile Romance'?"], *Jiaoyan xiehua: qing haishi dafu zhongjian xiao 45 zhounian wenji*, November (2004): 58–62.
53. Leng Haiyue, "Hai 'zaolian' yige yuanshai: zaolian taolun de jieshu yu" ["The Positive Side of 'Premature Love'"], *Hao fumu*, no.11 (2003): 10–11; and Wang Le, "Buxu chaochao mumu, zhiqiu cengjing yong you," *Hao fumu*, no.11 (2003): 10.
54. This came from a personal conversation with Andrew Kipnis about his discussions with Mainland Chinese students at the Chinese University of Hong Kong in 2010.
55. He Yonghai, "'Zaolian bao zheng ji' de zhengdang xingzhi de huaiyi" ["The Legimimacy of 'Premature Love Deposits' are Questionable"], *Zhongguo jiaoyu bao*, September 20, 2007, *Zhongguo jiaoyu xinwen wang*: http://news.xinhuanet.com/edu/2007–09/20/content_6757629.htm (accessed January 28, 2013).
56. Geng Yinping "Zaolian kekai chuxue jishi zhi baoli" ["Premature Love Leading to School Dismissal is an Abuse of the Education Regulations"], *Hubei jiao (shizheng xinwen) bianjibu youxiang*, vol.527 (2009): 47.

57. Qiao Xinsheng, "Chong xin dingyi zaolian de gainian" ["Redefining Premature Love"], May 2003: http://news.xinhuanet.com/newscenter/200310/25/content_1142231.htm (accessed January 28, 2013).
58. Bax, *Youth and Internet Addiction in China*, 138.
59. CNNIC, "24th China Internet Development Situation Statistical Report," *China Internet Network Information Center* (CNNIC), July 2009: http://www.cnnic.net.cn/en/index/index.htm (accessed January 28, 2013).
60. Wu Zengqiang and Zhang Jianguo, *Prevention and Intervention of Adolescent Internet Addiction* (Shanghai: Shanghai Education Publishers, 2008), quoted from Bax, *Youth and Internet Addiction in China*, 29.
61. Bax, *Youth and Internet Addiction in China*, 32.
62. Ibid.
63. Ibid., 16.
64. American Psychiatric Association, *Diagnostic and Statistical Manual of Mental Disorders: DSM-IV* (Washington, DC: American Psychiatric Association, 1994), xxi–xxii.
65. Wu Fan, "Institutional Roots of Ageism and Public Policy Reconstruction for the Elderly in China," *Chinese Journal of Sociology*, vol.31, no.5 (2011): 190–206.
66. Goode and Ben-Yahuda, *Moral Panics*.
67. Mary Douglas, *Purity and Danger: An Analysis of Concepts of Pollution and Taboo* (London: Routledge, 1991 [1966]).
68. Bakken, *The Exemplary Society*.
69. Karl Marx, "Manifesto of the Communist Party," in *Capital: The Communist Manifesto and Other Writings of Karl Marx*, ed. Karl Eastman (New York: Carlton House, 1932), 315–355.

6 Contagious Wilderness

Avian Flu and Suburban Riots in the French Media

Frédéric Keck

INTRODUCTION: 'SENTINELS'

What does it mean to consider pandemic influenza as a bioterrorist threat? At least since 1997, with the outbreak of highly pathogenic avian influenza (H5N1) in Hong Kong, two global threats became increasingly conflated: emerging disease and terrorism. The anthrax letters following the 9/11 terrorist attacks on New York and Washington and the global spread of SARS that coincided with the invasion of Iraq in March 2003, further reinforced this entanglement of imaginaries, as did the pronouncements of politicians who were prone to analogize obscure networks of terror with the invisible diffusion of predatory viruses.[1]

Over the last two decades, a number of actors, scattered across different institutional sites—in what might be called a "global assemblage"—have focused their research on the pandemic flu.[2] Public health experts have framed its emergence as a 'biosecurity' issue: that is, as an event that jeopardizes the political, social, and economic stability of the nation, necessitating a comprehensive preparedness plan.[3] Epidemiologists have investigated the way viruses spread through migratory birds, the conveyance of livestock, and the movement of human populations in an era of mass transportation. And, finally, virologists have examined the pathways through which the flu virus 'hijacks' the cell by using its mechanisms of reproduction to replicate at the expense of its host.[4]

But how did an audience of non-experts come to understand and respond to the threat posed by the flu? Before its articulation in popular culture—in pandemic thrillers such as Steven Soderbergh's *Contagion* (2011), in the numerous novels featuring 'virus hunters' in a race to thwart the 'killer virus,' or in 'popular' publications by concerned academics of the likes of Mike Davis—the media had widely promoted the notion that the world was under threat of attack by emerging viruses.[5] Indeed, the role of the media is to inform the public about the challenges and breakthroughs of science, as well as commenting on their political significance. Even with minimal grasp of biology and no background in public health, journalists quickly understood the resonances between a bird carrying a virus lethal to humans and a terrorist carrying a bomb.

This striking analogy has been much criticized, particularly after the H1N1 2009 pandemic that followed a different scenario from the one that had been anticipated: a mild virus emerging from Mexican swine, rather than a lethal virus emerging from Asian birds. It has been argued that this analogy created a general atmosphere of fear and panic, which was detrimental to preparing for the next pandemic.[6] Such an argument juxtaposes an emotive public, fed by a sensationalist media, against the rational sobriety of public health organizations. In other words, it ignores the fact that the ontology of the flu virus (its capacity to break boundaries and move through new pathways) fascinates journalists, as well as scientists. Moreover, by retrospectively condemning the hyped reaction to avian flu, which was in part fueled by the disease-as-terror analogy, the argument fails to take into account the historical contexts of this analogizing and the social, cultural, and political processes by which pandemics have come, historically, to be imagined as terrorist attacks (and, reciprocally, terrorist attacks imagined as disease outbreaks).

Recently, Brigitte Nerlich and Christopher Halliday have undertaken a review of articles on the flu published in the British press between February and March 2005 in order to explore how scientific evidence was framed for the general public.[7] The focus of their research is on the ways in which the public responded to metaphors of the virus as storm, earthquake, and terrorist act. According to the researchers, these metaphoric formulations have a performative function and create "negative expectations or predictions in the form of 'early warnings.'"[8] A statement such as 'birds are infected with a virus potentially lethal to humans' has an illocutionary force, drawing on a prehistory of earlier disease threats, including the epidemic of bovine spongiform encephalopathy (BSE) in Britain in the late 1980s and 1990s. Conversely, when an epidemic fails to materialize, these 'warnings' produce fear, cynicism, and complacency.

Elucidating viral metaphors on the linguistic level in this way, however, fails to take into account the manner in which such signals actually transform the world in which they operate by detecting unperceived threats, functioning as 'sentinels.'[9] To understand how journalists also perform as kinds of sentinels, we need a more pragmatic description of their work: how they obtain information, relate it to other information, and build a general structure of expectation. Rather than claiming that journalists work at the service of scientists, promoting fear—which is a general critique of the mediatization of pandemic flu—it is important to acknowledge that journalists operate much like scientists when they act as sentinels. Even if they do not work under the same publishing and funding constraints, journalists and scientists can be compared in the way they conceptualize 'new' phenomena, including emerging infections.

The work of scholars such as Priscilla Wald on the historical representations of disease emergence provides a useful point of departure for exploring how contemporary scientists and journalists report on disease and crime before they are qualified, in effect, to do so. Examining the cultural prehistory of what she terms "the outbreak narrative"—a literary form common to public health and criminology—Wald tracks back to the end of the nineteenth century, when the notion of 'contagion' was a major trope used to describe social relations. In particular, she considers the work of social psychologists and sociologists, such as Gabriel Tarde, whose reflections on the "invisible contagion of the public" by mass-circulation newspapers were later modified in Robert Park's method of social inquiry. One consequence of this 'contagionist' understanding of modern cultural processes, Wald writes, is "to transform an unhealthy contagion into a generative and transformative communication." And she concludes, "Through microbes, in other words, Park the sociologist envisions—makes visible as he imagines—the bonds of communication and community that are the material of social transformation and social inquiry."[10]

While nineteenth-century journalists were impugned for spreading contagious ideas, today social inquirers are more concerned with how individuals communicate despite their social and cultural differences. This shift can be explained by a 'new' emphasis on immigration as an object of sociological inquiry and by an interest in immunity as an object of biological study. In both instances the focus has moved to the border where new forms of (threatening) life emerge. Wald is interested in narratives where the index case is a stigmatized human—the 'patient zero' in the case of SARS or HIV/AIDS; however, avian flu produces narratives about the animal reservoir where new diseases emerge. Rather than looking at how some humans are cast out of humanity by social inquiry, it becomes possible to look at how some animals are humanized when considered as 'sentinels.' Social inquiry is then motivated by the link between wilderness and contagion: how wildlife produces new beings that do not have a place in the categories of domestication. This opens the space for another genealogy of the social sciences, from Lévy-Bruhl and Lévi-Strauss to Mary Douglas.[11]

Leaving aside the theoretical aspects of this discussion, the aim of this chapter is to explore how this double genealogy allows for a more nuanced account of what journalists do when they report on avian flu. In so doing, the chapter addresses the following questions: How and why have journalists played the role of social inquirers in their reporting of avian flu? How did they relate the flu to other forms of contagion that did not have a place in public categories? What was the structure of expectation that organized the work of these journalists? The focus, here, is on France, which offers a comparative case to the one studied by Nerlich and Halliday. The expectation of avian flu in early 2005 was fulfilled by another event: civil unrest in the suburbs between October and November (known in French as *les émeutes des banlieues*). If, in Britain, avian flu was described by the media as a virtual catastrophe that never became real, and if, in Vietnam and Egypt, it was a real catastrophe leading to a "war against the virus," France represents an intermediary case: a deadly virus was expected from Asia, but 'real' contagion came from the Parisian suburbs.[12] In what follows, we will investigate how metaphors of contagion and wilderness were transferred from avian flu to suburban riots in the French media, and we will consider how these transferences may shed light on the specific situation of France in relation to the global spread of avian flu.

Borrowing methods from the pragmatic sociology of media, this chapter draws on an analysis of 204 articles published in the French press between September and December 2005, together with interviews conducted with press journalists covering avian flu and the suburban riots, and a TV forum held on October 31, which treated these two events—pandemic threat and riots—in the same format.[13] A pragmatic sociology of the media allows us to understand why the media were criticized for having caused the 'contagion' they were supposed to be reporting. It addresses this criticism by suggesting that journalists were interested precisely in the fact that these two events did not have a place in collective representations and looked at the new forms of communication or signaling they produced. In short, by examining the media treatment of avian flu and suburban riots in the French media in 2005, the chapter contributes to two ongoing debates: first, to debates about the role of the media in skewing the 'facts' and, second, to debates about the intertwining of public health with security, of disease with crime.

FROM AVIAN FLU TO SUBURBAN RIOTS

On September 1, 2005, Socialist Deputy Jean-Marie Le Guen returned from the US to advise Jacques Chirac, President of the French Republic, that avian flu posed a major threat. Le Guen was mayor of a district of Paris with the largest Chinese community (the 13th arrondissement), as well as being the spokesperson on health issues for the Socialist Party.[14] The H5N1 virus had recently been identified in Siberia and Kazakhstan and was spreading towards Europe. After the discovery of a major outbreak among migratory waterfowl in Lake Qinghai in April, controversies were raging as to whether the virus spread through wild birds or via smuggled poultry on the Trans-Siberian route. In the US, the Bush administration, smarting from criticism of its inadequate humanitarian response in the aftermath of Hurricane Katrina, had declared that it was stockpiling masks and Tamiflu as a precautionary measure against avian flu.[15] When this information was relayed by Jean-Marie Le Guen, it provoked a consensus in France among both right-wing and left-wing officials that France should take the European lead in the fight against avian flu, which had already be prioritized in China and the US.

On September 8, Minister of Health Xavier Bertrand, a former insurance trader, declared, "On this issue, funding cannot be a consideration. All the experts, especially those of the World Health Organization, agree that pandemic flu poses a major risk. We have to be prepared."[16] On September 20, a representative of the World Health Organization (WHO) at a congress in La Baule-Escoublac, a fashionable French seaside resort declared, "If a pandemic occurs this winter, no country is prepared."[17] The notion of 'preparedness' had been taken by flu experts from the field of nuclear war to address the risk of an inter-human strain of H5N1. As international experts frequently reiterated, the question was not when the pandemic would occur, but whether the country was prepared? After the success of the global mobilization against SARS, WHO had issued a new International Health Regulation in 2004, which promoted standards of preparedness in the drawing up of national contingency plans and initiated a competition with the support of the pharmaceutical industry between developed countries as to which was the best prepared.

In October, the first cases of H5N1 were reported in Rumania, Turkey, and Greece. Maps were produced, plotting the progress of the virus, and blame was leveled at Asian countries for their failure to keep contagion in check. Soon the viral threat and the riots were becoming entangled. On October 27, for example, the French Minister of Interior published a map of the 10 most dangerous French departments based on the numbers of cars burned in the riots, while the Minister of Agriculture published a list of five departments on the path of migratory birds where the government ordered backyard poultry confined. These maps announced the conflation of avian flu with the suburban riots as two external threats that jeopardized the nation's security. In the case of avian flu, pandemic preparedness plans came from the US, and sick birds came from Asia; in the case of suburban riots, examples of car-trashing came from the US (reference was made in the newspapers to the Los Angeles riots of 1992, triggered by the beating of Rodney King), while China proposed its own model of authority as it "advised its citizens not to travel to that dangerous country, France, and denounced the curfews randomly imposed by autocratic police chiefs."[18] France was in an intermediary space between two waves of 'contagion': a social violence coming from the US and a biological virulence emanating from Asia.

The suburban riots began on October 29, when two adolescents in Clichy-sous-Bois, an eastern suburb of Paris, died in a power station where they were hiding from the police. In the nights following this event, thousands of cars were burned. Based on the testimony of the rioters, the spark that triggered the riots was the visit of Nicolas Sarkozy, the then Minister of Interior, to Argenteuil, where he asserted in front of the media: "Are you fed up with this riffraff (*racaille*)? Well, we are going to eradicate them!" The word *racaille* was then used by the rioters to define themselves in opposition to the French elites. *Racaille* is a derivative of the old English 'racker,' meaning a slaughterer.[19] The description of rioters as wild animals needing to be tamed was subsequently to become a major trope in the media.

In the 204 articles selected for this chapter, the word 'contagion' appears 11 times: seven in the articles about flu and four in the articles about the riots.[20] The word 'wild' appears 64 times: 60 about avian flu and four about suburban riots. The head of a departmental office in charge of hunting was quoted on October 18 in *Le Monde* as saying: "The risk of contagion from wild fauna and domestic animals is low but it exists. Hunters should pay attention and apply the rules without getting crazy. Forbidding hunting won't abolish risks of contagion."[21] And an editorial in *Le Monde* on November 3 declared, "Is there not, in these riots that seem to spread, as by contagion, without organization or rules, the birth of a consciousness? This *canaille*, in contrast with that of the songs of the revolutionaries of the Commune, has neither memory nor dreams."[22] Journalists borrowed the terminology of 'experts' and politicians because they did not know how to describe what was going on in any other way than as a form of 'contagion' from the wild.

The riots provided a backdrop to the political confrontation between Sarkozy and the then Prime Minister Dominique de Villepin, who were competing to be the candidate for the right-wing party at the presidential election two years later; this competition created a political void that fueled the riots. Sarkozy appeared repeatedly on TV to reiterate that he was supporting the police who arrested hundreds of young rioters. Meanwhile, the Socialist Party blamed the government for cutting the budgets of local associations, and they criticized the police for their complicity. On November 7, Villepin announced a curfew and a social plan to support the economy in the suburbs. The daily number of cars burned was no longer publicized since it was understood that the rioters were burning cars expressly to make the evening news broadcast on TV at 8:00 p.m.[23] However, the riots continued for the whole month of November, with cars burned every night. If the number of casualties remained low, the economic impact was huge. It is estimated that 10,000 cars were burned and 250 public buildings torched. Two hundred and eight people were brought before the court at Bobigny, mostly from immigrant African families.[24]

The conflation of avian flu with suburban riots found a last twist at the end of February 2006, when the H5N1 virus was identified for the first time in France on a wild duck in the wetland area of La Dombes near Lyon. Prime Minister Villepin went to the area the very next day to show that the government was concerned, and he was followed there by journalists. After the visit to the wetlands, a poultry farm was infected by H5N1. All the poultry had to be killed and incinerated, while the farms within a perimeter of three kilometers were quarantined for three weeks. Rumor spread among the farmers and veterinarians that the H5N1 virus had been transmitted from the wild duck to the poultry farm on the shoes of the politicians and journalists.[25] An analogy was implicit here: politicians and journalists had diffused the viral contagion they were supposed to be containing, just as they had intensified the 'contagion' of the riots. Two widely disseminated cartoons made this analogy explicit: poultry farms were depicted being burned when journalists arrived, as if they were in competition with the rioters for the headlines.

HEALTH AND SOCIETY: JOURNALISTS AT *LE MONDE*

Metaphors of contagion and wilderness, which pervaded the French media in the fall of 2005, suggest that something new was emerging that journalists sought to capture. Criticism against the media for fueling the contagion they were reporting fails to recognize the space between social representations and emerging forms of life. It is necessary to go beyond the arresting analogy between burning cars and poultry farms—an analogy that suggests violence is contagious and requires sequestration from mainstream society and relegation to the social fringes.[26] On the contrary, an analysis of news coverage shows that journalists were intrigued precisely by what was emerging on these borders as new forms of communication. When the headline in a news story or a cartoon in a newspaper draw analogies between two forms of 'contagion,' different kinds of work have been involved in the 'Health' and 'Society' sections to produce the 'news.' We will take, here, examples from *Le Monde,* one of France's main newspapers of record (with *Le Figaro* and *Libération*).

The 'Health' pages of *Le Monde* were instituted in 1956 by the physician Claudine Escoffier-Lambiotte, who was particularly interested in reporting on the consequences of medical progress for women, such as contraception techniques. She was a prominent voice in the contaminated blood scandal, accusing the left-wing journal *Libération* of supporting the Socialist government that was concealing the number of hemophilic patients infected with HIV/AIDS after receiving transfusions.[27] In 1980, she was joined at *Le Monde* by another physician-journalist, Jean-Yves Nau, who continued the tradition Escoffier-Lambiotte had established at the paper in connecting health concerns with socio-political issues of the day. During the scandal of mad cow disease after 1996, when the British government revealed that the new variant of Creuzfeldt-Jakob disease found in humans was caused by transmission of BSE, Nau published *Journal de la vache folle* [*Journal of the Mad Cow*] in which he chronicled unfolding health issues in a context of uncertainty.[28] He adopted this genre and style of writing because he held that reporting on health issues should not only be about technological progress but should also follow a narrative of political suspense and moral blame.

After gaining experience in the world of animal health, Nau was also the lead journalist in charge of the articles on avian flu in 2005. He wrote about migratory birds, backyard poultry, scientific research, and public behavior. His articles followed the same narrative as his account of mad cow disease but with a new focus on the 'unknown' aspects of the wild life where the virus mutated. He wrote in *Le Monde*: "After mad cow disease, the H5N1 epizootic allows us to see how science and medicine are helpless in the fight against a pathogenic agent that is able to cross the species barrier."[29] He later observed, reflecting on this period:

Information is contagious: one piece of information triggers another. Readers discovered a world they had previously ignored: wild birds, their migrations, their contact with domestic birds . . . It was really mysterious. These two worlds were intersecting: the wild and the domestic. And then we saw the structuration of this plan inspired by Jacobinism, a whole machinery of vaccination supported by the pharmaceutical industry.[30]

The classical trope of 'information as contagious' is here in tension with the investigative impulse of the journalist to understand and elucidate these 'wild' areas where pathogens emerge—the so-called 'species barriers,' revealed in the very moment when they are crossed. Nau is critical, too, of the state apparatus (Jacobinism) that fails to comprehend the newness of this event but instead falls back on Pastorian modes of vaccination.

Another physician, Paul Benkimoun, had joined *Le Monde* a few years earlier, and proposed another approach to avian flu. Having published papers about SARS in Hong Kong and Toronto, he was more interested in the global reach of the flu. "What is fascinating about epidemics," he declared, "is their geographical dimension: a localized phenomenon extends like an oil spill."[31] In October 2005, he published articles about chikungunya, a new disease transmitted by mosquitoes in the French overseas department of La Réunion. He argued with his colleague Nau on the comparative importance of a few swans dying from avian flu in Europe and thousands of humans crippled with chikungunya in La Réunion. In 2008, the Health section of *Le Monde* was renamed 'Planet,' and pandemics were one of its major themes, along with global warming and endocrine disruptors. Avian flu was no longer considered to be a mysterious phenomenon of the 'wild' that defied the logic of the Pastorian state. Instead, it was held up as an example and warning of the new environmental threats posed by an increasingly interlinked global ecology. According to Benkimoun, a journalist acted as a 'sentinel' when she or he reported on the environmental causes of emerging diseases before they had diffused globally into a pandemic.

Regarding the riots, only one journalist in *Le Monde*, Luc Bronner, reported directly from the suburbs. As a 29-year-old in 2005 who came from the 'Education' section of *Le Monde*, Bronner did not share the views of his older colleagues in the 'Society' section who considered that young men in the suburbs were unpoliticized hooligans destroying their own neighborhood. These journalists reported on social movements when they had a political dimension and were stunned by the fact that suburban riots had no spokesperson or collective message—particularly as the riots in 2005 took place in the former 'red suburbs' held by the Communist Party.[32,33]

Bronner initiated a mode of inquiry at *Le Monde* that drew on the English model of investigative journalism. He went regularly to Aulnay-sous-Bois, at a good distance from Argenteuil and Clichy-sous-Bois, where the major outbreaks occurred. From there, he could interview the rioters, their families, and the local political elites, at a time when other journalists, in *Le Parisien* for instance, were only reporting the number of cars burned or the frequency of police attacks. Even though he refused to use the analogy of contagion in connection with the riots, he later conceded, "It is true that, geographically, there is one outbreak that then extends in a viral-like mode, through SMS exchanges. Burning cars is an extraordinary game, with irrational, even feral aspects. Groups of rioters emulated each other in the number of cars burnt."[34] Rather than compensating for lack of knowledge, the metaphor of contagion here connotes the uses of new communication technologies that render obsolete the set-piece manifestos and demonstrations of the past.

In 2007, Bronner was awarded the Albert-Londres Prize for his reports on the riots in the Parisian suburbs. In 2010, he published *La loi du ghetto. Enquête dans les banlieues françaises* [*The Law of the Ghetto: Investigation on the French Suburbs*] in which he describes ordinary life in the suburbs, relying on the research of sociologists and drawing a link "between global crises—urbanism, unemployment, precarity, underemployment— and individual destinies."[35] The word 'ghetto' was used provocatively to criticize the failure of the French elites to recognize the existence of social 'margins,' in which the tensions of French society were condensed and intensified. Where politicians see an outbreak of violence, Bronner discerns the logical consequences of marginalized existences. "After every outbreak, politicians, the media and experts ask: will the 2005 scenario, with its three weeks of violence, be repeated? Probably not. For in the shadows of the media and politics, 2005 happens every day."[36]

The outbreak of avian flu and the violence of the suburban riots in 2005 were described as 'contagious' precisely because their causes were not yet deciphered and could not be expressed through the old symbols of the French Republic, such as Pastorian vaccination or political revolution. 'Contagion' became a shorthand for the unknown as journalists sought to investigate new zones produced by novel, globalized environments: animal wildlife, exotic diseases, and urban ghettos. An 'outbreak' marks the beginning of an inquiry that cannot rely on normative principles, such as disease or crime, but follows the paths of contagion to discover new forms of communication between living beings.

TV AND THE PRINCIPLE OF PARTICIPATION

There is one obvious difference between avian flu and suburban riots, of course. Birds cannot choose to become infected, whereas rioters can decide whether or not to burn cars. In other words, there is an issue, here, of intentionality. This is a classical distinction between disease and crime: the body does not decide to get sick, whereas the criminal can choose not to commit a crime and break the law. Sociologists who studied the cities where riots broke out in 2005 have demonstrated that there were clear strategies to participate or not in the violence, depending on age and group structure.[37] Their findings raise a more general question: How are different actors described as participating in a contagious event? Expressed differently: can we compare media depictions of how sick birds and rioters participated in the respective 'outbreaks'?

We have seen how press journalists investigate the social spaces where new forms of life emerge and relate them to global causes. We can now see how television journalists put these different actors together in public forums. Whereas the press journalist focuses on one actor after the other, as they are revealed through the unfolding process of contagion, TV forums seek to produce a general image that makes sense of a given event for the public.[38] They restore an order that has been contested by the outbreak, and in so doing they are obliged to exclude actors who are too closely linked with contagion. Through the mise-en-scène of a debate in which everyone notionally participates, they in fact exclude some actors from political participation.[39]

To understand the significance of the conflation of avian flu with suburban riots in France in 2005, I turn, here, to examine the TV program *Mots croisés* [*Crossed Words*] where both events were simultaneously discussed. This forum, where experts debate about public issues, is broadcast every Monday on Channel 2 at 10:30 p.m., with an estimated audience rating of 13 percent. In October 2005, the journalist who presented the program, Olivier Mazerolles, had just been removed because of his support for Sarkozy. To replace him, the head of France 2 News section, Arlette Chabot, who was reported to be close to President Chirac, chose the young journalist Yves Calvi. Since then, Calvi has become renowned for the unrelenting and often provocative way he cross-questions politicians and experts, raising public awareness and often breaking the conventional questions-answer format. In the politicized world of French TV forums, Calvi is the closest thing to an investigative journalist.[40]

On October 31, Calvi was presenting one of his first programs. He had planned to devote the program to avian flu, but the events in Clichy-sous-Bois forced him to present a debate on suburban riots in the first part of the program. Several politicians and sociologists were invited to participate, but only one represented the suburbs.[41] Samir Mihi, who was a specialized educator in a lycée in Clichy-sous-Bois, was not considered as a spokesman for the complaints of the rioters but rather as a mediator who could appease the violence. He was the only participant who did not talk about the suburban violence explicitly but rather expressed this violence in the manner with which he answered Calvi. Here is an extract from the interview:

YVES CALVI: Could you ask the youths in Clichy who are watching us not to torch their neighborhood tonight?
SAMIR MIHI: But we've already said that, we say it every day . . .
YVES CALVI: Well, we want to hear you say it!
SAMIR MIHI: Besides, I want to say to Mr. Sarkozy . . .
YVES CALVI: Excuse me, I would like you to answer my question!
SAMIR MIHI: But I will answer your question!
YVES CALVI: Please do!
SAMIR MIHI: Just as Mr. Sarkozy has paid homage to his men who have done a great job in the *cités*, I want to pay homage . . . I won't say to my men but to the men who work on the ground and who have done a great job of mediation and have stayed calm while all that was dearest to us was attacked: our families who were inside the mosque, and our religion.[42]

Mihi introduced a confrontational logic in the debate where all points of view were supposed to be represented. He employed a language redolent of war—"my men"—where experts used a language of contagion. The reference to Sarkozy allowed him to say that the riots did not start as an outbreak of irrational violence but as a deliberate response to a provocation. The reference to Islam—"our religion"—contested the principles of the French Republic defended by other experts. Although he was accustomed to watching TV, Mihi refused to accept the conventions of the TV forum including answering the host's questions in a prescribed order. "You have to take the opportunity to speak without waiting for it to be given to you."[43]

This eruption of a non-standardized mode of speech contrasted with the smooth presentation of avian flu in the second part of the program. Experts on the transmission of bird to human infection were represented, although there was no representative present from the poultry industry.[44] The program aired the worrying news from Asia and the fall of poultry consumption in France, while the debate that followed centered on whether there had been an over-reaction to the threat coming from abroad. Calvi asked Didier Houssin, who was in charge of contingency planning for avian flu at the Ministry of Health, if people had reason to be afraid. Houssin sought to reassure the audience: France had a plan, and poultry only needed to be cooked to prevent the risks of infection.

YVES CALVI: Our security depends on you. Are we prepared?
DIDIER HOUSSIN: Your security doesn't depend only on me, thank God, there are other people who take care of it. We are getting prepared.
YVES CALVI: Is there a plan against avian flu?

DIDIER HOUSSIN: There is a plan.
YVES CALVI: What does the plan consist of?
DIDIER HOUSSIN: First: delay the coming of any possible infected person into France. Second: treat the sick as best as possible; third, vaccinate everyone as quickly as possible.
YVES CALVI: How do you delay the coming of any possible infected person into France?
DIDIER HOUSSIN: We watch and inform the tourists about the danger of getting close to poultry.
YVES CALVI: But in Asia there is poultry everywhere!
DIDIER HOUSSIN: That's the difficulty . . .
YVES CALVI: Are we frightening people unduly?
DIDIER HOUSSIN: People can eat poultry without fear. On the condition that it is well cooked.[45]

There was thus a clear distinction between the ways in which avian flu and the suburban riots were debated on TV. In the case of the riots, those who burned cars could participate in a public discussion but only on condition that they claimed they would stop their criminal activities. When they protested that the riots were a response to the violent action of the French state, they lost the opportunity to speak. For avian flu, the debate pivoted on whether the French state was over-reacting, while poultry breeders were given no voice, and the representative of the state closed the discussion saying there was a plan. In both cases, the state sought to disrupt the paths of contagion through a fictitious participation: bringing back rioters to reason through education and controlling sick chickens through preparedness and thorough cooking.

CONCLUSION

This chapter has analyzed the ways in which emerging diseases and forms of criminal violence have become entangled in the twenty-first century. The responses of the French state to the threat of avian flu and to the violence of the riots in the suburbs of Paris in 2005 provide a case study that sheds light, not only on the ways in which analogies are produced, but also on the consequences of these analogies in the world. If the association between avian flu and terrorism acquired different meanings elsewhere (roughly, preparedness for a catastrophe in America and war with an enemy in Asia), in France the association led to a suspension of the rules of participation and a re-definition of who is able to speak politically and who is not at a time of political instability and self-reflection on France's position in an increasingly interconnected world. The analogy between crime and disease could be made precisely because no collective principle defined the paths of contagion: cars were trashed and farms were burned, without the espousal of any political claim or public health rationale. The ways of contagion opened up a space of uncertainty in the search for an overarching and integrating principle.

Hence, the role of journalists, as investigators in these social spaces where new forms of normativity were emerging, developed. If the French state perceived a contagion that contested its principles, journalists discovered a viral communication (transmitters between species barriers and messages between urban neighborhoods) that disclosed new forms of public activity. Journalists acted as sentinels when they discovered warning signals in the zones where politicians saw only irrational behavior. However, as I have argued above, a distinction needs to be made between press journalists and TV presenters. TV forums reintroduced the rules of participation to the French Republic and imposed standardized frames of speech to these warning signals. In effect, they closed the space of uncertainty by trying to reassure the public with certainties.

Rather than denouncing journalists for promoting panic through the use of analogies of torched cars with farms aflame and of 'sick' rioters with diseased birds, I suggest in this chapter that the study of such analogies might be taken as a starting point for a more far-reaching examination of the ways in which normative principles become contested and reformulated by journalists in a situation of outbreak. Disease and crime, as other contributors to this volume show, were conceptualized and explained in the nineteenth century through research on the causalities, both natural and social, of extraordinary events: contagion and participation functioned as critical categories through which these causalities were stabilized.[46] In today's interconnected world, however, where public spaces appear to be undermined by new forms of migration and novel technologies of communication, it has become more difficult to link contagion with participation in any meaningful way. The French case of 2005 can be seen as a modest but vivid attempt to do so.

NOTES

1. See Melinda Cooper, "Pre-empting Emergence: The Biological Turn in the War on Terror," *Theory, Culture & Society*, vol.23, no.4 (2006): 113–135.
2. See Stephen Collier and Aiwah Ong, *Global Assemblages: Technology, Politics, and Ethics as Anthropological Problems* (Malden, MA: Blackwell, 2005).
3. See Andrew Lakoff, "Preparing for the Next Emergency," *Public Culture*, vol.19, no.2 (2007): 247–271; and Andrew Lakoff and Stephen J. Collier, ed., *Biosecurity Interventions: Global Health and Security in Question* (New York: University of Columbia Press, 2008).
4. Malik Peiris, Menno de Jong, and Yi Guan, "Avian Influenza Virus (H5N1): A Threat to Human Health," *Clinical Microbiology Review*, vol.20, no.2 (2007): 243–267.
5. Mike Davis, *The Monster at Our Door: The Global Threat of Avian Flu* (New York: Henry Holt, 2006).

6. Nick Muntean, "Viral Terrorism and Terrifying Viruses: The Homological Construction of the 'War on Terror' and the Avian Flu Pandemic," *International Journal of Media and Cultural Politics*, vol.5, no.3 (2009): 199–216. I deliberately use the notion of analogy rather than homology as it reflects the author's argument. The analogy supposes four terms to be defined (birds are to viruses what humans are to bombs), whereas homology leaves one term undefined (the ontology of viruses remaining an enigma).

7. Brigitte Nerlich and Christopher Halliday, "Avian Flu: The Creation of Expectations in the Interplay between Science and the Media," *Sociology of Health and Illness*, vol.29, no.1 (2007): 46–65.

8. Ibid., 48.

9. On the notion of 'sentinels' in relation to emerging disease, see Frédéric Keck, "Une sentinelle sanitaire aux frontières du vivant. Les experts de la grippe aviaire à Hong Kong," *Terrain*, no.54 (2010): 26–41; and Keck and Andrew Lakoff eds. "Sentinel Devices," *Limn*, no.3 (2013): 38–40.

10. Priscilla Wald, *Contagious: Cultures, Carriers, and the Outbreak Narrative* (Durham, NC: Duke University Press, 2008), 135, 138.

11. See Frédéric Keck, "On the Limits of Classification: Claude Lévi-Strauss and Mary Douglas," in *Cambridge Companion to Lévi-Strauss*, ed. Boris Wiseman (Cambridge: Cambridge University Press, 2009), 139–155.

12. Matthieu Fintz, "Emerging Viruses, State of Emergency and the Manufacture of Health Crises," in *Chroniques égyptiennes/Egyptian Chronicles 2006*, ed. Enrique Klaus and Chaymaa Hassabo (Cairo: Cedej, 2007), 275–305; and Annick Guénel and Sylvia Klingberg, "Press Coverage of Bird Flu Epidemic in Vietnam," in *Liberalizing, Feminizing and Popularizing Health Communications in Asia*, ed. Liew Kai Khiun (Farnham, UK: Ashgate, 2010), 77–93. For an account of the ways in which the 2009 H1N1 pandemic became conceptually entangled with a 'contagious' financial crisis, see Robert Peckham, "Economies of Contagion: Financial Crisis and Pandemic," *Economy and Society*, vol.42, no.2 (2013): 226–248.

13. This method is attentive to the 'pragmatic' reasons given by actors in their course of action and the conflicts of normativities that emerge out of their practices. It borrows from Robert Park's school of sociology idea that the sociologist is not more objective than journalists since both groups can be defined as social inquirers. It assumes that the role of the sociologists is to clarify normative conflicts that remain implicit in journalists' practices. See Cyril Lemieux, *Mauvaise presse. Une sociologie compréhensive du travail journalistique et de ses critiques* (Paris: Métailié, 2000).

14. See Jean-Marie Le Guen and Jean-Pierre Door, *Le H5N1: une menace durable pour la santé animale* (Paris: Rapport de l'Assemblée Nationale, vol.2, no.2833 (2006)).

15. Lakoff, "Preparing for the Next Emergency."

16. "Interview de Xavier Bertrand, Ministre de la Santé et des solidarités," *Le Point*, no.1721, September 8, 2005, 64.

17. Sandrine Cabut, "Grippe aviaire: les spécialistes préfèrent imaginer le pire," *Le Figaro*, no.19015, September 22, 2005, 12.

18. "Audience et sidération," *Libération*, no.7622, November 10, 2005, 2.

19. The Wikipedia entry for this word in French states that it was used by Albert Camus in his novel *La peste* (1947) to describe the reactions of French people to the arrest of a man who had killed an Arab on the beach: "If we put all this *racaille* in prison, we could at last breathe." Of course, Sarkozy was not making reference to Camus, but the occurrence of this word defining humans on the margins of society in a book about contagion is worth noting. See also,

Laurence Allard and Olivier Blondeau, "La racaille peut-elle parler? Objets expressifs et émeutes des cités," *Hermès*, vol.47 (2007): 79–87.

20. I thank Gaël Villeneuve for helping with the selection of articles and for his guidance using the software Europresse.
21. Joseph Daul, "Une pandémie de grippe aviaire émergera un jour ou l'autre," *Le Monde*, October 18, 2005, 10.
22. "Un petit Mai-68 des banlieues," *Le Monde*, November 5, 2005, 15. "*Canaille*" is literally a wild dog, but it is used to describe outlaws. The resonance with "*racaille*" is deliberately exploited here.
23. From "Audience et sidération": "Television would have fanned the flames. It would have been like oxygen for fire, the indispensable element for the propagation of 'urban violence.' Should we have showed as many burnt cars and devastated owners?"
24. Fabien Jobard, "Rioting as a Political Tool: The 2005 French Riots," *Howard Journal of Criminal Justice*, vol.48, no.3 (2009): 235–244; see, also, Laurent Mucchielli and Véronique Le Goaziou, *Quand les banlieues brûlent . . . Retour sur les émeutes de novembre 2005* (Paris: La Découverte, 2007).
25. See Vanessa Manceron, "Les oiseaux de l'infortune et la géographie sanitaire: La Dombes et la grippe aviaire," *Terrain*, no.51 (2008): 160–173.
26. This is the thesis of René Girard, partially endorsed by Priscilla Wald.
27. See Dominique Marchetti, *Contribution à une sociologie des transformations du champ journalistique dans les années 80 et 90. A propos d'"événements sida" et du "scandale du sang contaminé"* (Paris: EHESS, 1997); and Dominique Marchetti, *Quand la santé devient médiatique: les logiques de production de l'information dans la presse* (Grenoble, France: Presses universitaires de Grenoble, 2010).
28. Jean-Yves Nau, *Journal de la vache folle* (Paris: Georg, 2003). He later published *A(H1N1) journal de la pandémie* with Antoine Flahaut in 2009.
29. Jean-Yves Nau, "Grippe aviaire: aider le Sud pour protéger le Nord," *Le Monde*, September 30, 2005, 1.
30. Interview, November 2009.
31. Interview, November 2009.
32. See Sandrine Lévêque, *Les journalistes sociaux. Histoire et sociologie d'une spécialité journalistique* (Rennes, France: Presses universitaires de Rennes, 2000).
33. See Julie Sedel, *Les médias et la banlieue* (Lormont, France: INA/Le bord de l'eau, 2009).
34. Interview, February 2012.
35. Luc Bronner, *La loi du ghetto. Enquête dans les banlieues françaises* (Paris: Calmann-Lévy, 2010), 31.
36. Ibid., 253.
37. See Marwan Mohammed, "Youth Gangs, Riots and the Politicisation Process," in *Rioting in the UK and France, 2001–2008: A Comparative Analysis*, ed. David Waddington, Fabien Jobard, and Mike King (Cullompton, UK: Willan, 2009): 157–172.
38. Gaël Villeneuve, *Faire parler le public. Une ethnographie comparée des débats politiques à la télévision* (Unpublished PhD thesis, Université de Paris 8, 2008).
39. Fabien Jobard notes that the participation to elections in the suburbs increased after the riots but then fell again; see "Rioting as a Political Tool."
40. See Jérôme Bourdon, *Haute fidélité. Pouvoir et télévision (1935–1994)* (Paris: Seuil, 1994).
41. Azouz Begag, Delegate Minister for Equality of Chances; Claude Dilain, socialist mayor of Clichy-sous-Bois; Manuel Valls, socialist mayor of Évry;

Manuel Aeschimann, conservative mayor of Asnières; Sébastien Roché, researcher at CNRS on "urban violences"; Bruno Beschizza, police officer and head of the union Synergie Officiers.

42. Transcript of the program *Mots croisés* on October 31, 2005.
43. "Prendre la parole sans attendre qu'on vous la donne." Interview with Gaël Villeneuve, November 2005.
44. They are Jean-Philippe Derenne, head of pneumatology at La Pitié-Salpetrière in Paris; Vincent Carlier, Professor of Food Hygiene at the Veterinary School of Maisons-Alfort; Claude Allègre, physicist and former Minister of Research; Jean Claude Jaillette, vice-head of the newspaper *Marianne*. The first two warned against Avian Flu, and the second two considered the warning as exaggerated.
45. Transcript of the program *Mots croisés* on October 31, 2005.
46. See Stephen Kern, *A Cultural History of Causality: Science, Murder Novels, and Systems of Thought* (Princeton: Princeton University Press, 2004); and Luc Boltanski, *Enigmes et complots. Une enquête à propos d'enquêtes* (Paris: Gallimard, 2012).

7 The Criminalization of Industrial Disease
Epidemiology in a Japanese Asbestos Lawsuit

Paul Jobin

INTRODUCTION: INDUSTRIAL CRIME

Many of the chapters in this volume explore the ways in which definitions of 'disease' and 'crime' have been—and continue to be—deployed institutionally, and often in state-sponsored initiatives, to control and manage populations. Medicalization or 'pathologization' is understood, in this context, as the process by which particular social behaviors are framed by dominant actors as 'conditions' or 'disorders' that require specific interventions: medical study, diagnosis, prevention, and treatment. The critical focus is on the discursive formation of 'crime' and 'disease' as contingent juridical and biological categories.

In this chapter, however, I shift the emphasis away from this sociological and historical critique of the 'medicalization of deviance' to consider 'disease' and 'crime' from an altogether different perspective: that of victims of industrial pollution and occupational disease in contemporary Japan. In so doing, my aim is to suggest how the symbolic violence inflicted by these categories ('crime' and 'disease') at the hands of dominant actors (either the state or large corporations) may be inverted by 'victimized' social groups seeking redress for 'unfair' treatment. Innocent people are not treated *as* sick, they *are* truly sick. But they have an imperative to prove it. In their attempts to obtain formal apologies and compensation, they meet with tremendous difficulties in defining their affliction and then demonstrating that it results from corporate or state negligence. This chapter, then, is about victims of industrial disease who bring their charges to court in order to prove such negligence. It is concerned with the 'positive' side of medicalization and criminalization, and examines the tests that people must endure in the process of defining a specific industrial crime.

The notion of 'industrial disease' is generally used to denote work-related illness.[1] The definition adopted in this chapter embraces both occupational and environmental hazards, either resulting from an industrial process (industrial pollution) or the consequence of an industrial output (for example, food poisoning or product liability).[2] Between the end of the nineteenth century and the mid-1950s, industrialized countries developed various forms of compensation systems for the victims of occupational hazards, which often resulted from historic compromises between labor movements and the executives of industry, with the state acting as mediator. Conceived as insurance schemes, they were established to limit costly litigations.[3] In other words, employers agreed to pay a premium to cover occupational injuries and a limited number of occupational diseases, in exchange for not being sued by their employees. A number of countries, including Japan in the 1970s, also established compensation schemes for the victims of industrial pollution. However, occupational or environmental compensation systems often set overly strict conditions that dissuaded many people from applying (the phenomenon of 'under-declaration') or limited the number of successful applicants to a fraction of those who applied. A striking example is the case of Minamata disease (a mercury poisoning of the food chain, the largest industrial pollution of postwar Japan, which, as of July 2012, has prompted over 50,000 applicants.)[4]

Although compensation systems make it unnecessary to prove corporate or state negligence, sometimes the victims of industrial disease turn to the courts for redress, through individual or class actions. Since this requires sufficient evidence, few cases are ever brought to court. Despite this, such litigations have been a key focus in studies of the history and sociology of risk, science studies, and the anthropology of law.[5] Some scholars, drawing on the work of Foucault, have emphasized the power relations and 'disciplinary' impulse that underpin and shape the law and the judicial system. Others have focused on the social impact of these lawsuits and their part in what Bruno Latour has called "the making of law."[6] Finally, there has been an emphasis in such studies on the decisive role of 'cause lawyers.'[7] My interest in this chapter, however, focuses rather on the motivations of the plaintiffs themselves, on their own formulation of industrial disease, and by extension, on what I term 'industrial crime.'

It is important to stress from the outset that industrial disease lawsuits present significant differences, depending on the legal framework in question. In common law systems (practiced primarily in anglophone countries), 'crime' is a broad category composed of felonies (major offenses such as murder, rape, and arson) and misdemeanors or petty crimes. In this context, industrial disease lawsuits fall into the non-criminal category of torts—in this case, 'toxic torts'—which are handled by civil courts, with conviction resulting in compensation, rather than imprisonment. In continental legal systems (such as those used in Europe, Japan, Taiwan, South Korea, and Brazil), 'crime' is the heaviest category that will tend to bring the case to 'criminal' rather than 'civil' court. The large majority of litigations related to industrial diseases are brought in civil court, but in some circumstances, the victims feel the need to deepen the symbolic meaning of their pledge through a criminal complaint so as to explicitly condemn their offenders as 'criminals.' For example, in Japan, in the wake of the 2011 Fukushima Daiichi nuclear disaster, while several civil complaints are being drawn up, a group of 1,324 Fukushima residents has filed a criminal complaint against executives of TEPCO (Tokyo Electric Company), as well as certain government officials.[8]

Beyond these variations embedded in different legal frameworks, universal questions remain, such as why some victims opt to go to court, while others do not. In my fieldwork in Japan and Taiwan, I have been repeatedly puzzled by the way victims tend to focus on the symbolic nature of the crime itself, in contrast to their lawyers who deal with specific judicial concepts.[9] The plaintiffs sometimes perceive industrial hazards not as the consequence of an accident but rather as the logical result of corporate cynicism (in other words, 'they *knew* this was toxic and would cause harm, but their priority was their profits'). Rather than compensation for damages, plaintiffs then argue that their main motivation in taking action is to avoid the repetition of that sort of crime: in some cases, the 'no more' ('no more Minamata' and 'no more Bhopal') might sound like a mere slogan, but for some plaintiffs, it is a sincere obsession, a Deleuzian *ritournelle* ('refrain').[10]

The lawsuit that I present in this chapter is a civil case filed by victims of asbestos poisoning in the Japanese city of Sennan in the Osaka prefecture. The toxicant at issue here—asbestos—deserves some explanation, as in many ways it presents the perfect 'candidate' to define industrial crime. Asbestos' status is now close to that of lead and other old pollutants, whose dangers are less hotly disputed than they used to be, being now well established in the international medical literature. The World Health Organization (WHO) has clearly pronounced its absolute toxicity, regardless of the type of asbestos. And yet, as of 2012, many countries continue to use asbestos in large quantities, with Asia accounting for more than half of the world's production, led by China with more than 1,000,000 tons per year, of which less than a half is locally produced. The main producer countries (Russia, China, Brazil, Kazakhstan, and Canada), which constantly work to undermine any attempt at 'controlled usage,' have even managed to prevent the addition of asbestos to the United Nations Rotterdam Convention's list of dangerous substances. While not banning asbestos outright, Canada has reduced its own use to negligible amounts but continues to produce it for export to Asia. The history of asbestos thus presents an emblematic accumulation of double standards, benefiting from governmental laxness, and even state complicity, whether tacit or explicit (for example, in the name of conserving jobs).[11]

Industry's sluggishness in undertaking preventative measures or in substituting toxic agents is a critical question, since the most cynical explanation might be that they profit from protracted delays. When a toxic agent is a cost-effective product like asbestos—given the low cost of its extraction and production—even though its prohibition seems ultimately inevitable, any extra years of production are welcome additions to the bottom line; no thought is given to the years of life lost to those exposed to the toxins. These culpable delays are brought before the courts with a variety of procedures and conclusions, not just due to the great diversity of judicial systems, but also to the diversity of the victims' reactions and organization. For example, the 700,000 civil suits filed in the US have never resulted in a legislative decision to ban asbestos, while, in France, criminal charges remain in abeyance. In Italy, however, the Turin courts in February 2012 convicted the managers of the Swiss-Belgian firm Eternit, following charges brought by more than 2,000 plaintiffs, both former employees and nearby residents. This established a precedent, which could impel industry to think twice before deliberately ignoring a confirmed danger.

While the Turin trial did not address the possible complicity of state authorities, the Sennan episode remains one of the very rare cases to focus its charges against the state. From this perspective, the Sennan trial can bring useful elements to the conceptualization of industrial crime. Another significant element is the specific role of epidemiology in the trial. Here, epidemiology is not only a central element of the causation debate (as is more and more the case in toxic torts), but it also motivated the launching of the complaint in the first place, in an attempt to criminalize the state.

THE ASBESTOS TRIALS IN JAPAN

Japan was the first Asian country, in 2005, to move toward a complete ban of asbestos, though it was rather late compared to other industrialized countries. The decision to do so was motivated by the shockwave produced by the Kubota scandal.[12] Kubota is a manufacturer of asbestos cement pipes in Osaka, which, in July 2005, admitted that its heavy use of chrysotile asbestos (or white asbestos) and crocidolite (blue asbestos, even more noxious) was responsible for numerous cases of mesothelioma—a cancer of the pleura and of the peritoneum clearly linked to asbestos—among its former workers and nearby residents of the factory. Within a couple of days, negotiations between the firm and the victims' families had triggered an avalanche of similar claims across the whole of the archipelago, transforming the matter into a national cause, in a manner comparable to the situation in France 10 years earlier.[13] As long as the victims are limited to workers, even in considerable numbers, asbestos is the cause of an 'occupational' disease; as soon as the disease extends beyond the gates of the factory through 'environmental' exposure, the toxic agent is then considered a danger to the public.

This was not, however, the first time that the alarm bells had sounded. Previously, in 1986, the discovery of asbestos waste from the American aircraft carrier Midway at Yokosuka, a US military base in Tokyo Bay, had led to a similar crisis. A further scandal then erupted when asbestos was detected in the flooring of kindergartens. After a wave of panic, however, media attention abated and social or labor activists focusing on asbestos struggled to gain support for the issue. By contrast, since 2005, the Kubota scandal has forced public authorities to take more radical measures. Cases of mesothelioma, a relatively rare form of cancer, constituted proof all the more damning for the company since they were geographically circumscribed, forming a cluster on the map, and thus serving as graphic evidence to mobilize around.[14]

In addition to progressing towards the complete prohibition of asbestos use, a law compensating asbestos victims was adopted the following year, drawing on the Indemnification Fund for Victims of Asbestos (*Fonds d'indemnisation des victimes de l'amiante*, or FIVA), instituted in France in 2002. Unlike the case of FIVA, however, a significant number of victims of environmental exposure were eligible to receive compensation. Until the July 2010 revision, pleural plaques caused by exposure to asbestos were not included in Japan, which is hardly surprising since France is the only country in the world to offer this possibility (FIVA's director even confided to me that she 'regretted' the legislation which 'costs France dearly').[15] Asbestosis (a pulmonary disease related to silicosis) was also not taken into account by the new Japanese law, despite the fact that the causal link to asbestos had been established by the medical literature before that of mesothelioma, but it primarily affects workers, and this 'occupational' connotation limited its political influence. Asbestos also causes various types of lung cancer, in even greater numbers than mesothelioma. But until a recent modification (February 2012), the allocation criteria set out by the new law for asbestos victims dissuaded most of the potential claimants; contrary to mesothelioma and pleural plaques, which are recognized 'biomarkers' of exposure to asbestos, lung cancer can be attributed to other factors, such as smoking, which the evaluation committees use as a pretext to eliminate most of the claims. For the victims' associations and unions involved in this struggle, these flaws attest to the hypocrisy of the system set up by the state.

To date, some 30 suits have been filed against companies that exposed their employees to asbestos. These trials, the majority of which involve companies in the region of Osaka, have garnered far more media coverage than the 18 court cases that preceded the Kubota scandal. Three of these suits target the state. The first is that of Sennan, which began in 2006; a second suit, filed in 2007, concerns two victims from the Kubota company; the last, which is taking place in Tokyo, is the largest as far as the number of victims (172 to date), but the state plays just a complementary role, the principal defendants being a group of some 40 construction companies.[16]

The Sennan case is particularly interesting for several reasons. First, the plaintiffs are employees or nearby residents of now-defunct small companies, who, unable to take on a manufacturer, turn against the state. If their action succeeds, the consequences would extend well beyond the case of asbestos, establishing a precedent for other cases of industrial disease, and opening up the possibility of redress being sought by other groups, including temporary or subcontracted workers who continue to be exposed to all sorts of chemical substances. Second, and it is this point to which we will devote the rest of this chapter, for the victims' attorneys, the state is not a defendant by default: its responsibility is clearly demonstrated by the numerous epidemiological studies that have been carried out, nearly all of which were commissioned and financed by the state.

THE 'VILLAGE OF ASBESTOS'

Sennan is located in the southern outskirts of Osaka, between the coast bordering Osaka Bay and the mountains on the Ise peninsula on Japan's main island of Honshu. Despite its asbestos-laden past, the area is picturesque, and the air apparently unpolluted. It is there that the Japanese asbestos industry started in 1907, when Seiki Sakaeya, one of the founders of the joint-stock company Nihon Asubesuto, now Nichias, decided to establish the first woven asbestos factory, taking advantage of local know-how from cotton growing, which had developed there, and of the proximity of Sakai, the old port of Osaka, for mineral imports. The asbestos industry took off quickly, especially during World War I, in order to meet the needs of the army, and then again in the 1930s, with the invasion of China. But, above all, it was in the aftermath of World War II that the business experienced its meteoric growth. The Osaka region (and in large part Sennan) absorbed roughly two-thirds of all Japanese asbestos imports, reaching a first peak of 350,000 tons in 1974 and another of 300,000 tons in 1988, before beginning a slow decline until 2004.

In Sennan, up until the 1980s, a scattering of small firms worked as subcontractors for giant producers, such as Nichias.[17] Starting at the end of the 1960s, as Japanese legislation regarding asbestos became more restrictive, Nichias gradually relocated its factories to Taiwan and South Korea. Circumventing the total ban on asbestos usage adopted by Japan in 2005, the company continues to process asbestos in Indonesia and China, under conditions similar to those formerly known at Sennan.

Sennan was commonly called the 'village of asbestos' (*ishiwata mura*), the separation between workplace and home was often porous. When there was a rudimentary system of aeration, it spat out dust on the adjoining houses and schools, right up to the 1990s. In the case of asbestos, this blurring of boundaries in relation to the conditions of exposure is not unusual. At first, this dispersion of small enterprises made it more difficult to clearly identify one polluter as was the case for Kubota. When, in 2005, some residents of Sennan were alerted by the Kubota scandal, they first considered suing the major contractors like Nichias, but that would have involved locating all the invoices of the now-defunct small subcontractors. The chain of responsibility meant that there ought to be some bigger institution at the root of the story. Together with their lawyers, they then started to consider the origins of the asbestos mono-industry in that specific location and therefore the role of the state in its development.

The fact that the state is the sole defendant might obscure the responsibility of private industry, but the charges underline the economic character of this state crime, with the public authorities having systematically supported and even encouraged the asbestos industry to the end of the 1960s. Subsequently, the state continually delayed the adoption of stricter regulations, clearly giving priority to the 'competitive edge' gained by the entire Japanese economy from the low cost of asbestos importing and processing—apart, of course, from the consequences for the health of certain population groups.

Without going so far as to accuse the state of an overall conspiracy, the plaintiffs suggested that a criminal act had been committed through the negligence of the Ministry of International Trade and Industry (MITI) in disregarding the warnings issued by the Ministry of Health.[18] This was, for example, the argument developed by Hiroyuki Mori, a specialist in economic history who testified in court at the request of the attorneys for the plaintiffs.[19] The responsibility of the state is all the heavier, since the ministries had not only received a great number of medical warnings from abroad, they had themselves financed several sanitary and medical studies conducted in Sennan, which had come to explicit and alarming conclusions, beginning in the 1940s. From this, there emerged a unifying slogan for the plaintiffs: the state "knew it could [change the situation], but it did nothing" (*shitteta, dekita, yaranakatta*). Here, the charges were established around a body of evidence put together by the state itself but systematically ignored, an *a priori* error of omission all the more damning for the state since the companies involved were, in the great majority, very small operations, with no access themselves to international knowledge about the known dangers of asbestos. Ironically, at the very same time, their working population was the subject of in-depth studies on an international level.

A SUCCESSION OF MEDICAL AND EPIDEMIOLOGICAL STUDIES

Beginning in December 1937, Hiroshi Sukegawa, a doctor who had been recently appointed adjunct director of the Osaka Bureau of Health Insurance, an arm of the Home Ministry, launched a study on the state of workers' health, initially involving 19 asbestos producers and a cohort of 1,024 employees, later reduced to 689 individuals at 14 companies.[20] The Sennan district was well represented with 406 individuals from 11 companies. The final report, dated February 1940, revealed a 12 percent rate of asbestosis, irrespective of age or sex, which in itself should have been enough to alert the public authorities. A more explicit finding was the drastic increase in incidence proportional to years of seniority: 20 percent rate of asbestosis after three and five years of work, 60 percent between 10 and 15 years, and a full 100 percent after 20 and 25 years of service.[21] Despite this study having a scope and rigorousness practically unequaled at that time, even at the international level, not only do the workers seem not to have been informed of the results, but none of the measures recommended by Sukegawa and his colleagues for improving labor conditions were adopted.[22] As Hiroyuki Mori underscores, this behavior contrasts sharply with the British government's adoption of preventative measures following the publication of the Merewether and Prince report in 1930.[23] It is true, that Japan was on the verge of entering into war with the US and these figures, while on a par with battlefield casualties, would hardly have impressed the senior officials of the Home Ministry—particularly since the workforce affected was largely made up of immigrants from the Korean Peninsula, at the time a Japanese colony.[24] More than 60 years later, for Akio Shibahara, the lead lawyer for the plaintiffs, this information was to constitute the cornerstone of their case: "The day that I got my hands on this report at the library, I realized that we had a chance of winning this suit."[25]

Further studies were undertaken after the war, this time in a far more democratic and humanitarian context. Pressured by the miners, the Ministry of Labor launched a campaign for the prevention of occupational disease, which resulted in an initial decree, in 1955, recognizing silicosis and in the adoption, in 1960, of a law recognizing various forms of pneumoconiosis (*jinpai*), the generic term for all the pulmonary ailments related to silicosis.[26]

As for asbestosis, Yoshitsugu Hōrai, a student of Sukegawa, initiated his own study in Sennan beginning in 1949. The early results reported by the Hōrai team in 1952 showed a relatively small rate of 5 percent asbestosis, or 10 individuals in a cohort of 203; however, young people were over-represented in this group.[27] Further studies increased the cohort size to 679 workers spread among no less than 131 companies and addressed the cumulative effects of asbestosis and tuberculosis.[28] Starting in 1956, Hōrai and his team were entrusted with an investigation financed by the Ministry of Labor, the purpose of which was to examine the "diagnostic criteria of asbestosis."[29] The initial study, conducted between 1957 and 1959 and covering a cohort of 814 employees at 30 asbestos factories in Sennan and two in Osaka, arrived at results nearly identical to those of the Sukegawa report of 1940. The study reported a total of 10 percent incidence of asbestosis and a mortality rate which rose exponentially with seniority: 25 percent for the group with five to 10 years seniority, 50 percent for those with 10 to 15 years, and 100 percent at 20 to 25 plus years.

Yoshizumi Sera, who ran a clinic near Sennan and took part in a series of surveys headed by Hōrai, conducted three other studies at the request of the Ministry of Labor, carried out between 1974–1978 and 1983–1984.[30] If the studies by Hōrai and Sera made a decisive contribution towards asbestosis being included in the 1960 law, follow-up studies of these cohorts during the following decade did not show any improvement.[31] Sera was the first in Japan to delineate, through an autopsy, the possible degradation of asbestosis into cancer.[32] His disciple, Ken'ei Kan (alias Kŏn-yŏng Kang in its Korean transcription) would be the first to observe the connection between asbestosis and pleural mesothelioma.[33] In a recent work, he recalls workers who, up until the early 1970s, spent their days literally covered in asbestos and who, after several years of such work, almost all ended up dying at Sakai City Hospital—of asbestosis, lung cancer, or mesothelioma.[34] Traces of this can be seen in the increase, starting in the 1970s, of studies on cancers linked to asbestos.

In a report to the Environmental Agency, Sera and his team concluded that, not only was asbestosis doing as much harm as ever, but even among people who declared that they had had no direct contact with asbestos in their work, asbestos dust could be found in their lungs and airways.[35] Moreover, the number of lung cancers diagnosed in patients already suffering from asbestosis was on the rise, be they retired asbestos workers, their relatives, or residents of Sennan with no history of working with asbestos. Kenji Morinaga, at the time another student of Sera, led his own study on a cohort of 791 Sennan workers from 1974 to 1981; he observed an increase in cancer incidence four times higher than the national average.[36] He would later produce other similar studies, publishing his results—in greater numbers than his predecessors—in English-language journals, a sign of the growing inclusion of Japanese research in the international medical community, a factor that is likely to bring additional pressure on the Japanese authorities with regard to preventative measures.[37]

In an effort to evaluate the sanitary consequences of asbestos beyond the population of workers directly exposed and starting from the position that the presence of pleural plaques attests to a definite exposure to asbestos, the Central Hospital of Kinki (the region surrounding the district of Sennan) carried out two targeted studies together with the Osaka Cancer Registry and the Osaki Health Center: the first between 1972 and 1974, with a cohort of 791; the second between 1978 and 1981, with a much larger cohort of more than 27,000 individuals. If the number of people suffering from pleural plaques, 159, was then rather limited, it was set to explode in the 1990s.[38]

An examination of the medical literature carried out in the mid-1980s by the National Association for Measures against Pneumoconiosis listed 125 publications directly linked to asbestos-related pathologies observed throughout Japan, from the first research report by Sukegawa in 1938 up to the most recent studies of the 1980s.[39] The Ministry of Labor commissioned no less than five studies between 1956 and 1984 (all centered on the region of Osaka, Sennan, and Nara); six others were ordered by the Ministry of Health beginning in 1971 and eight by the Environmental Agency (which was established in 1971). Even the Ministry of Education got involved, starting in 1980, when it commissioned two studies on the development of means to reduce exposure to asbestos. All of these studies seem to have resulted in a limited number of decisions regarding preventative measures, their sponsors mostly opting instead for the pursuit of further studies in order to evaluate the risks and consequences with greater precision.

Seiji Kajimoto practiced general medicine in Sennan for some 40 years, beginning in 1953. Alarmed by the high number of pulmonary pathologies, he researched asbestos alongside Sera and afterwards continually pushed the factory managers in Sennan to improve aeration and furnish workers with face masks. Often turned away, he even had thousands of leaflets printed at his own expense in order to alert workers of the danger, mentioning that he had warned the state, local authorities, and researchers but had received no reply.[40] His efforts were in vain, judging by a 1989 report by the Kishiwada Bureau of Labor Inspection, which stated that many workers still failed to wear face masks because they considered the risks from asbestos to be similar to the risks from tobacco.[41]

MEDICAL EXPERTISE IN THE DOCK

Under such conditions, how are we to understand the purpose of these numerous studies? Setting aside the initial survey of 1938–1949 with its unique context of a looming world war, what could have motivated their compilation? According to a pragmatic sociology of action, which informs my approach to these industrial controversies, it is a mistake to assign specific actors with strategic intentions in order to accuse them *a priori* of some action.[42] In other words, the question as to what purpose these studies had, can only be legitimate if it is articulated by the actors involved and not imposed from the outside by sociologists. Surprisingly, neither the plaintiffs nor their lawyers seemed to wonder about the purposes of the many medical studies that were conducted. In other contexts, notably at Minamata and in Taiwan—or more recently in the criminal complaint launched by Fukushima residents against TEPCO, NISA (Nuclear Industry Safety Agency) executives and scientists involved in the 'safety campaign' on radiation risks—the victims of pollution, refusing to serve as 'guinea pigs,' increasingly question the intentions of the science itself and not just its role in political decision-making.[43,44] In so doing, the plaintiffs and their lawyers make use of the existing medical studies in order to compete in the medico-legal jousting that is the trial format. The experts and scientists called to testify thus relinquish what Latour calls the "pre-modern innocence" of industrial pollution's victims.[45]

In the Sennan trial, these questions about the purpose of the studies were not put forward, and when I brought them up with the plaintiffs and their attorneys, they did not show much interest. The lawyers were primarily preoccupied with getting the commitment of the various witnesses and with what they would say, given that the experts tend to separate themselves into researchers in the pay of the state and those who agree to testify in favor of the plaintiffs. The commitment of the latter is all the more impressive, because they risk tarnishing their reputations with the very government agencies upon which they might depend for research projects or prestigious positions on various committees.

Among the experts called by the defense, the pneumologist Takumi Kishimoto testified on four different occasions. During the first session, he was asked to challenge the results of the report by Sukegawa and his colleagues, and the conclusions drawn from it by the doctor called by the plaintiffs. To do so, Kishimoto argued that the study lacked objectivity, judging that Sukegawa and his colleagues had been influenced by their low-quality radiology equipment, which prevented them from clearly distinguishing asbestosis from contagious diseases such as tuberculosis or pneumonia, or from other pneumoconioses, such as silicosis. As we saw above, the workers were dying one after another, but Kishimoto nonetheless believed that in Sukegawa's place, he would have refrained from drawing the same conclusions and would have recommended the commissioning of further studies.[46] At the next session, questioned point by point by the attorneys for the plaintiffs, Kishimoto was forced to retract his previous statements, admitting, for example, that given the available information, a case of asbestosis after 10 years of exposure would have called for a rapid intervention in working conditions.[47]

During the two sessions that followed, the questions centered on the medical file of two plaintiffs, one of whom was Yōko Okada, born in 1956, who spent her childhood alongside her mother, an asbestos weaver, and who now shows symptoms of asbestosis. In the meantime, Kishimoto, who was a member of the College of Physicians that rules on the recognition of pneumoconiosis as an occupational disease (*jinpai shinsa i*), was promoted from the regional to the national level. Questioned by the defense, this time he contested the diagnosis of asbestosis for the two plaintiffs, based solely on the CT scans provided by the defense, disregarding the clinical files and plaintiff depositions. In the case of Okada, despite traces of pleural plaques attesting to asbestos exposure, complicated by pulmonary emphysema which he deemed "very mild" (although she is never without an oxygen tank), Kishimoto disagreed that she had asbestosis, attributing her pulmonary problems to tobacco use.[48] While it is true that Okada conceded that she had smoked a packet of cigarettes a day between 1976 and 2004, that does not diminish the effect of the first 13 years of her life spent in a perpetual cloud of asbestos. During the second session, the cross-examination of the plaintiffs' attorneys succeeded in confusing Kishimoto, notably by presenting medical certificates which had been requested from him and whose existence he had forgotten.[49] His stance rested on two assumptions: first, that asbestosis is strictly an occupational disease; second, that pleural plaques never cause pain or impairment. In effect, Kishimoto maintained that if it is not discussed in the medical literature, the problem does not exist. The doctors who worked on the pleural plaques study in the 1970s and 1980s seemed to be looking at verifying the environmental character of the asbestos pollution emanating from the Sennan factories, rather than looking for asbestosis, a disparity which the defense counsel highlighted to its advantage. In the case of Okada and the other incidents of environmental exposure, the plaintiffs would not, finally, be successful.

The ruling by the Osaka District Court on May 19, 2010, largely favored the plaintiffs by recognizing the responsibility of the state for 29 victims (out of 33); it imposed damages of 946 million yen (approximately US$11 million) against the state, underlining the state's negligence in failing to use its regulatory powers. The defense was not unprepared for such a ruling, and the state appealed the decision, while still intimating that a settlement was possible. The attorneys for the plaintiffs then lobbied lawmakers in Tokyo, arguing that the state should not again shirk its responsibility while waiting for the plaintiffs to die off. Up until now, in most of these cases, the state has made victims wait through trials all the way up to the Supreme Court only to end up ultimately avoiding conviction. In some cases, however, especially those involving atmospheric pollution, settlements have been arrived at—an example being the adoption of a law in July 2009 to compensate victims of Minamata—thus holding out the hope of a political solution for ongoing lawsuits, such as Sennan.[50] In February 2010, however, the state refused in the Court of Appeal to meet the settlement demands of the Osaka District Court judge. Then, in August 2011, against all expectations, the Osaka Court of Appeal reversed the lower court's decision and rejected the plaintiffs' case on all grounds. The letdown was enormous. However, although their chances for success remain slim, the plaintiffs have resolved to pursue the matter at the Supreme Court level. In March 2012, the Osaka District Court announced another decision for a second group of 55 plaintiffs that, once again, largely favored the plaintiffs and recognized the responsibility of the state.

CONCLUSION

The people of Sennan and their lawyers decided to sue the Japanese state after they found several public health surveys that were conducted as early as the 1940s. In this sense, epidemiology played a decisive role in their attempts to criminalize the state. I would like to conclude this chapter by exploring some of the ways in which epidemiology was used in the courtroom, specifically in relation to the formulation of 'industrial crime' as a distinct category in Japan.

Thanks largely to the work of Ulrich Beck, which has foregrounded 'risk' as a key notion to apprehend modernity, there has been vigorous debate within science and technology studies about the status of risk as regards controversies (through litigation or within various forms of public sphere) and policy-making. Today, there is a theoretical framework in place for elucidating the respective roles of scientists, experts, and lay citizens, as well as the different contested 'knowledges' implicated in 'science': from 'known unknowns' and 'unknown unknowns' to 'undone science'—that is, research areas that may be unfunded and overlooked by the state or private business, but which civil society organizations deem nonetheless to be critical.[51] The question of scientific uncertainty plays a particularly crucial role as concerns medico-legal controversies over the causal links between pollutants and pathologies, the respective roles of epidemiology and clinical observation, and the balance of power between different groups of actors and fields of study. Such controversies have become increasingly dominated by epidemiology with the following consequences: first, the reduction of industrial disease to a matter of 'risk management' to be treated in a technocratic fashion, according only to the criteria of the quantifiable evaluation of risk (hence, a fascination for statistical tools, like geographic information systems, for example); second—and conversely—the promotion of a rhetoric about scientific uncertainty, which may serve as a pretext for political inaction. Between these two poles, the notion of 'industrial crime' reframes industrial disease as a matter of ethics.

During the last few decades, the blatant discrepancy between the victims of industrial pollution and the impunity enjoyed by their offenders has motivated the development of 'environmental ethics,' as well as proactive research subfields like 'popular epidemiology,' and 'environmental justice.'[52,53,54] The work of social scientists, ethicists, and historians such as David Rosner and Gerald Markowitz, and their commitment to testifying for the victims, remains an important source of inspiration for the contemporary study of industrial disease and industrial crime.[55] These scholars do not produce science purely for the sake of science; they are explicitly motivated by what they perceive to be blatant injustices, and they clearly empathize with the people they write about. Although they have been criticized, in this respect, for their lack of objectivity, it could be argued, on the contrary, that it is precisely this affinity that has enabled them to produce such groundbreaking work on industrial disease, influencing debates about health and safety, and the implementation of health policy.

While American scholars such as Rosner and Markowitz have produced key works and formulated critical concepts for understanding industrial disease and industrial crime, during the same period, US court decisions on toxic torts have shown a rather regressive tendency, with various consequences for policy-making and other litigation at the global level. The 1993 US Supreme Court ruling of *Daubert v. Merrell Dow Pharmaceuticals* drastically limited the admissibility of scientific testimony in court. The trial judge was assigned an impossible mission as 'gatekeeper' in an effort to eliminate 'junk science.' The application of the Daubert Standard has resulted in a drastic reduction of toxic tort cases, and several industries have seized on this opportunity to weaken environmental and public health regulations concerning their industrial process or output.[56] As suggested by Taiwanese sociologist Hsin-Hsing Chen, the 'epidemiological principles' (*ekigaku gensoku*) used in Japanese pollution trials, and the 'precautionary principle' used in the EU industrial chemical regulations (REACH), offer challenging alternatives to the US Daubert Standard.[57] The decision of the criminal court of Turin in February 2012 related to the asbestos company Eternit, and the expected decision of the

Japanese Supreme Court regarding the Sennan trial, could also be important challenges to the Daubert Standard.

Another problem is the growing dominance of epidemiology over other scientific knowledge in industrial disease litigation. In the US, Sheila Jasanoff has shown through her work on several toxic torts that judges, and even more so juries, have generally favored clinical over epidemiological evidence, as the clinical presentation of a disease appears more concrete than epidemiological statistics.[58] However, as stressed by David Michaels, because of the Daubert Standard, in recent years US judges have also tended to favor epidemiology over other disciplines, notably toxicology: the latter relies mainly on animal studies, which can be conducted at limited cost and within a rather short period of time, while epidemiology must work with large cohorts of humans, requiring long periods of research and considerable financing. Big industry, therefore, when it anticipates possible attacks from groups of victims, might prefer to finance expensive epidemiological studies as a means to control the results. But it does not favor toxicological research that challenges the safety of the manufacturing process or industrial products.[59]

As regards the dominant position of epidemiology in industrial crime litigation, we might question the recent promotion of 'epidemiological criminology.'[60] As other contributors to *Disease and Crime* have noted, this subfield of criminology reflects the legacy of the physician and criminologist Cesare Lombroso (considered in Chapter 2 by Chiara Beccalossi), as well as the new avatars of behaviorism and genetic determinism discussed briefly by Robert Peckham in the Introduction. From the perspective of popular epidemiology, this hybrid subfield represents another aspect of a legal framework that has been increasingly favorable to deregulation in areas from environment to public health.

Finally, if we consider the likelihood of the victims of industrial disease having their offenders punished through litigation, we should discuss the role of expertise at large. We have seen that in the US, the Daubert Standard has limited the use of expertise in court to challenge the polluters, while it has encouraged big industries to promote biased epidemiology. In continental law jurisdictions, such as Japan, the absence of a jury in civil cases tends to push judges to lean more heavily on expert testimony, which is more and more reliant on epidemiology.

Since epidemiology requires long term and expensive research, its dominant use is therefore also to the disadvantage of the victims-plaintiffs. As shown in the case of Sennan, the victims are often reduced to an *ex-post* protestation of the risks, long after the facts (in an echo of the latency period between exposure to asbestos and the onset of pathologies), and within the framework of a judicial system with ever-greater techno-scientific constraints. Or, as sociologist Luc Boltanski notes:

> counter-expertise is necessarily dominated and invariably the loser, since it can only seek to attain expertise [. . .] by conforming to the

test forms laid down by the latter and adopting its formalism and, more generally, its way of encoding reality.[61]

Indeed, the 'expert' plaintiffs are often compelled to adopt the positivist historical test or the 'large numbers' of epidemiology.[62]And by focusing on the disputes inherent in the uncertainties of ongoing scientific inquiry, the defendants can lead the judge to disregard the certainties and the asymmetry of power between the plaintiffs and the defendants.

This asymmetry between dominant offenders and dominated victims has been criticized in the concept formulated by Michel Callon and others of "hybrid forums," and wrongly so, since the authors of this concept were aiming above all to observe how popular knowledge challenges the knowledge of experts or scholars.[63] In this sense, the court resembles a "hybrid forum"; a public space, that is, where 'experts,' lay citizens, and policy-makers come together, as opposed to the sequestered spaces of specialists or professional politicians. As a process, a trial allows for the re-examination of the full history of a case of industrial pollution and, thus, for the formulation of fundamental questions that go beyond the sole exercise of proving causal links.

Moreover, if it does not eliminate the asymmetry of power, which often favors the language of experts, the trial is also a test for scientists, since it requires a translation from 'pure' science to 'expertise.' In order for the judge to reach a decision, the 'expert' researcher must temporarily suspend the doubt that is inherent in the scientific process and agree to compromise himself by issuing an expert opinion.[64] In rendering decisions regarding the recognition of occupational diseases or who should receive the indemnity funds for victims of industrial pollution, the medical experts can present their conclusions with no explanation, so that their denial of their duty of care remains hidden from the public. Conversely, the great advantage of the medico-legal battles waged in the courtroom, especially when open to the public, is that the doctors and scientists are forced to justify their decisions and actions.

So the plaintiffs' expertise is not always disappointed, far from it. The Sennan trial demonstrates this chaotic journey, as it was marked by a victory in the lower courts and a defeat on appeal, and it is impossible to say which of these two decisions is more likely to prevail in the Supreme Court. As stated by the jurist and reiterated by Jasanoff in her account of the legal development in the US since *Daubert v. Merrell Dow Pharmaceuticals*, particularly in relation to "fundamental assumption about law, science, and their interactions," the question is not "how judges can best do justice to science; the more critical concern is how courts can better render justice under conditions of endemic uncertainty and ignorance."[65] Or, as the sociologist Laurent Thévenot explains, although the judgment aims to end the dispute, there is nonetheless a fine line "between the expert called to establish the facts" and the judge's role in pronouncing on the basis of these facts, with the result that "the authority of the *res judicata* does not prevent the dispute from being taken up again outside of the judicial forum."[66] In the case at hand, even if the Japanese Supreme Court does not find in favor of the Sennan plaintiffs, it may well be that the movement gains new momentum and, taking inspiration from the Turin trial and the residents of Fukushima, perhaps even leads to a criminal charge.

In short, the asbestos controversies in Japan provide insights into the ways in which state and corporate institutions attempt to manage technosocial controversies. The case of Sennan, in particular, raises issues about the meaning and scope of participatory democracy, even as it underscores the role of scientific and biomedical knowledge in the production of technical 'expertise,' and the extent to which lay citizens are increasingly contesting the domains of specialists. In contemporary Japan, as elsewhere, 'disease' and 'crime' have become critical categories for those who seek to reconcile a world of uncertainty with justice by invoking the authority of 'science.'

ACKNOWLEDGMENTS

This chapter is based on field research undertaken between 2009 and 2011 as part of a Franco-Japanese program, "Silicosis and asbestos-related diseases in France and Japan; cartography, sociology, history and ethical reflection" supported by grants from the Agence Nationale de la Recherche and the Japanese Society for the Promotion of Sciences, for which I was the coordinator (with logistical support from Marine Sam and Alfred Aroquiame of the Asia Network, CNRS). For my fieldwork on the Sennan trial, I am indebted to my colleagues at the University of Kobe for their hospitality, in particular Professor Tsuyoshi Matsuda and his doctoral students. My study of the trial would have been impossible without access to the archives and advice offered by the plaintiffs' attorneys, notably Itō Akiko, Muramatsu Akio, and Shibahara Akio. My thanks to Rebecca Fite for her editorial input. Aspects of the argument were first presented in French in a journal article ["L'Etat, c'est personne! Ou l'Etat (japonais) à l'épreuve des catastrophes industrielles," *Quaderni*, no.78 (2012): 45–66] and my thanks to the editors.

NOTES

1. For a historical approach, see Christopher Sellers, *Hazards of the Job: From Industrial Disease to Environmental Health Science* (Chapel Hill: University of North Carolina Press, 1997).
2. Paul Jobin, *Maladies industrielles et renouveau syndical au Japon* [*Industrial Disease and Renewal of Trade Unionism in Japan*] (Paris: EHESS Editions, 2006).
3. See David Rosner and Gerald Markowitz, *Dying for Work: Workers' Safety and Health in Twentieth-Century America* (Bloomington: Indiana University Press, 1987); *Deadly Dust: Silicosis and the Politics of Occupational*

Disease in Twentieth-Century America (Princeton: Princeton University Press, 1991); Annie Thébaud-Mony, *La reconnaissance des maladies professionnelles en France. Acteurs et logiques sociales* (Paris: La Documentation française, 1991); Stéphane Buzzi, Jean-Claude Devinck, and Paul-André Rosental, *La santé au travail 1880–2006* (Paris: La Découverte, 2006); and Paul-André Rosental, "Health and Safety at Work: An Issue in Transnational History—Introduction," *Journal of Modern European History*, vol.7, no.2 (2009): 169–173.

4. See Timothy George, *Minamata and the Struggle for Democracy* (Cambridge, MA: Harvard University Press, 2001); and Jobin, *Maladies industrielles.*
5. See Sheila Jasanoff, *Science at the Bar: Law, Science, and Technology in America* (Cambridge, MA: Harvard University Press, 1995); Gerald Markowitz and David Rosner, *Deceit and Denial: The Deadly Politics of Industrial Pollution* (Berkeley: University of California Press, 2002); David Rosner and Gerald Markowitz, "The Trials and Tribulations of Two Historians: Adjudicating Responsibility for Pollution and Personal Harm," *Medical History*, vol.53, no.2 (2009): 271–292; Madeleine Akrich, Yannick Barthe, and Catherine Rémy, *Sur la piste environnementale. Menaces sanitaires et mobilisations profanes* (Paris: Presses des Mines, 2010); and Barbara Allen, "A Tale of Two Lawsuits: Making Policy-Relevant Environment Health Knowledge in Italian and U.S. Chemical Regions," in *Dangerous Trade: Histories of Industrial Hazard across a Globalizing World*, ed. Christopher Sellers and Joseph Melling (Philadelphia: Temple University Press, 2012), 154–167.
6. I borrow this expression from Bruno Latour, *The Making of Law: An Ethnography of the Conseil d'Etat* (Cambridge: Polity, 2010 [2002]). An eminent advocate of the innovative character of law is Mireille Delmas-Marty, chair professor at the College de France; see her book series *Les forces imaginantes du droit* (all published in Paris by Seuil): 1) *Le relatif et l'universel* (2004); 2) *Le pluralisme ordonné* (2006); 3) *La refondation des pouvoirs* (2007); 4) *Vers une communauté de valeurs* (2011).
7. This concept has gathered many scholars around the journal *Law and Society*. See the series of books edited by Austin Sarat and Stuart Scheingold: *Cause Lawyering: Political Commitments and Professional Responsibilities* (Oxford: Oxford University Press, 1998); *Cause Lawyering and the State in a Global Era* (Oxford: Oxford University Press, 2001); *Cause Lawyers and Social Movements* (Stanford: Stanford University Press, 2006); and *The Cultural Lives of Cause Lawyers* (Cambridge: Cambridge University Press, 2008).
8. Tomomi Yamaguchi, "Muto Ruiko and the Movement of Fukushima Residents to Pursue Criminal Charges against Tepco Executives and Government Officials," *The Asia-Pacific Journal*, no.27 (July 2, 2012). http://japanfocus.org/ (accessed January 28, 2013)
9. See Paul Jobin, "The Tragedy of Minamata: Sit-in and Face-to-Face Discussion," in *Making Things Public, Atmospheres of Democracy*, ed. Bruno Latour and Peter Weibel (Cambridge: MIT Press, 2005), 988–993; Jobin, *Maladies industrielles*; Paul Jobin, "The Postwar for Labour Unionism and Movements against Industrial Pollution," in *Japan's Postwar*, ed. Michael Lucken, Anne Bayard-Sakai, and Emmanuel Lozerand, trans. James A. Stockwin (London: Routledge, 2011 [2006]), 268–282; Paul Jobin and Yu-Hwei Tseng, "Guinea Pigs Go to Court: Epidemiology and Class Actions in Taiwan," [in Chinese] *Taiwanese Journal for Studies of Science, Technology and Medicine*, vol.12, no. 4 (2011): 159–203; and Soraya Boudia and Nathalie Jas, eds., *Powerless Science? Science and Politics in a Toxic World*, (Oxford: Berghahn, in press).

10. On the concept of the *ritournelle*, see Gilles Deleuze and Félix Guattari, *A Thousand Plateaus: Capitalism and Schizophrenia*, trans. Brian Massumi (London: Continuum, 1987 [1980]), 342–386.

11. Barry Castleman, *Asbestos: Medical and Legal Aspects* (Englewoods Cliffs, NJ: Prentice Hall Law & Business, 1990); Geoffrey Tweedale, *Magic Mineral to Killer Dust: Turner & Newall and the Asbestos Hazard* (Oxford: Oxford University Press, 2001); and James Rice, "The Global Reorganization and Revitalization of the Asbestos Industry, 1970–2007," *Occupational and Environmental Health Policy*, vol.41, no.2 (2011): 239–254. For a contradictory view, see Peter Bartrip, *The Way from Dusty Death: Turner and Newall and the Regulation of Occupational Health in the British Asbestos Industry, 1890–1970* (London: The Athlone Press, 2001) and *Beyond the Factory Gates: Asbestos and Health in Twentieth-Century America* (London: Continuum, 2006).

12. Called the "Kubota Shock" in Japanese.

13. Emmanuel Henry, "How the Environment Came to the Rescue of Occupational Health: Asbestos in France c. 1970–1995," in *Dangerous Trade: Histories of Industrial Hazard across a Globalizing World*, ed. Christopher Sellers and Joseph Melling (Philadelphia: Temple University Press, 2012), 140–150.

14. Norio Kurumatani and Shinji Kumagai, "Mesothelioma Due to Neighborhood Asbestos Exposure: A Large-Scale, Ongoing Disaster among Residents Living near a Former Kubota Plant in Amagasaki, Japan," in *Asbestos Disaster: Lessons from Japan's Experience*, ed. Kenichi Miyamoto, Kenji Morinaga, and Hiroyuki Mori (Tokyo: Springer, 2011), 75–91.

15. Interview in Paris, May 2011.

16. Katsumi Matsumoto, "Asbestos Litigation in Japan: Recent Trends and Related Issues," in *Asbestos Disaster*, 281–302.

17. In 1987, there were 79 such businesses with between one and 30 employees (most had less than 10) and four with over 30 employees.

18. On the Japanese adoption of a 'Bismarckian' model during its modernization—an influence reflected in the creation of the Japanese Ministry of International Trade and Industry, see Chalmers Johnson, *MITI and the Japanese Miracle* (Stanford: Stanford University Press, 1982).

19. For a presentation of his statements in English, see Hiroyuki Mori, "Asbestos Disaster and Public Policy: From the Prewar Era through the Postwar Economic Boom," in *Asbestos Disaster*, 93–126.

20. *Hereafter the documents preceded by an asterisk are those entered into evidence in the Sennan asbestos trial in the district of Osaka. *Hiroshi Sukegawa et al., *Asubesuto kōjō ni okeru sekimenhai no hassei jōkyō ni kansuru chōsa kenkyū [Research on the Conditions of Asbestosis Occurrence in Asbestos Factories]* (Tokyo: Naimushō, Hoken iji eisei [Home Ministry, Department of Insurance, Medicine and Public Hygiene], 1940), 109. Regarding the establishment of institutions concerned with issues of occupational health in pre-war Japan, see Bernard Thomann, "L'hygiène nationale, la société civile et la reconnaissance de la silicose comme maladie professionnelle au Japon (1868–1960)," *Revue d'histoire moderne et contemporaine*, vol.56, no.1 (2009): 142–176.

21. *Sukegawa, *Asubesuto kōjō*.

22. As stressed by Fujio Oikawa, Kōsuke Ōta, Keinosuke Kaburagi, Kikuji Kimura, Hiroyuki Sakabe, Shōgo Shima, et al., *Nihon no jinpai taisaku*

[*Measures against Pneumoconiosis in Japan*], vol.4 (Tokyo: Chūō rōdō saigai bōshi kyōkai [National Association for the Prevention of Labor Casualties], 1985), 125.

23. Mori, *Asbestos Disaster*, 116–117. Mori's view is congruent with Bartrip, *The Way from Dusty Death*.

24. Regarding the lawsuits brought in the 1990s by Koreans and Chinese 'recruited' to work in Japanese mines and steel mills during World War II, see Jobin, *Maladies industrielles et renouveau syndical Japon*, 420–424.

25. Interview in Osaka, July 2009.

26. Bernard Thomann, "Yoroke: la silicose au Japon," in *Santé au travail: approches critiques*, ed. Annie Thébaud-Mony, Véronique Daubas-Letourneux, Nathalie Frigul, and Paul Jobin (Paris: La Découverte, 2012), 59–82.

27. *Yoshitsugu Hōrai, *Sekimenhai ni kansuru kenkyū (1) sekimen kōjō ni okeru sekimenhai kenshin seiseki shōwa 27nendo seiseki* ["Research on Asbestos 1; Results for 1952 at an Asbestos Factory"], *Nara igaku zasshi* [*Nara Medical Journal*], (1957); Oikawa, *Nihon no jinpai taisaku*, 127; and Mori, *Asbestos Disaster*, 117.

28. *Yoshitsugu Hōrai et al., "Shōhichi ni okeru keihai kenshin to sono keika" ["The Sites of Consumption and Results of Silicosis Exams"], *Rōdō kagaku kenkyū* [*Research on Science of Labor*], vol.29, no.4 (1953): 237; and *Yoshitsugu Hōrai et al., "Sekimenhai kekkaku no shōrei" ["The Symptoms of Asbestosis and Tuberculosis"], *Nara igaku zasshi*, vol.7, no.4 (1956): 309.

29. *Yoshitsugu Hōrai et al., *Sekimenhai no shindan kijun ni kansuru kenkyū* [*Research Relative to Diagnostic Criteria for Asbestosis*] (Tokyo: Rōdōshō, Rōdō eisei shiken kenkyūjo [Ministry of Labor, Center for Experimental Research on Hygiene], 1957 and 1958); and *Yoshitsugu Hōrai et al., *Sekimenhai nado no jinpai ni kansuru kenkyū* [*Research Relative to Diagnostic Criteria for Asbestosis and Other Pneumoconiosis*] (Tokyo: Ministry of Labor, Rōdōshō shiken kenkyū [Experimental Hygiene Research], 1960).

30. Oikawa, *Nihon no jinpai taisaku*, 144.

31. The general average of people affected is around 12 percent: 48 of 633 in 1960; 27 of 240 in 1963; 29 of 260 in 1966; 42 of 231 in 1970; and 53 of 444 in 1972 (*Akio Shibara, Akio Muramatsu, Yukio Kamata, et al., *Sojō* [Bill of Indictment], May 26, 2006, Archives of the Sennan Trial, North Osaka General Law Office, Nishitenma 3–14–16 (hereafter AST).

32. *Yoshizumi Sera, et al., "Haigan o gappei shita sekimenhai no 1 bōkenrei" ["First Autopsy of a Case of Asbestosis Combined with Lung Cancer"], *Sangyō igaku* [*Industrial Medicine*], vol.2, no.4 (1960): 326.

33. Ken'ei Kan, Yoshizumi Sera and Kunihiko Yokoyama, "Sekimen hai ni gappei shita kyōmaku chūhishu no ichi rei" ["Initial Case of Asbestosis Combined with Pleural Mesothelioma"], *Nihon kyōbu shikkan zasshi* [*Japan Journal of Thoracic Diseases*], vol.12 (1974): 458–464.

34. Ken'ei Kan, *Asubesuto kōgai to gan hassei* [*Asbestos Pollution and the Onset of Cancer*] (Tokyo: Shuchōsha, 2006).

35. *Yoshizumi Sera, et al., *Sekimenhai to haigan no kanren ni kansuru ekigakuteki rinshōteki byōri soshikigakuteki kenkyū, "Hitohai no byōri soshikigakuteki kenkyū" hōkoku* [*Research on the Relationship between Asbestosis and Lung Cancer: Epidemiology, Clinic, and Histopathology, "Histopathology of Human Lung" Report*] (Tokyo: Kankyōchō kōgai chōsa kenkyū itaku jigyō [Environment Administration, Public Nuisances Survey Office], 1973).

36. Oikawa, *Nihon no jinpai taisaku*, 134–135.

37. For example, Kenji Morinaga, I. Hara, S. Yutani and Yoshizumi Sera, "Use of Population-Based Cancer Registration in Occupational Epidemiology: Experience in Osaka," *Journal of the University of Occupational and Environmental Health,* vol.5 (1983): 215–223; Kenji Morinaga, Kunihiko Yokoyama, Satoshi Yamamoto, Yoshinobu Matsuda and Yoshizumi Sera, "Mortality and Survival of Workers Receiving Compensation for Asbestosis in Osaka, Japan," in *Proceedings of the 6th International Pneumoconiosis Conference* (Geneva: International Labor Office, 1984), 768–774; and Kenji Morinaga, Takumi Kishimoto, Mitsunori Sakatani, Masanori Akira, Kunihiko Yokoyama and Yoshizumi Sera, "Asbestos-Related Lung Cancer and Mesothelioma in Japan," *Industrial Health,* vol.39, no.2 (2001): 65–74.

38. Shibahara, *Sojō,* 33.

39. Oikawa, *Nihon no jinpai taisaku.*

40. Kazuyoshi Yuoka, "Kakusareta higai no genba o aruku" ["Walking around the Site of Hidden Damages"], in *Asubesuto sanka o kuni ni tou [Questioning the State about Asbestos Disasters],* ed. Osaka jinpai asubesuto bengodan [Osaka Attorneys' Group on Asbestos Silicosis] and Sennan chiiki no sekimen higai to shimin no kai [Asbestos Victims' and Citizens' Association for the Region of Sennan], (Kyōto: Kamogawa, 2009), 68–69. Dr. Kajimoto's testimony was recorded by Kazuyoshi Yuoka in the company of Kajimoto's wife and eldest son, who are active supporters of the plaintiffs. A graduate in literature from the University of Kyōto, Yuoka's grandfather had founded an asbestos cloth company in Sennan in the 1920s. Following the Kubota scandal, his grandson became one of the main leaders of the citizens' movement behind the Sennan trial.

41. Yuoka, "Kakusareta higai," 67–68.

42. Luc Boltanski and Laurent Thévenot, *On Justification: Economies of Worth,* trans. Catherine Porter (Princeton: Princeton University Press, 2006 [1991]); Laurent Thévenot, *L'action au pluriel. Sociologie des régimes d'engagement* (Paris: La Découverte, 2006); Laura Centemeri, *Ritorno a Seveso. Il danno ambiantale, il suo riconoscimento, la sua reparazione* (Milano: Bruno Mondadori, 2006); Laura Centemeri, "Retour à Seveso. La complexité morale et politique du dommage à l'environnement," *Annales. Histoire, Sciences Sociales,* vol.1 (2011): 213–240; and Laura Centemeri, "What Kind of Knowledge is Needed about Toxicant-Related Health Issues? Some Lessons Drawn from the Seveso Dioxin Case," in *Powerless Science?*

43. Jobin, *Maladies industrielles;* Jobin and Tseng, "Guinea Pigs."

44. Yamaguchi, "Muto Ruiko."

45. See Bruno Latour, *We Have Never Been Modern,* trans. Catherine Porter (Cambridge, MA: Harvard University Press, 1993 [1991]; see, also, *On the Modern Cult of the Factish Gods* (Durham, NC: Duke University Press, 2010).

46. *Takumi Kishimoto, Minutes of Witness Testimony, October 1, 2008 (AST).

47. *Takumi Kishimoto, Minutes, November 19, 2008 (AST).

48. *Takumi Kishimoto, Minutes, May 27, 2009 (AST).

49. *Takumi Kishimoto, Minutes, June 24, 2009 (AST).

50. Jobin, *Maladies industrielles,* chap. 2.

51. Ulrich Beck, *The Risk Society: Towards a New Modernity,* trans. by Mark Ritter (London: Sage, 1992 [1986]). For a synthesis on risk, uncertainty, and unknowns, see Ulrike Fecht, Brian Wynne, Michel Callon, Maria E. Gonçalves, Sheila Jasanoff, Maria Jepsen, et al., *Taking European Knowledge Society Seriously. Report of the Expert Group on Science and Governance*

to the *Science, Economy and Society Directorate, Directorate-General for Research* (Brussels: European Commission, 2007). On 'undone science,' see Scott Frickel, Sahra Gibbon, Jeff Howard, Joanna Kempner, Gwen Ottinger and David J. Hess, "Undone Science: Charting Social Movement and Civil Society Challenges to Research Agenda Setting," *Science, Technology, & Human Values,* vol.35, no.4 (2010): 444–473.

52. For example, Kristin Schrader-Frechette, *Environmental Justice: Creating Equity, Reclaiming Democracy* (New York: Oxford University Press, 2002).

53. Led by Phil Brown. See his seminal article "Popular Epidemiology: Community Response to Toxic Waste Induced Disease in Woburn, Massachusetts," Science, Technology, & Human Values, vol.12, nos.3–4 (1987): 76–85; and his last edited collection *Contested Illnesses: Citizens, Science, and Health Social Movements* (Berkeley: University of California Press, 2012).

54. For example, Barbara Allen, *Uneasy Alchemy: Citizens and Experts in Louisiana's Chemical Corridor Disputes* (Cambridge, MA: MIT Press, 2003).

55. As historians of polluting industries, they have been called many times by plaintiffs to stand at the bar as expert witnesses, then facing all forms of harassment from the accused industries. See Rosner and Markowitz, "The Trials and Tribulations of Two Historians."

56. Carl F. Cranor, *Toxic Torts: Science, Law, and the Possibility of Justice* (New York: Cambridge University Press, 2006); David Michaels, *Doubt Is Their Product: How Industry's Assault on Science Threatens Your Health* (Oxford: Oxford University Press, 2008).

57. Hsin-Hsing Chen, "How Does Legal Justice Meet Scientific Fact? A View on Law, Science and Society through the *Daubert* Controversy," [in Chinese] *Taiwanese Journal for Studies of Science, Technology and Medicine,* vol.12, no.4 (2011): 44–48. Japanese epidemiological principles were developed in the 1970s, when several cases of industrial pollution were brought to court through class action (the first being the case of Minamata disease). These established that the plaintiffs only have to prove the *general causation* (the toxicity of the defendant's manufacturing process or the consumption of its products has been proven in general), while the charge of the proof for the *specific causation* (the plaintiff has been exposed to the defendant's process or its product and not another company's) relies on the defendant. Furthermore, when the causal links are weaker, the judge can reduce the amount of compensation, although he does not necessarily have to disregard the charges.

58. See Jasanoff, *Science at the Bar*, chap. 6. For a fascinating description of this process, see also Jonathan Harr's novel *A Civil Action* (New York: Vintage, 1996); and, on the reception of this book, see Sarat and Scheingold, *The Cultural Lives of Cause Lawyers*, 351–358.

59. Michaels, *Doubt Is Their Product*, 170; on epidemiology and toxicology, see Jobin and Tseng, "Guinea Pigs."

60. Timothy Akers and Mark M. Lanier, "'Epidemiological Criminology': Coming Full Circle," *American Journal of Public Health,* vol.99, no.3 (2009): 397–402; and Mark M. Lanier, "Epidemiological Criminology (EpiCrim): Definition and Application," *Journal of Theoretical and Philosophical Criminology,* vol.2, no.1 (2010): 63–103.

61. Luc Boltanski, *On Critique: A Sociology of Emancipation*, trans. Gregory Elliott (Cambridge: Polity, 2011), 137. The strategic 'modesty' of experts is another interesting aspect of this problem; see Thomas Scheffer, "Knowing How to Sleepwalk: Placing Evidence in the Midst of an English Jury Trial," *Science, Technology, & Human Values,* vol.35, no.5 (2010): 620–664. For Bruno Latour, expertise is an obsolete intermediary between politics and

science that cannot but offer the wrong answers to controversies on scientific governance, although Latour does not specifically address the particular framework of litigation expertise; see his *Cogitamus: six lettres sur les humanités scientifiques* (Paris: La Découverte, 2009).

62. See Alain Desrosières, *The Politics of Large Numbers: A History of Statistical Reasoning*, trans. Camille Naish (Cambridge, MA: Harvard University Press, 1998 [1993]).

63. Michel Callon, Pierre Lascoumes, and Yannick Barte, *Acting in an Uncertain World: An Essay on Technical Democracy* (Cambridge, MA: MIT Press, 2009 [2001]).

64. I am indebted to Laurent Thévenot for helping me clarify this fundamental point regarding a case study in Taiwan (Jobin and Tseng, "Guinea Pigs").

65. Sheila Jasanoff, "Law's Knowledge: Science for Justice in Legal Setting," *American Journal of Public Health*, vol.95, no.S1 (2005): 49–58 (quoted by Michaels, *Doubt Is their Product*, 173).

66. Thévenot, *L'action au pluriel*, 178, 180.

8 Crime Between History and Natural History

Mark Seltzer

We might begin—in setting out some of the relays between crime and malady in a modern society—with Bertolt Brecht's dictum that "human beings learn no more from catastrophe than a laboratory rabbit learns about biology." The immediate field of reference for Brecht's remark is, of course, the catastrophic violence of World Wars I and II. But I take the reference from the German writer W. G. Sebald's extended reconsiderations of what he calls "the natural history of destruction," centered on the obliterating air war over Germany. This is an account of a total destruction that, for Sebald, takes place "between history and natural history."[1]

The sense of crime, or war crime, between social and natural history in effect leads thinking in a circle. It does so not merely because, as Sebald concisely expresses it, "collective catastrophe marks the point where history threatens to revert to natural history."[2] There is at this point a sudden reversion of high modernity to the hunting and gathering stage of species life. And there is, put simply, a horrific collapse of the social organization into the biological order of things. Sebald's account of the aftermath of the obliteration from the air proceeds in these terms: After the destruction of the city, "people had lit small fires in the open, as if they were in the jungle, and were cooking their food or boiling up their laundry on those fires . . . trodden paths appear across the rubble, linking up to a faint extent with earlier networks of paths, for it is not yet certain whether the surviving remnants of the population will emerge from this regressive phase of evolution as the dominant species, or whether that species will be the rats or the flies swarming everywhere in the city, instead."[3]

In this way the "inorganic" destruction of life by the bombs from the air and fire on the ground is joined by destruction of an organic form: the takeover, and horrifying teeming, of new life from beneath the fresh rubble architecture of the ruined city. Hence, it leads thinking in a circle, above all, because it would seem that, far from being opposed or distinct, the "perspective of human history and natural history are one and the same, so that destruction and the tentative forms of new life that it generates act like biological experiments in which the life of the species is concerned."[4] This is not least the case in that the species conducting the experiment, and the one submitting to it, are one and the same, too.

Both the destruction and the reflexes set off in response to it are like laboratory experiments in species life conducted by the species on itself. Here, we enter into the self-conditioned character of our modernity. The defining attribute of catastrophes in what has come to be called a reflexive modernity is the manner in which they are and are more and more reported to be—from climate change to epidemic outbreaks to crimes against humanity—"catastrophes generated by [the species] itself."[5] These are the control conditions—the laboratory life—proper to an autotropic and self-induced world, one that comes to itself by producing and reporting its own conditions, such that each enters into the other.

If the perspectives of human and natural history are one and the same, this is to posit, on the one side, the strictly artificial and autonomous character of a reflexive modernity (what the sociologist Emile Durkheim described as a modern society's almost sui generis character). But it is to posit, on the other, that the autonomy of the species in the face of the real, or potential, devastation it has caused is "no greater in the history of the species than the autonomy of the animal in the scientist's cage."[6] (We recall that Durkheim's inaugural study of an almost sui generis modernity is in fact focused on the sociology of suicide and its statistical regularities.)

Consider, for example, this passage early on in the American writer Patricia Highsmith's remarkable novel *Ripley's Game* (1974), a novel in which a young picture-framer, dying of leukemia, is drawn into committing a series of murders, such that crime and disease each hold the place of the other:

> The hospital was a vast assembly of buildings set among trees and pathways lined with flowers. Karl had again driven them. The wing of the hospital where Jonathan had to go looked like a laboratory of the future—rooms on either side of a corridor as in a hotel, except that these rooms held chromium chairs or beds and were illuminated by fluorescent or variously coloured lamps. There was a smell not of disinfectant but as of some unearthly gas, something Jonathan had known under the X-ray machine which five years ago had done him no good with the leukaemia. It was the kind of place where layman surrendered utterly to the omniscient specialists, Jonathan thought, and at once he felt weak enough to faint. Jonathan was walking at that moment down a seemingly endless corridor of sound-proofed floor surface.[7]

A laboratory of the future—its pathways outlined with a transplanted nature. This is, as it were, a working model of an antiseptic modernity. To borrow the social psychologist Erving Goffman's description of the interaction rituals that define modern institutions, it is a working model of our "indoor social life."[8]

There is, first, the "vast assembly" of buildings with their endless corridors, sound-proofed and utterly self-conditioned. There is, second, the reassembling of the social as a laboratory for conducting experiments. There is, third, the manner in which a designed nature (planted with trees and lined with flowers) is there entirely for the purpose of being framed, seen, and staged: the demarcation zone of an experimental nature or second life.

These together mark the boundary lines of a totally unreal kind of reality, one in which the staging of world within the world, and its outlining, have become a precondition of life itself. It is an "unearthly" and alien life—no more one's own than the body that enters into the vast assembly of its administration. We might recall here Stanislaw Lem's statement that "your genuinely immediate world is the outside world"—"that body of yours, which to some extent obeys you, says nothing and lies to you."[9] It reports instead directly to the omniscient specialists who populate a laboratory of the future.

The patient is led into an unnatural, unearthly, posthuman maze of corridors; into an entire closed world of light, sound, and smell; the senses are surrendered to experts conducting biological experiments so that death and life appear as "readouts," "reports," blood counts, statistics—baseline conditions of a self-posited and self-describing world, one that endlessly generates a commentary on itself as it goes along. This is to say, if the commentary stops, life stops. To take one example of many from Highsmith's novel: "All the while, the doctor murmured in German to a nurse who was taking notes"[10]—and, of course, both the language and the notes are indecipherable to the object of this commentary. That is, death and life— and, in this case, deadly crime and deadly disease, life-support systems and life-taking ones—epitomize an autotropic world. This world is at once self-reporting, self-inciting, and self-conditioned.

Self-reporting. At the advent of this type of society, the psychiatrist Jean-Martin Charcot (Freud's predecessor) applied the name "l'homme du petit papier" to those neurasthenic patients who "frequently appeared with slips of paper or manuscripts endlessly listing their ailments." Like those other victims of fin-de-siècle maladies of energy and will, the patients suffering from "fatigue-amnesia"—that is, the condition of "being too tired to remember to feel tired"—Charcot's men with little pieces of paper, have only external access to their interior states, as if they know how they feel only by reading about it.[11] This is one of the conditioned reflexes of the official world and its experimental zones—its autonomic nervous system and its coupling of life to its registration.

Self-inciting. In his recent account *On Deep History and the Brain*, the historian Daniel Lord Smail traces in some detail the emergence and spreading of autotropic commodities in the long eighteenth century:

self-stimulants such as alcohol, caffeine, chili pepper, opiates, tobacco, chocolate, sugar, gossip, sports, music, new media, religiosity, recreational drugs, sex for fun, and pornography. Last and not least—or most—is novel reading and related forms of literary leisure: what in the nineteenth century came to be called "a reading world." These are versions of what he calls "the controlled use of the uncontrollable."[12] This is, as it were, the biological component of collective self-incitation. Smail is entranced by the example of the snorting horse: "Horses who get bored or lonely while isolated in a paddock sometimes take pleasure in startling themselves. A lively snort causes a chemical feedback that induces a startle reflex and an exciting wash of neurochemicals." He, the horse, mimics the conditions that would naturally stimulate a startle reflex. For Smail, this feedback pleasure is like the self-stimulative history he traces, with the difference, of course, that "the horse cannot say to himself, 'I feel like getting startled,'" or say it or report it to others. Hence, the autotropic world is between history and natural history (at once *deep* history and deep *history*).[13]

Self-conditioned. The sui generis and so self-exposed character of a strictly reflexive world is nowhere more clearly anatomized than in Cormac McCarthy's recent post-apocalyptic novel, *The Road.* But the novel takes the measure of this self-conditioning by way of its subtraction or denudation. It strips away one by one by one the self-contained nature of a modern world. It is as if, made to its own ends, this is a world intent too on putting an end to itself—or as McCarthy puts it, the tautologically coherent work of a "creation perfectly evolved to meet its own end."[14] It achieves the extreme formality of its own world entire.

For one thing, the landscape of *The Road* is suspended between biology and geology. The landscape is, more exactly, a woundscape. In *The Road*, body and terrain refer back to each other at every point—external and internal realities meet and fuse: "They were days fording that cauterized terrain . . ." "It took two days to cross that ashen scabland."[15] The world of the novel, like the world of the horror genre that it borders on, realizes inner and bodily states in external reality. The connection is not analogical but real such that the terrain that the characters cross is their own torn body, scarred, and cauterized.

The stripped world has been contracted to a father and son—"each the other's world entire"—who push down the road a battered shopping cart, containing their bare provisions, in a thoroughly consumed world—as if, then, going down the same road that led to the disaster in the first place. It is as if the reflexes of a form of life that not merely preceded the disaster but led to it continue on in the absence of the obliterated world that was the prerequisite for them.

And that was the prerequisite for the form of the novel itself, to the very extent that the novel as genre at once depends on and epitomizes a mutually observed and self-reported form of life. But the post-apocalyptic world of *The Road* is stripped of self-observation and so of news of itself. The world of *The Road* is one shorn of secondary qualities. It is a barely observable world.

The point not to be missed is that observation and self-observation are the very presuppositions of our modernity. This is the case from the moment that Galileo, in 1610, turned his telescope on the heavens and reported on "news from the stars," and, at the very same moment, reported on how the lens of the telescope and the lens of the eye worked and worked together. The turning outward to a new world and the great outside was at one and the same time a turning inward, a self-reflection on how we see and the perspective on the world as worldview—a constellation and a constellation of views, observation, and self-observation.[16]

This is the systole and diastole of modernity. If (as the systems theorist Heinz von Foerster put it) "reality appears as a consistent reference frame for at least two observers," this is to posit reality as the correlation of the world and its mutual (or triangulated) observation.[17] But here, in the eclipsed world of *The Road*, for instance, this shared frame of observation and observers has vanished: "Night dark beyond darkness and the days more gray each one than what had gone before. Like the onset of some cold glaucoma dimming away the world."[18] It is as if this glaucomic dimming were at once physiological and geological, uncertainly a property of the eye and the state of the world. Hence, the dependence of reality on its reflexive observation continues after that has ended, too. There are, here and there in the novel, talismans of a lost world, the remnant small technologies—the binoculars, the sextant, the folded and torn map, the small lamp—that not merely locate a way of seeing but ways of seeing: the world as it looks to us. *The Road* thus reenacts the form of the novel at its meridian: it is a thought experiment of sorts and one that compares the world as it looks to us to the world as it looks without us.

Hence, too, the novel crosses the scene of the crime (a crime against humanity) as if crossing a diseased body, glaucomic, scarred, and cauterized. In doing so, it models the demarcation zones of a strictly autogenic, and so autocidal, world. *The Road* is an experiment—one almost unbearably moving, and so at times almost unbearably gimmicky—in testing out the conditions of a self-conditioned world. As in horror stories, biology and topography, history and natural history, and the end of life and the end of the world—change places with each other. Or, in case we missed it, "We're the walking dead in a horror film."[19]

THE WALKING DEAD

I want, in the pages that follow, to fill in a bit more—and via a series of fictional and factual examples—what this world between history and natural history looks like. I take up these matters by way of these fictional examples in part because, as may already be evident, there is no better way to report on a self-reporting world. These new experimental novels are part of a world that more and more moves toward its own autonomous form; and these fictional accounts register and blueprint that world as it goes along—they epitomize a self-epitomizing world and (as we have seen) are one of its self-inciting forms. The experimental novel takes up the limit cases of this world, existential matters of life and death in cases of deep pathology and fatal crime.

The contemporary fascination with "the walking dead"—the refugee populations of a war uncertainly natural and technological, and one in which crime and disease meet and fuse—provides something like a field guide to death and life in this world at its limit. This fascination provides a way to track the crossing points of biology and history: a violence that has "long been foreshadowed by the complex physiology of human beings, the development of their hypertrophied minds, and their technological methods of production."[20]

Consider, then, this example of that strange postwar form of life: one at the lower range of both life and form, and so a baseline way to take the pulse, such as it is, of these general conditions. Here is the opening of Max Brooks's recent bestseller, *World War Z*, an unexpectedly compelling novel subtitled, *"An Oral History of the Zombie War"*:

Greater Chongquing, the United Federation of China

[At its prewar height, this regime boasted a population of over thirty-five million people. Now there are barely fifty-thousand. Reconstruction funds have been slow to arrive in this part of the country, the government choosing to concentrate on the more densely populated coast. There is no central power grid, no running water besides the Yangstze River. But the streets are clear of rubble and the local "security council" has prevented any postwar outbreaks. The chairman of that council is Kwang Jing-shu, a medical doctor who, despite his advanced age and wartime injuries, still manages to make house calls to all his patients.]

The first outbreak I saw was in a remote village that officially had no name. The residents called it "New Dachang," but this was more out of nostalgia than anything else. Their former home, "Old Dachang," had stood since the period of the Three Kingdoms, with farms and houses and even trees said to be centuries old. When the Three Gorges Dam was completed, and reservoir waters began to rise, much of Dachang had been disassembled, brick by brick, then rebuilt on higher ground. This New Dachang, however, was not a town anymore, but a "national historic museum." It must have been a heartbreaking irony for those poor peasants, to see their town saved but then only being able to visit it as a tourist. Maybe that is why some of them chose to name their newly constructed hamlet "New Dachang" to preserve some connection to their heritage, even if it was only in name . . . Officially, it didn't exist and therefore wasn't on any map.[21]

World War Z is, like Bram Stoker's *Dracula* a century before, a chronicle, or better a chronologically ordered dossier, made up of documents, files, numbers; grids, maps, committees, and officialism; the administratively located, named, and recorded—and the unnamed and unrecorded, and so officially inexistent. (It is also, like *Dracula*, or its early silent film version F. W. Murnau's *Nosferatu* [1922], a story in which plague and crime indicate each other in circular form.) The written records of an oral history have the neutrality of a series of collated reports. This makes for a foreign or alien reality, one in which the familiarity with cultural and social circumstances that the writing and reading of novels depends on has been (as in *The Road*) abrogated or suspended.

The reporter on the new state of life on the planet in this case is a doctor and regional medical officer. That makes perfect sense, given the ongoing transformation of human conditions into treatable disorders in modernizing society.[22] We know—for instance, from the work of the philosopher of disease Georges Canguilhem on the normal and the pathological, and that of his student Michel Foucault—that the medicalization of the social body is one of the defining characteristics of modernity, accelerative from the later eighteenth century on.[23]

But here the relays between sociology and biology and between crime, or war crime, and disease have mutated. The coupling of biology and its administration is, for one thing, the mode of the experimental novel. This could not be more explicit: the novelist and the doctor stand in for each other in Zola's manifesto for the experimental novel: "usually it will be sufficient for me to replace the word 'doctor' by the word 'novelist' in order to make my thought clear and to bring to it the rigor of scientific truth."[24]

The experimental novelist conducts "experiments on man," that is, on autotropic "man living in the social milieu which he himself has produced."[25] The recent turn to neuro-history and the neuro-novel, cognitive biology and evolution-premised histories, marks a certain return of a sociobiological dispositif. Or, as Zola bluntly put it: "The social circle is identical to the vital circle: in society as in the human body there is a solidarity which links the different members, the different organs together so that if an organ becomes infected many others are tainted, and a very complex illness becomes evident. Thus in our novels when we experiment on a grave infection which poisons society we proceed like the experimental doctor."[26]

This is what makes it possible, in Zola's fiction from *Thérèse Raquin* (1867) on, for disease (the disorder of structure or function at the level of the organism) and crime (the disorder of structure or function at the level of social organization) to reciprocally index each other. We may recall with that the function of fictions, or thought experiments, in the natural sciences, in pupating truth.

The new experimental novel returns to these premises, now on worldwide and species-wide scale. Here, in the collated journal pages of the zombie plague years in *World War Z*, history and natural history crisscross each other, thinning the line between them. The zombie plague itself seems, in *World War Z*, to have had its origins in an experimental medical laboratory in China. It is initially broadcast as a "mysterious natural disaster" and spreads via the black market organ trade and migrant or refugee populations. The boundaries, political and physical, come down between war and disease, between organic and inorganic catastrophes, and between the physiology of human beings and their technological methods of production and destruction.

The opening account takes place at the dark intersection of all these strands. The opening report by the medical examiner implicitly compares scales of time and place and natural and social forms of life and death. It compares, more exactly, the newly constructed, or reconstructed, to the long span of natural life (trees centuries old). But at the same time, it compares that to the yet even longer span of unnatural or political life (the Three Kingdoms, two millennia old). The Three Kingdoms and the Three Gorges Dam are in effect 'floated' in relation to each other, in an ongoing comparison of man-made and geological measures. That is the case because, as we have noted, collective catastrophe marks the point where social life overturns into the life of nature. As Sebald notes in *On the Natural History of Destruction*: "Is the destruction not, rather, irrefutable proof that the catastrophes which develop, so to speak, in our hands and seem to break out suddenly are a kind of experiment, anticipating the point at which we shall drop out of what we have thought for so long to be our autonomous history and back into the history of nature?"[27]

The official world is of necessity always patrolling the dikes of made culture, and in doing so, managing the catastrophes their construction sets in motion. The unspecified 'outbreak' lies then in the interval between controlled and uncontrollable life, and the walking dead, like the displaced in a war zone, carry their restlessness around like a sickness.[28]

But it is another and apparently gratuitous observation that in fact centers these opening pages. It does so not in diegetic but in extremely formal terms and so italicizes its centrality. I am referring to the reenactment project that preoccupies the opening: the brick-by-brick disassembly and reconstruction of a small world, one irremediably in the code of reported discourse—"New Dachang"—a world suspended in quotation marks. This is, then, not exactly a constructed, or even a reconstructed, place. It is the staging of one—a life-size model of itself as a "national historic museum." The town that is not exactly a town and place that is not exactly a place centers this entry into the postwar world of the novel and its counterfactual realism. Hence, it is where the novel describes its own "experimental" conditions. Hence, too, this is how it frames a space of reenactment in which its own artificial reality applies. In this way, the world appears in the world—it demarcates "the official world" as observation and experiment zone, a space of reenactments.[29]

THE INTERNATIONAL NECRONAUTICAL SOCIETY

"Zombiedom," the English novelist Tom McCarthy has recently noted, "is just re-enactment without content."[30] McCarthy's novel *Remainder* (the focus of the last part of this chapter) is a novel about reenactment (not least reenactments of the scene of the crime). The sponsor of these reenactments is the novel's human-like narrator, a first-person narrator who is not exactly a person but, as he puts it, a "robot or zombie," and one who is irremediably alien or "second-hand" with respect to the world.[31]

Reenactment without content. If a modern world comes to itself by staging its own conditions, then the prototype for that is no doubt the nature of the experiment. For one thing, the experiment is the defining form of observation, and the observation of observation, in the modern age. For another, observation via continuous reenactment, and commentary on it, are the presuppositions of the official world. That means the staging and repetition of natural processes via technical means, and the continuous alternation of observation, denotation, and report, such that observing, denoting, reporting, and their repetition, may itself be observed. "The experiment," as Hannah Arendt presents it, "repeats the natural process as though man himself were about to make nature's objects, this not for practical reasons of technical applicability but exclusively for the 'theoretical' reason that certainty in knowledge could not be gained otherwise."[32] In Kant's terms (which inform Arendt's): "Give me matter and I will build a world from it, that is, give me matter and I will show you how a world developed from it."[33] The experiment repeats the natural process by technical means, not for practical but formal reasons: it makes a world and shows that.

This—reenactment without content—is also, as McCarthy makes clear enough, the logic of the official world at its purest. These reenactments, and their extreme formality, take place, quite literally, "under the weight of officialism" and realize it to the letter. (Whether to the breaking point or to their point of installation: we recall that, in Kafka's fiction, official decision-makers are as shamefaced as young girls.)

Figure 8.1 INS London Declaration on Inauthenticity, General Secretary Tom McCarthy and Chief Philosopher Simon Critchley. (Richard Eaton/Tate) © Richard Eaton/Tate/INS.

McCarthy serves as General Secretary of the International Necronautical Society, which he co-founded. (One of its meetings or performances—featuring, of course, reenactors—is pictured above.) The Founding Manifesto of the Society (1999)—an "official document" authorized by the "First Committee, INS"—sets out its mission in these terms:

> We, the First Committee of the International Necronautical Society, declare the following:
>
> 1. That death is a type of space, which we intend to map, enter, colonize and, eventually, inhabit.
> 2. That there is no beauty without death, its immanence. We shall sing death's beauty—that is, beauty.
> 3. That we shall take it upon us, as our task to bring death out into the world. We will chart all its forms and media: in literature and art, where it is most apparent; also in science and culture, where it lurks submerged . . .
> 4. Our ultimate aim shall be the construction of a craft that will convey us into death in such a way that we may, if not live, then at least persist.[34]

These are the contours of what I have elsewhere called death and life in our wound culture—but in the terms of a "bureaucratic comedy, trimmed out in red tape."[35] The General Secretary's Report to the INS has as its ground zero, it may be noted, "Berlin: World Capital of Death." It is, that is, the world capital for the submission of the planetary life of the species to an unnatural selection and extinction process and its bureaucratic forms of death and life. (This is, after all, a world in which a piece of furniture—the bureau—takes command.)

The report is replete with forensic detail, dossiers, archives, aerial surveys, and sites of "marking and erasure, transit and transmission, cryptography and death." It choreographs its own intent, with a hyperbolic and deadpan officialism: in its combination of a statement and a practice, it is sort of practical joke—and the practical joke (it can be seen) is one of the dress rehearsal routines of the official world. The central place in McCarthy's account is in fact a place that's not quite a place. It is in fact a transit and transmission zone and the modern world's "primary reenactment space":

"I'd like to hire a room," I told him.
"What kind of room?" he asked.
"A space. An office."
"Right."[36]

THE UNCANNY VALLEY

It is not hard to see that the novel—and not least what I have called the new experimental novel—is bound up through and through with the primary reenactment zones of the official world and its autotropic practices. If a modern world continuously reenacts its own situation, the new experimental novel reports and epitomizes that. The experimental novel, from the later nineteenth century on, sets out the at once routine and unearthly spaces—the space of the office, the hospital, the laboratory, and the scene of the crime—that perform, record, and transmit these conditions. In short, the experimental novel—from, say, Zola to McCarthy—at once blueprints and performs the unity of the official world and draws white chalk lines along its edges.

"The novel itself had found its leitmotifs in the bodies of its protagonists," the sociologist Niklas Luhmann notes in *The Reality of the Mass Media*, and it does so "especially in the barriers to the controllability of bodily processes." The dominance of dangerous or erotic adventures—crime and sex—in the novel is explained, he further suggests, in that they provide ways "in which the reader can then participate voyeuristically using body-to-body analogy": the "tension in the narrative is 'symbolically' anchored in the barriers to controllability in each reader's body."[37] It is not simply then that readers imitate characters in novels. Instead, they enter into situations of incitation and their observation—which is to say, situations of self-incitation and self-observation.[38]

One complement to novel reading, on this account, is the boundary condition of bodily control to be found in the viewing of sporting events. Such events, to the extent that they are intended for spectation, provide body-to-body analogies, too. The spectacular sporting event—like the return to the scene of the crime or the scene of the wound, the world of *CSI* or that of *ER*—then provides not merely occasions for excitation by proxy but fitness to a reenacting, risk-driven, and self-reporting world.

These are the demarcation zones of the official world, a world that continuously stages its conditions and reports on that. The primary zones of distinction here are these: the space of the game, the scene of the crime, and the form of the work of art. In them, there is an ongoing coupling of act and observation, reenactment, and commentary. We should not lose sight of the improbability of this type of self-inciting society. As the great science fiction writer Stanislaw Lem neatly expressed it, "in the Eolithic age there were no seminars on whether to invent the Paeolithic."[39]

Let me, via a small detour, clarify what these body-to-body analogies look like and how they work in a self-reporting world. Consider, for example, one of the most popular forms of representation over the last century or so—the illuminated books of the second machine age, comic books. In what Scott McCloud has called "the invisible art" of comics, "most characters were designed simply, to assist in reader-identification."[40] These are the crude simplifications and forms of line, character, and ground in this work—and we are very familiar with these outlines: think of the simplicity of the emoticon. "Just as our awareness of our biological selves are simplified conceptualized images," the minimalism of the comics means that the world is turned outside in: "when you look at a photo or realistic drawing of a face—you see it as the face of *another* . . . the world outside of us . . . But when you enter into the world of the *cartoon*—you see *yourself* . . . the world within."[41] The simplification of figures in the direction of line and outline means that "those same lines became *so* stylized as to almost have a *life* and physical presence *all their own*."[42]

The drive to identification here has a counterside, however. For one thing, the intrusion of realism (a realism relative to line or diagram) interrupts or spoils it. The deviation from line and outline into irregularity, or asymmetry, not merely interrupts but overturns that identification. This is the moment when the stylized "body-to-body analogies" that make identification possible mutate.

These mutant figures inhabit what robotics engineers, from the 1970s on, call "the uncanny valley"—that abrupt transit point in realist representation at which identification with the simulation of human face or body abruptly reverses into revulsion, and the nearly human overturns into the barely human. The uncanny valley charts that moment when the incitation to identification (via say puppet, clown, or doll) becomes horrific. Here, it is perhaps appropriate to let the diagram stand in for a more extended explanation:

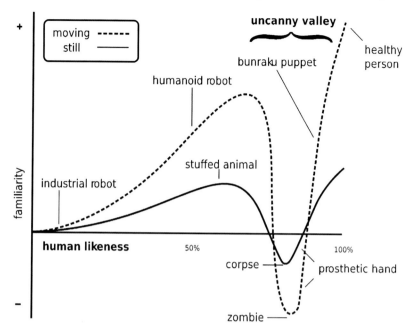

Figure 8.2   The Uncanny Valley.

This is the moment when over-identification turns to horror and body-to-body analogy to pathology. The zombie, we note, moves and lives, or persists, at the bottom of the uncanny valley. The walking dead, motion without life, undoes the fundamental principle (as Hobbes expressed it) that "life itself is but motion." Hence, the simplified analogy between bodies upon which identification is founded becomes too real to be sustained. These are the formal conditions for the uncontrollable identifications—and disidentifications—we have been setting out. They are too the preconditions for self-conditioning and autotropic practices like novel reading—and its excitations—in the first place.

The experimental novelist Tom McCarthy (who has written a book on comic books, *Tintin and the Secret of Literature*) sets out in *Remainder* (2005) the pedagogical principles of this type of society in pure form. For one thing, it sets out its demarcation zones—crime, game, and art. This is a zoned world that vibrates with violence; it is the world as forensic zone:

> Forensic procedure is an art form, nothing less. No, I'll go further: it's higher, more refined, than any art form. Why? Because it's real. Take just one aspect of it—say the diagrams: with all their outlines, arrows and shaded blocks they look like abstract paintings, avant-garde ones from the last century—dances of shapes and flows as delicate and skillful as the markings on butterflies' wings. But they're not abstract at all.

They're records of atrocities. Each line, each figure, every angle—the ink itself vibrates with an almost intolerable violence, darkly screaming from the silence of white paper: something has happened here, someone has died.[43]

The fascination of the forensic is that it is at once "extremely" formal and "real." But the point not to be missed is that this fascination, and the bodily analogs it solicits, are what makes the crime scene like the space of the game and both like the reenactment zone of the work of art too: "'It's just like cricket . . .' 'In what sense?' 'Each time the ball's been past,' I said, 'and the white lines are still zinging where it hit, and the seam's left a mark, and . . .' 'Each ball is like a crime, a murder. And then they do it again, and again and again, and the commentator has to commentate, or he'll die too.'"[44]

Remainder, in short, sets out a simplified world of reenactment and commentary. The narrator, or, more exactly, commentator, of the novel has, prior to the events he relates, had an accident that has eliminated his memory of the accident, among many other things. Limited to the bits and pieces of consciousness and act available to him, the commentator is under continuous medical care and continuously stages scenarios that ultimately take the form of lethal crime scenes, "vaporizing"—or, as he also puts it, "transubstantiating" life.

The accident makes it impossible for the damaged commentator to do anything, like walking, or, to take his most extended example, picking up a carrot, without breaking down every move into its component parts, putting them back together in sequence, consciously pre-enacting and formatting them, and then in effect putting in practice what has been practiced again and again, so that acting is reenacting them. Or, as he puts it, "We weren't doing them: they were being done."[45]

In effect, it is necessary to plan, rehearse, stage, and comment on an act as it takes place—and these positions run in a continuous loop. The commentator is, in fact, fixated on the figure of the loop, or figure eight. And here we are reminded, as Diedrich Diederichsen neatly puts it, that the endless loop has become the contemporary rhetorical figure par excellence: "The reason the loop became such a successful rhetorical trope in the effort to describe, narrate, and even organize experiences is that it harbours possibilities ranging from regression to self-reflection without ever becoming arbitrary: a conspicuous constellation that subsumes ever more (sub)cultural territory, organizing very different things that would have otherwise been mere narrative. And no one really trusts narrative anymore."[46]

Along these broken lines, the narrator's reenactments move from the scene of the hospital to the scene of the crime, spaces of an existential and forensic intensity without reserve. Yet, if it appears that "the act itself" "turns out to be more complicated than you thought"—if one needs to "visualize" or "picture" it before putting in motion the "twenty-seven separate manoeuvres involved," until you "understand how it all works"—then it turns out too that the situation he is in does not break with the usual conditions of action in the official world, it epitomizes it.[47]

Another way of saying this is that these motions, and the running commentary on them, are like the moves on a game field or the forensic reconstructions of the scene of the crime, or more generally still, like the systemic reorganization of industrial and technological processes, from the principles of scientific management and time-motion studies at the end of the nineteenth century, through the control revolution and the control society and the nature of the systems epoch today. (In the institutions of the second modernization, as Harry Braverman notes, "the process of production is replicated in paper form before, as, and after it takes place in physical form."[48] The paradox then is that things have to be "replicated" before, as, and after they take place; in this way, act and description alternate with each other in rotary fashion.)

One of the analogs of these technical processes is the serial photograph or filmic cuts. One of its obsessions is stop action, replay, and slow motion. And it is worth recalling that the origin of the filmic work is not exactly the art of photography but the research laboratory. It was in research labs that experimenters proceeded in breaking down motion into parts and calibrating it to the worker's body or the soldier's body (for example, in the pioneering motion studies of Etienne-Jules Marey or Paul Gilbreth, a student of the father of systematic management in the workplace, Frederick Winslow Taylor). In the research laboratory, bodies are cut in pieces for the military and for industry—and for their combination in industrialized warfare—reassembled into the productive (or destructive) apparatus. The intimacy with machines that defines the second machine age, its body-machine complex, takes the form of the human apparatus cut to pieces, reassembled, and played back on a loop. (We may recall too then, as Bernhard Siegert summarizes it, that stop-action and slow motion "actually preceded the motion picture projected at normal speed." Time-motion studies preceded motion pictures, as the laboratory origins of that form of art.)[49]

THE LOYALTY CARD

These are the moving parts of what the novel calls "the logistics industry." They are also, I have been suggesting, the terrain of the experimental novel and its bodily mechanisms—the scene of the crime or the hospital, the autopsy table and forensic science, and the robot or zombie are its zones and its subjects.

Yet, if reports on crime, wound, and disease—forensics, criminal, and medical—serve as melodramatizations of the official world, it is again and again the everyday spaces of this world—spaces like the office itself—that are its working models: models of an autotropic world between history and natural history. (The etymological root of "life"—*lib*—it will be recalled, means the remainder: what continues, or persists, particularly after battle or war, and so what goes on after life, and as its aftermath. Life is, or was, the remains of the day.)

It is in these laboratory spaces that experiments in the daily forms of life and death are conducted, repeated, and denoted. These spaces make up the circuitry of an autotropic and reenacting world, its operating system. These are the sites in which it becomes possible to rotate persons through positions and to repeat the process.

Here, in closing, is one of those iconic sites, one that epitomizes an auto-inciting and reenacting world and how its bodies and institutions are synched to run on an endless loop:

> After a while I tired of watching all these amateur performances [that is, people interacting on the street] and decided to buy a coffee from a small concession a few feet away. It was a themed Seattle coffee bar where you buy caps, lattes, and mochas, not coffees. When you order they say *Heyy!* to you, then they repeat your order aloud, correcting the word *large* into *tall, small* into *short.* I ordered a small cappuccino.
>
> "Heyy! Short cap," the man said. "Coming up! You have a loyalty card?"
>
> "Loyalty card?" I said.
>
> "Each time you visit us, you get a cup stamped," he said, handing me a card. It had ten small pictures of coffee cups on it. "When you've stamped all ten, you get an extra cup for free. And a new card."
>
> "But I'm not here that often," I said.
>
> "Oh, we have branches everywhere," he told me, "It's the same deal. . . ."
>
> If I got all ten of its cups stamped then I'd get an extra cup—plus a new card with ten more cups on it . . . The idea excited me.[50]

The loyalty card is a little technology that is business as usual to everyone, except the narrator who, due to his accident, is, as he puts it, more usual than usual. The loyalty card blueprints, comments on, and records what it does, and reinstates itself as it goes. It does so here via one of the auto-tropic drugs bound up through and through with the daily grind, as if via breaks from it. Not only that, it incites loyalty—that is, reenactment—in the process. And that's, as the nameless narrator puts it, "the beauty of it. It became real while it was going on."[51]

NOTES

1. Brecht, as cited (loosely) in Winfried Georg (W. G.) Sebald, *Campo Santo,* trans. Anthea Bell (New York: Modern Library, 2005), 89. I am here drawing on Sebald, *Campo Santo,* "Between History and Natural History," 65–96; and

Sebald, *On the Natural History of Destruction*, trans. Anthea Bell (New York: Modern Library, 2004).

2. Sebald, *Campo Santo*, 80.
3. Hans Erich Nossack, *Der Untergang* (Hamburg: E. Kabel, 1981), as quoted in Sebald, *Campo Santo*, 80–81.
4. Sebald, *Campo Santo*, 77.
5. Ibid., 90. My account of an autotropic and self-induced modernity—what I redescribe as the official world—is drawn from my forthcoming book, *The Official World*. Parts of that book have appeared in my "Parlor Games: The Apriorization of the Media," *Critical Inquiry*, vol.36, no.1 (2009): 100–133; "Die Freie Natur," in *Gefahrensinn: Archiv für Mediengeschichte*, ed. Lorenz Engell, Bernhard Siegert and Joseph Vogl (München: Wilhelm Fink, 2009): 127–138; and "The Official World," *Critical Inquiry*, vol.37, no.4 (2011): 724–753; and "The Daily Planet," *Post45*: http://post45.research.yale.edu/2012/12/the-daily-planet (accessed May 29, 2013).
6. Sebald, *Campo Santo*, 90.
7. Patricia Highsmith, *Ripley's Game* (New York: Vintage, 1999 [1974]), 59.
8. Erving Goffman, *The Presentation of Self in Everyday Life* (New York: Doubleday, 1959), 244.
9. Stanislaw Lem, *Imaginary Magnitude* (New York: Harcourt Brace, 1984), 75.
10. Highsmith, *Ripley's Game*, 59.
11. On Charcot, I am indebted to Anson Rabinbach, *The Human Motor: Energy, Fatigue, and the Origins of Modernity* (New York: Basic, 1990), 154–163.
12. Daniel Lord Smail, *On Deep History and the Brain* (Berkeley: University of California Press, 2008).
13. Ibid., 127, 144.
14. Cormac McCarthy, *The Road* (New York: Vintage, 2006), 59.
15. Ibid., 14, 16.
16. On the Galileic turn and its implications, see Quentin Meillassoux, *After Finitude: An Essay on the Necessity of Contingency*, trans. Ray Brassier (New York: Continuum, 2008). I am here drawing too on Joseph Vogl, "Becoming-Media: Galileo's Telescope," *Grey Room*, vol.29 (2007): 14–25.
17. Heinz von Foerster, *Observing Systems* (Seaside, CA: Intersystems Publications, 1981).
18. McCarthy, *The Road*, 3.
19. Ibid., 55.
20. Sebald, *Campo Santo*, 95.
21. Max Brooks, *World War Z: An Oral History of the Zombie War* (New York: Three Rivers, 2006), 4–5.
22. See Peter Conrad, *The Medicalization of Society: On the Transformation of Human Conditions into Treatable Disorders* (Baltimore: Johns Hopkins University Press, 2007).
23. See, for example, Georges Canguilhem, *The Normal and the Pathological*, with an introduction by Michel Foucault (New York: Zone Books, 1991). Canguilhem's account centers on the nineteenth-century medical theorist Claude Bernard's breakthrough work in experimental pathology; Bernard's experimental method, it will be seen, enters, via Emile Zola, into the form and method of the experimental novel—which makes explicit, it will be seen too, the location of the novel at the crossing point of physiology and social pathology, history and natural history.
24. Emile Zola, "The Experimental Novel," in *Documents of Modern Literary Realism*, ed. George J. Becker (Princeton: Princeton University Press, 1963), 162.
25. Ibid., 177.
26. Ibid., 179.

27. Sebald, *On the Natural History of Destruction*, 66.
28. See Alexander Kluge's accounts of the aftershocks of dislocation in the time of war, *Unheimlichkeit der Zeit* (Frankfurt: Edition Surhkamp, 1977).
29. See my "The Official World."
30. http://dossierjournal.com/read/interviews (accessed on January 28, 2013).
31. "Re-enactment brings about a kind of split within the act itself . . . on the one hand it's something you do, and on the other it's not something you're actually 'doing': it's a citation, a marker for another event that this one isn't." McCarthy, quoted in Simon Reynolds, *Retromania: Pop Culture's Addiction to Its Own Past* (New York: Faber and Faber, 2011), 54. This citation—this one—reminds you that events are possible and only because they happened before.
32. As quoted in Hannah Arendt, *The Human Condition* (Chicago: University of Chicago Press, 1998), 295.
33. "Gebet mir Materie, ich will eine Welt daraus bauen! das ist, gebet mir Materie, ich will euch zeigen, wie eine Welt daraus entstehen soll." Kant's Preface to his *Allgemeine Naturgeschichte und Theorie des Himmels*, as quoted in Arendt, *The Human Condition*, 295.
34. http://www.necronauts.org/manifesto1.htm (accessed on January 28, 2013).
35. Saul Bellow, *Dangling Man* (New York: Penguin, 1971 [1944]), 10.
36. Tom McCarthy, *Remainder* (New York: Vintage, 2005), 93.
37. Niklas Luhmann, *The Reality of the Mass Media*, trans. Kathleen Cross (Stanford: Stanford University Press, 2000), 59.
38. Embarrassment, and its self-observed observation, is only the most everyday-life version of that; one cannot imagine the first two centuries of the European novel without it—what Edith Wharton, in her novel *The House of Mirth* (1905), calls the "art of blushing at the right time." The "novel of manners" is anchored by these daily social forms felt on the body. Crime or sex novels, novels of uncontrollable bodies—torn, wounded, driven, fallen, idealized, or pathologized—are then analogs of these body-to-body analogies, at the limits of bodily control, and in this way sensationalize (in both senses) a self-inciting world.
39. Lem, *Imaginary Magnitude*, 131.
40. Scott McCloud, *Understanding Comics: The Invisible Art* (New York: Harper, 1994), 44.
41. Ibid., 40–41.
42. Ibid., 111.
43. McCarthy, *Remainder*, 185.
44. Ibid., 186. Or, as McCarthy elsewhere expressed it, "I think there's three modes in which being in the world, being towards death and so on is most intensely staged and I'd say that's war, sport, and poetry." http://dossierjournal.com/read/interviews/the-radical-ambiguity-of-tom-mccarthy (accessed on January 28, 2013).
45. McCarthy, *Remainder*, 216.
46. Diedrich Diederichsen, "Living in the Loop," *Fillip*, vol.14 (2011). Accessed from http://fillip.ca/content/living-in-the-loop (accessed on January 28, 2013).
47. McCarthy, *Remainder*, 40.
48. Harry Braverman, *Labor and Monopoly Capital: The Degradation of Work in the Twentieth Century* (New York: Monthly Review Press, 1998), 58.
49. See Bernhard Siegert, "There Are No Mass Media," in *Mapping Benjamin: The Work of Art in the Digital Age*, ed. Hans Gumbrecht and Michael Marrinen (Stanford: Stanford University Press, 2003), 30–38.
50. McCarthy, *Remainder*, 28, 52.
51. Ibid., 296.

Bibliography

Ackroyd, Peter. "Introduction." In *Jack the Ripper and the East End*, ed. Alex Werner. London: Chatto & Windus, 2008.

Adler, Hans G. *Theresienstadt, 1941–1945. Das Antlitz einter Zwangsgemeinschaft*, 2nd ed. Tübingen: J. C. B. Mohr (Paul Siebeck), 1960.

Agamben, Giorgio. *Homo Sacer: Sovereign Power and Bare Life*. Translated by Daniel Heller-Roazen. Stanford: Stanford University Press, 1998.

———. *Means without End: Notes on Politics*. Translated by Cesare Casarino and Vincenzo Binetti. Minneapolis: University of Minnesota Press, 2000.

Allen, Arthur. *Vaccine: The Controversial Story of Medicine's Greatest Lifesaver*. New York: W.W. Norton, 2007.

Akers, Timothy and Mark M. Lanier. "'Epidemiological Criminology': Coming Full Circle." *American Journal of Public Health*, vol.99, no.3 (2009): 397–402.

Akrich, Madeleine, Yannick Barthe, and Catherine Rémy. *Sur la piste environnementale. Menaces sanitaires et mobilisations profanes*. Paris: Presses des Mines, 2010.

Allard, Laurence and Olivier Blondeau. "La racaille peut-elle parler? Objets expressifs et émeutes des cites." *Hermès*, vol.47 (2007): 79–87.

Allen, Barbara. *Uneasy Alchemy: Citizens and Experts in Louisiana's Chemical Corridor Disputes*. Cambridge, MA: MIT Press, 2003.

———. "A Tale of Two Lawsuits: Making Policy-Relevant Environment Health Knowledge in Italian and U.S. Chemical Regions." In *Dangerous Trade: Histories of Industrial Hazard across a Globalizing World*, ed. Christopher Sellers and Joseph Melling. Philadelphia: Temple University Press, 2012.

Allen, Rick. *The Moving Pageant: A Literary Sourcebook on London Street Life, 1700–1914*. London: Routledge, 1998.

American Psychiatric Association. *Diagnostic and Statistical Manual of Mental Disorders: DSM-IV*. Washington, DC: American Psychiatric Association, 1994.

Amrith, Sunil S. *Migration and Diaspora in Modern Asia*. Cambridge: Cambridge University Press, 2011.

Arendt, Hannah. *The Human Condition*. Chicago: University of Chicago Press, 1998.

Arnold, David. "Cholera and Colonialism in British India." *Past & Present*, vol.113, no.1 (1986): 118–151.

Bakken, Børge. "Prejudice and Danger: The Only Child in China." *Childhood*, vol.1, no.1 (1993): 46–61.

———. *The Exemplary Society: Human Improvement, Social Control, and the Dangers of Modernity in China*. Oxford: Oxford University Press, 2000.

Baldwin, Peter. *Contagion and the State in Europe, 1830–1930.* Cambridge: Cambridge University Press, 2005.

Bartrip, Peter. *The Way from Dusty Death: Turner and Newall and the Regulation of Occupational Health in the British Asbestos Industry, 1890–1970.* London: The Athlone Press, 2001.

———. *Beyond the Factory Gates: Asbestos and Health in Twentieth-Century America.* London: Continuum, 2006.

Bashford, Alison, ed. *Medicine at the Border: Disease, Globalization and Security, 1850 to the Present.* London: Palgrave, 2006.

Bax, Trent. *Youth and Internet Addiction in China.* New York: Routledge, in press.

Beccalossi, Chiara. "The Origin of Italian Sexological Studies: Female Sexual Inversion ca. 1870–1900." *Journal of the History of Sexuality,* vol.18, no.1 (2009): 103–120.

———. "Nineteenth-Century European Psychiatry on Same-Sex Desires: Pathology, Abnormality, Normality and the Blurring of Boundaries." *Psychology & Sexuality,* vol.1, no.3 (2010): 226–238.

———. *Female Sexual Inversion: Same-Sex Desires in Italian and British Sexology, ca. 1870–1920.* Basingstoke: Palgrave Macmillan, 2012.

Beck, Ulrich. *The Risk Society: Towards a New Modernity.* Translated by Mark Ritter. London: Sage, 1992 [1986].

Becker, Howard S. *Outsiders: Studies in the Sociology of Deviance.* New York: The Free Press of Glencoe, 1963.

Bell, Suzanne. *Crime and Circumstance: Investigating the History of Forensic Science.* Westport, CT: Greenwood Press, 2008.

Bellow, Saul. *Dangling Man.* New York: Penguin, 1971 [1944].

Bender, Sara. *The Jews of Bialystok During World War II and the Holocaust.* Translated by Yaffa Murciano. Waltham, MA: Brandeis University Press, 2008.

Benjamin, Walter. *The Arcades Project.* Cambridge, MA: The Belknap Press, 1999 [1982].

———. *Walter Benjamin: Selected Writings, Vol.2, Part 2, 1931–1934,* ed. Michael W. Jennings, Howard Eiland, and Gary Smith. Cambridge, MA: Harvard University Press, 2005 [1999].

Berkowitz, Michael. *The Crime of My Very Existence: Nazism and the Myth of Jewish Criminality.* Berkeley: University of California Press, 2007.

Bernstein, Philip S. "Displaced Persons." In *The American Jewish Year Book, Vol.49, 1947–1948.* New York: American Jewish Committee, 1947.

Blake, Judith. *Family Size and Achievement.* Berkeley: University of California Press, 1989.

Blendon, Robert J., et al. "The Public's Response to Severe Acute Respiratory Syndrome in Toronto and the United States." *Clinical Infectious Diseases,* vol.38, no.7 (2004): 925–931.

Boltanski, Luc. *On Critique: A Sociology of Emancipation.* Translated by Gregory Elliott. Cambridge, MA: Polity, 2011.

———. *Enigmes et complots. Une enquête à propos d'enquêtes.* Paris: Gallimard, 2012.

Boltanski, Luc and Laurent Thévenot. *On Justification: Economies of Worth.* Translated by Catherine Porter. Princeton: Princeton University Press, 2006 [1991].

Borris, Kenneth and George Rousseau, eds. *The Sciences of Homosexuality in Early Modern Europe.* London: Routledge, 2008.

Bourdon, Jérôme. *Haute fidélité. Pouvoir et télévision (1935–1994).* Paris: Seuil, 1994.

Brady, Sean. "Homosexuality: European and Colonial Encounters." In *A Cultural History of Sexuality in the Age of Empire*, ed. Chiara Beccalossi and Ivan Crozier. Oxford: Berg, 2011.

Braverman, Harry. *Labor and Monopoly Capital: The Degradation of Work in the Twentieth Century*. New York: Monthly Review Press, 1998.

Briggs, Asa. *Victorian Things*. London: Penguin, 1990 [1988].

Brill, Abraham A. *Psychoanalysis: Its Theories and Practical Applications*. Philadelphia: Saunders, 1917.

Bronner, Luc. *La loi du ghetto. Enquête dans les banlieues françaises*. Paris: Calmann-Lévy, 2010.

Broszat, Martin, Helmut Krausnick, and Hans-Adolf Jacobsen. *Anatomy of the SS-State*. Translated by Dorothy Long and Marian Jackson. Frogmore, UK: Palladin, 1968.

Brown, Bill. *A Sense of Things: The Object Matters of American Literature*. Chicago: University of Chicago Press, 2003.

Brown, Phil. "Popular Epidemiology: Community Response to Toxic Waste Induced Disease in Woburn, Massachusetts." *Science, Technology, & Human Values*, vol.12, nos.3–4 (1987): 76–85.

———, ed. *Contested Illnesses: Citizens, Science, and Health Social Movements*. Berkeley: University of California Press, 2012.

Browning, Christopher. *The Origins of the Final Solution: The Evolution of Nazi Jewish Policy, September 1939–March 1942 (Comprehensive History of the Holocaust)*. Lincoln: University of Nebraska Press, 2004.

Buzzi, Stéphane, Jean-Claude Devinck, and Paul-André Rosental. *La santé au travail 1880–2006*. Paris: La Découverte, 2006.

Callon, Michel, Pierre Lascoumes, and Yannick Barte. *Acting in an Uncertain World: An Essay on Technical Democracy*. Cambridge, MA: MIT Press, 2009 [2001].

Canguilhem, Georges. *The Normal and the Pathological*. With an introduction by Michel Foucault. New York: Zone Books, 1991.

Canter, David. *Criminal Shadows: Inside the Mind of the Serial Killer*. London: HarperCollins, 1994.

Cao Manzhi, ed. *Zhongguo qingshaonian fanzuixue* [*The Criminology of Chinese Juvenile Delinquency*]. Beijing: Qunzhong chubanshe, 1988.

Carroll, John M. *A Concise History of Hong Kong*. Lanham, MD: Rowman & Littlefield, 2007.

Castleman, Barry. *Asbestos: Medical and Legal Aspects*. Englewoods Cliffs, NJ: Prentice Hall Law and Business, 1990.

Castro, Teresa. "Scène de crime: la mobilisation de la photographie métrique par Alphonse Bertillon." In *Aux origines de la police scientifique: Alphone Bertillon, précurseur de la science du crime*, ed. Pierre Piazza. Paris: Karthala, 2011.

Centemeri, Laura. *Ritorno a Seveso. Il danno ambientale, il suo riconoscimento, la sua reparazione*. Milano: Bruno Mondadori, 2006.

———. "Retour à Seveso. La complexité morale et politique du dommage à l'environnement." *Annales. Histoire, Sciences Sociales*, vol.1 (2011): 213–240.

———. "What Kind of Knowledge is Needed about Toxicant-Related Health Issues? Some Lessons Drawn from the Seveso Dioxin Case." In *Powerless Science? Science and Politics in a Toxic World*, ed. Soraya Boudia and Nathalie Jas. Oxford: Berghahn, in press.

Chen Hsin-Hsing. "How Does Legal Justice Meet Scientific Fact? A View on Law, Science and Society through the *Daubert* Controversy." [in Chinese] *Taiwanese*

Journal for Studies of Science, Technology and Medicine, vol.12, no.4 (2011): 44–48.

Chiang, Wen-Yu and Ren-Feng Duann. "Conceptual Metaphors for SARS: 'War' between Whom?" *Discourse & Society,* vol.18, no.5 (2007): 579–602.

Christensen, Allan Conrad. *Nineteenth-Century Narratives of Contagion: "Our Feverish Contact."* London: Routledge, 2005.

Clark, Michael and Catherine Crawford, eds. *Legal Medicine in History.* Cambridge: Cambridge University Press, 1994.

Cohen, Ed. *A Body Worth Defending: Immunity, Biopolitics, and the Apotheosis of the Modern Body.* Durham, NC: Duke University Press, 2009.

Cohen, Stanley. *Folk Devils and Moral Panics.* Oxford: Blackwell, 1983 [1972].

Collier, Stephen and Aiwah Ong. *Global Assemblages: Technology, Politics, and Ethics as Anthropological Problems.* Malden, MA: Blackwell, 2005.

Conrad, Peter. *The Medicalization of Society: On the Transformation of Human Conditions into Treatable Disorders.* Baltimore: Johns Hopkins University Press, 2007.

Conrad, Peter and Joseph W. Schneider. *Deviance and Medicalization: From Badness to Sickness.* Philadelphia: Temple University Press, 1992.

Cooper, Melinda. "Pre-empting Emergence: The Biological Turn in the War on Terror." *Theory, Culture & Society,* vol.23, no.4 (2006): 113–135.

Corbett, David Peters. *The World in Paint: Modern Art and Visuality in England, 1848–1914.* Manchester: Manchester University Press, 2005 [2004].

Corbin, Alain. *The Foul and the Fragrant: Odor and the French Social Imagination.* Cambridge, MA: Harvard University Press, 1986.

Cornwall, Patricia. *Portrait of a Killer: Jack the Ripper—Case Closed.* New York: Berkeley/Penguin, 2002.

Cranor, Carl F. *Toxic Torts: Science, Law, and the Possibility of Justice.* New York: Cambridge University Press, 2006.

Crozier, Ivan. "The Medical Construction of Homosexuality and its Relationship to the Law in Nineteenth-Century England." *Medical History,* vol.45, no.1 (2001): 61–82.

———. "'All the Appearances Were Perfectly Natural': The Anus of the Sodomite in Nineteenth-Century Medical Discourse." In *Body Parts: Critical Explorations in Corporeality,* ed. Christopher E. Forth and Ivan Crozier. Lanham, MD: Lexington Books, 2005.

———. "Introduction." In *Sexual Inversion: A Critical Edition: Havelock Ellis and John Addington Symonds,* ed. Ivan Crozier. Basingstoke: Palgrave Macmillan, 2008.

———. "Pillow Talk: Credibility, Trust and the Sexological Case History." *History of Science,* vol.46, no.4 (2008): 375–404.

Curtis, Jr., L. Perry. *Jack the Ripper and the London Press.* New Haven: Yale University Press, 2001.

Daston, Lorraine. "Objectivity and the Escape from Perspective." *Social Studies in Science,* vol.22, no.4 (1992): 597–618.

Daston, Lorraine and Peter Galison. *Objectivity.* New York: Zone Books, 2007.

Davidson, Arnold I. "Closing Up the Corpses: Diseases of Sexuality and the Emergence of the Psychiatric Style of Reasoning." In *Meaning and Method: Essays in Honor of Hilary Putnam,* ed. George Boolos. Cambridge: Cambridge University Press, 1990.

Davie, Neil. *Tracing the Criminal: The Rise of Scientific Criminology in Britain, 1860–1918.* Oxford: Bardwell Press, 2005.

Davis, Mike. *The Monster at Our Door: The Global Threat of Avian Flu.* New York: Henry Holt, 2006.

Dawidowicz, Lucy S. *The War Against the Jews, 1933–1945*. New York: Bantam, 1975.

Delaporte, François. *Disease and Civilization: The Cholera in Paris, 1832*. Translated by Arthur Goldhammer. Cambridge, MA: MIT Press, 1986.

Delmas-Marty, Mireille. *Le relatif et l'universel*. Paris: Seuil, 2004.

———. *Le pluralisme ordonné*. Paris: Seuil, 2006.

———. *La refondation des pouvoirs*. Paris: Seuil, 2007.

———. *Vers une communauté de valeurs*. Paris: Seuil, 2011.

Deleuze, Gilles and Félix Guattari. *A Thousand Plateaus: Capitalism and Schizophrenia*. Translated by Brian Massumi. London: Continuum, 1987 [1980].

Deng Hongxun. "You'er jiaoyu shi peiyang yi ge xinren de diaoni gongcheng" ["Infant Education Is the Important Project of Fostering a New Person"]. *Hongqi* (1987): 30–33.

Desrosières, Alain. *The Politics of Large Numbers: A History of Statistical Reasoning*. Translated by Camille Naish. Cambridge, MA: Harvard University Press, 1998 [1993].

Ding Yu. "Tantan ruhe zhengque chuli zhongxuesheng 'zaolian' de wenti" ["On How to Handle Correctly the Problem of 'Premature Love' among Secondary School Pupils"]. *Renmin jiaoyu*, no.3 (1988): 21.

Douglas, Mary. *Purity and Danger: An Analysis of Concepts of Pollution and Taboo*. London: Routledge, 1991 [1966].

Dowbiggin, Ian A. "Back to the Future: Valentin Magnan, French Psychiatry, and the Classification of Mental Diseases, 1885–1925." *Social History of Medicine*, vol.9, no.3 (1996): 383–408.

Dyos, Harold J. "The Slums of Victorian London." In *Exploring the Urban Past*, ed. David Cannadine and David Reeder. Cambridge: Cambridge University Press, 1982.

Elbe, Stefan. *Virus Alert: Security, Governmentality, and the AIDS Pandemic*. New York: Columbia University Press, 2009.

Erikson, Kai T. *Wayward Puritans: A Study in the Sociology of Deviance*. New York: John Wiley, 1966.

Erni, John Nguyet. "Epidemic Imaginary: Performing Global Figurations of 'Third World AIDS.'" *Space and Culture*, vol.9, no.4 (2006): 429–452.

Evans, Richard. *Telling Lies about Hitler: The Holocaust, History and the David Irving Trial*. London: Verso, 2002.

Falbo, Toni and Denise F. Polit. "Quantitative Review of the Only Child Literature: Research Evidence and Theory Development." *Psychological Bulletin*, vol.100, no.2 (1986): 176–189.

Falbo, Toni, Dudley L. Poston, G. Ji, S. Jiao, Q. Jing, S. Wang, et al. "Physical Achievement and Personality Characteristics of Chinese Children." *Journal of Biosocial Science*, vol.21, no.4 (1989): 483–496.

Fecht, Ulrike, Brian Wynne, Michel Callon, Maria E. Gonçalves, Sheila Jasanoff, Maria Jepsen, et al. *Taking European Knowledge Society Seriously. Report of the Expert Group on Science and Governance to the Science, Economy and Society Directorate, Directorate-General for Research*. Brussels: European Commission, 2007.

Ferrell, Jeff, Keith Hayward, and Jock Young, eds. *Cultural Criminology: An Invitation*. London: Sage, 2008.

Fintz, Matthieu. "Emerging Viruses, State of Emergency and the Manufacture of Health Crises." In *Chroniques égyptiennes/Egyptian Chronicles 2006*, ed. Enrique Klaus and Chaymaa Hassabo. Cairo: Cedej, 2007.

Fishbein, Diana H. *Biobehavioral Perspectives on Criminology*. Belmont, CA: Wadsworth Publishing, 2001.

Flanders, Judith. *The Victorian House: Domestic Life from Childbirth to Death-bed*. London: HarperCollins, 2003.

Foucault, Michel. *The Birth of the Clinic: An Archaeology of Medical Perception*. London: Tavistock, 1976.

———. *Discipline and Punish: The Birth of the Prison*. Translated by Alan Sheridan. New York: Vintage, 1979.

Frickel, Scott, Sahra Gibbon, Jeff Howard, Joanna Kempner, Gwen Ottinger and David J. Hess. "Undone Science: Charting Social Movement and Civil Society Challenges to Research Agenda Setting." *Science, Technology, & Human Values*, vol.35, no.4 (2010): 444–473.

Friedlander, Henry. *The Origins of the Nazi Genocide: From Euthanasia to the Final Solution*. Chapel Hill: University of North Carolina Press, 1995.

Friedlander, Saul. *Nazi Germany and the Jews: Vol.1: The Years of Persecution*. New York: HarperCollins, 1997.

Fritzsche, Peter. *Life and Death in the Third Reich*. Cambridge, MA: Belknap Press of Harvard University Press, 2008.

Galsworthy, John. *The Forsyte Saga*, Vol.1–3. London: Penguin, 2001.

George, Timothy. *Minamata and the Struggle for Democracy*. Cambridge, MA: Harvard University Press, 2001.

Gibson, Mary. *Born to Crime: Cesare Lombroso and the Origins of Biological Criminology*. Westport, CT: Praeger, 2002.

Gilbert, Pamela K. *Cholera and Nation: Doctoring the Social Body in Victorian England*. Albany: State University of New York Press, 2003.

Gilman, Sander. *The Jew's Body*. New York: Routledge, 1991.

Gilroy, Paul. *Against Race: Imagining Political Culture Beyond the Color Line*. Cambridge, MA: Harvard University Press, 2000.

Gissing, George. *London and the Life of Literature in Late Victorian England: The Diary of George Gissing*, ed. Pierre Coustillas. Hassocks, UK: Harvester Press, 1978.

Goffman, Erving. *The Presentation of Self in Everyday Life*. New York: Doubleday, 1959.

Goode, Erich and Nachman Ben-Yahuda. *Moral Panics: The Social Construction of Deviance*, 2nd ed. Chichester, UK: Wiley-Blackwell, 2009.

Gould, Stephen Jay. *Ontogeny and Phylogeny*. Cambridge, MA: Harvard University Press, 1977.

Grier, Katherine C. *Culture and Comfort: Parlor Making and Middle-Class Identity*. Washington, DC: Smithsonian Institution Press, 1988.

Grossmann, Atina. *Jews, Germans and Allies: Close Encounters in Occupied Germany*. Princeton: Princeton University Press, 2007.

Grynberg, Michal, ed. *Words to Outlive Us: Eyewitness Accounts from the Warsaw Ghetto*. Translated by Philip Boehm. New York: Picador, 2002.

Guénel, Annick and Sylvia Klingberg. "Press Coverage of Bird Flu Epidemic in Vietnam." In *Liberalizing, Feminizing and Popularizing Health Communications in Asia*, ed. Liew Kai Khiun. Farnham, UK: Ashgate, 2010.

Gutmann, Philipp. "On the Way to Scientia Sexualis: 'On the Relation of the Sexual System to the Psyche in General and to Cretinism in Particular' (1826) by Joseph Häussler." *History of Psychiatry*, vol.17, no.1 (2006): 45–53.

Hacking, Ian. *The Social Construction of What?* Cambridge, MA: Harvard University Press, 1999.

Hamlin, Christopher. *Cholera: The Biography*. Oxford: Oxford University Press, 2009.

Harr, Jonathan. *A Civil Action*. New York: Vintage: 1996.

Hekma, Gert. "A History of Sexology: Social and Historical Aspects of Sexuality." In *From Sappho to De Sade: Moments in the History of Sexuality*, ed. J. Bremmer. London: Routledge, 1989.

————. "'A Female Soul in a Male Body': Sexual Inversion as Gender Inversion in Nineteenth-Century Sexology." In *Third Sex, Third Gender: Beyond Sexual Dimorphism in Culture and History*, ed. Gilbert Herdt. New York: Zone Books, 1994.

Henry, Emmanuel. "How the Environment Came to the Rescue of Occupational Health: Asbestos in France c. 1970–1995." In *Dangerous Trade: Histories of Industrial Hazard across a Globalizing World*, ed. Christopher Sellers and Joseph Melling. Philadelphia: Temple University Press, 2012.

Hepworth, Mike. "Privacy, Security and Respectability: The Ideal Victorian Home." In *Housing and Dwelling: Perspectives on Modern Domestic Architecture*, ed. Barbara Miller Lane. Abingdon, UK: Routledge, 2007.

Herf, Jeffrey. *The Jewish Enemy: Nazi Propaganda During World War II and the Holocaust*. Cambridge, MA: Belknap Press of Harvard University Press, 2006.

Hershatter, Gail. *Dangerous Pleasures: Prostitution and Modernity in Twentieth-Century Shanghai*. Berkeley: University of California Press, 1997.

Hewitt, Martin. "District Visiting and the Constitution of Domestic Space in the Mid-Nineteenth Century." In *Domestic Space: Reading the Nineteenth-Century Interior*, ed. Inga Bryden and Janet Floyd. Manchester: Manchester University Press, 1999.

Highsmith, Patricia. *Ripley's Game*. New York: Vintage, 1999 [1974].

Hôrai, Yoshitsugu, et al. "Shôhichi ni okeru keihai kenshin to sono keika" ["The Sites of Consumption and Results of Silicosis Exams"]. *Rôdô kagaku kenkyû*, vol.29, no.4 (1953): 237.

————, et al. "Sekimenhai kekkaku no shôrei" ["The Symptoms of Asbestosis and Tuberculosis"]. *Nara igaku zasshi*, vol.7, no.4 (1956): 309.

Horn, David G. *The Criminal Body: Lombroso and the Anatomy of Deviance*. New York: Routledge, 2003.

Howell, Philip. "Prostitution and Racialized Sexuality: The Regulation of Prostitution in Britain and the British Empire before the Contagious Diseases Acts." *Environment and Planning D: Society and Space*, vol.18, no.3 (2000): 321–339.

————. *Geographies of Regulation: Policing Prostitution in Nineteenth-Century Britain and the Empire*. Cambridge: Cambridge University Press, 2009.

Hu Hong. "De budao ai de haizi cai zaolian" ["Premature Love Children Are Those Who Cannot Get Love"]. *Shuo ni xingfu (zhixin)*, no.1 (2009): 9.

Jasanoff, Sheila. *Science at the Bar: Law, Science, and Technology in America*. Cambridge, MA: Harvard University Press, 1995.

————, ed. *States of Knowledge: The Co-Production of Science and Social Order*. London: Routledge, 2004.

————. "Law's Knowledge: Science for Justice in Legal Setting." *American Journal of Public Health*, vol.95, no.S1 (2005): 49–58.

Jiang Xin. "Jishi women shi jimo" ["Because We Are Lonely"]. *Hao fumu*, no.11 (2003): 10–11.

Jobard, Fabien. "Rioting as a Political Tool: The 2005 French Riots." *Howard Journal of Criminal Justice*, vol.48, no.3 (2009): 235–244.

Jobin, Paul. "The Tragedy of Minamata: Sit-in and Face-to-Face Discussion." In *Making Things Public, Atmospheres of Democracy*, ed. Bruno Latour and Peter Weibel. Cambridge, MA: MIT Press, 2005.

————. *Maladies industrielles et renouveau syndical au Japon* [*Industrial Disease and Renewal of Trade Unionism in Japan*]. Paris: EHESS Editions, 2006.

————. "The Postwar for Labour Unionism and Movements against Industrial Pollution." In *Japan's Postwar*, ed. Michael Lucken, Anne Bayard-Sakai, and Emmanuel Lozerand. Translated by James A. Stockwin. London: Routledge, 2011 [2006].

Jobin, Paul and Yu-Hwei Tseng, "Guinea Pigs Go to Court: Epidemiology and Class Actions in Taiwan." [in Chinese] *Taiwanese Journal for Studies of Science, Technology and Medicine*, vol.12, no.4 (2011): 159–220.

———. "Guinea Pigs Go to Court: Epidemiology and Class Actions in Taiwan." In *Powerless Science? Science and Politics in a Toxic World*, ed. Soraya Boudia and Nathalie Jas. Oxford: Berghahn, in press.

Johnson, Chalmers. *MITI and the Japanese Miracle*. Stanford: Stanford University Press, 1982.

Jonsson, Gustav. *Flickor på glid: en studie i kvinnoförtryck* [*Slipping Girls: A Study in the Oppression of Women*]. Borås: Tiden Folksam, 1977.

Jordan, David P. *Transforming Paris: The Life and Labors of Baron Haussmann*. Chicago: University of Chicago Press, 1996.

Kan, Ken'ei. *Asubesuto kôgai to gan hassei*. Tokyo: Shuchôsha, 2006.

Kan, Ken'ei, Yoshizumi Sera and Kunihiko Yokoyama. "Sekimen hai ni gappei shita kyômaku chûhishu no 1 rei" ["Initial Case of Asbestosis Combined with Pleural Mesothelioma"]. *Nihon kyōbu shikkan zasshi* [*Japan Journal of Thoracic Diseases*], vol.12 (1974): 458–464.

Kassow, Samuel. *Who Will Write Our History? Emanuel Ringelblum, the Warsaw Ghetto, and the Oyneg Shabes Archive*. Bloomington: Indiana University Press, 2007.

Katz, Janet and Charles F. Abel. "The Medicalization of Repression: Eugenics and Crime." *Contemporary Crises*, vol.8, no.3 (1984): 227–241.

Keck, Frédéric. "On the Limits of Classification: Claude Lévi-Strauss and Mary Douglas." In *Cambridge Companion to Lévi-Strauss*, ed. Boris Wiseman. Cambridge: Cambridge University Press, 2009.

———. "Une sentinelle sanitaire aux frontières du vivant. Les experts de la grippe aviaire à Hong Kong." *Terrain*, no.54 (2010): 26–41.

Keck, Frédéric and Andrew Lakoff, eds. "Sentinel Devices." *Limn*, no.3 (2013): 38–40.

Keith, Ronald C. and Zhiqiu Lin. *New Crime in China: Public Order and Human Rights*. London: Routledge, 2006.

Kern, Stephen. *A Cultural History of Causality: Science, Murder Novels, and Systems of Thought*. Princeton: Princeton University Press, 2004.

Kluge, Alexander. *Unheimlichkeit der Zeit*. Frankfurt: Edition Surhkamp, 1977.

Kontje, Todd Curtis. *Thomas Mann's World: Empire, Race, and the Jewish Question*. Ann Arbor: University of Michigan Press, 2011.

Krase, Andreas. "Archives du regard—inventaire des choses: *Le Paris D'Eugène Atget*." In *Paris Eugène Atget: 1897–1927*, ed. Hans Christian Adam. Cologne: Taschen, 2008.

Kurumatani, Norio and Shinji Kumagai. "Mesothelioma Due to Neighborhood Asbestos Exposure: A Large-Scale, Ongoing Disaster among Residents Living near a Former Kubota Plant in Amagasaki, Japan." In *Asbestos Disaster: Lessons from Japan's Experience*, ed. Kenichi Miyamoto, Kenji Morinaga, and Hiroyuki Mori. Tokyo: Springer, 2011.

Lakoff, Andrew. "Preparing for the Next Emergency." *Public Culture*, vol.19, no.2 (2007): 247–271.

Lakoff, Andrew and Stephen J. Collier, eds. *Biosecurity Interventions: Global Health and Security in Question*. New York: University of Columbia Press, 2008.

Lane, Christopher. *Shyness: How Normal Behavior Became a Sickness*. New Haven: Yale University Press, 2008.

Lanier, Mark M. "Epidemiological Criminology (EpiCrim): Definition and Application." *Journal of Theoretical and Philosophical Criminology*, vol.2, no.1 (2010): 63–103.

Larson, Reed W., Gerald L. Clore, and Gretchen A. Wood. "The Emotions of Romantic Relationships: Do They Wreak Havoc on Adolescents?" In *The*

Development of Romantic Relationships in Adolescence, ed. Wyndol Furman, Bradford Brown, and Candice Feiring. Cambridge: Cambridge University Press, 1999.

Latour, Bruno. *The Pasteurization of France*. Translated by Alan Sheridan and John Law. Cambridge, MA: Harvard University Press, 1993 [1984].

———. *We Have Never Been Modern*. Translated by Catherine Porter. Cambridge, MA: Harvard University Press, 1993 [1991].

———. *Cogitamus: six lettres sur les humanités scientifiques*. Paris: La Découverte, 2009.

———. *The Making of Law: An Ethnography of the Conseil d'Etat*. Cambridge: Polity, 2010 [2002].

———. *On the Modern Cult of the Factish Gods*. Durham, NC: Duke University Press, 2010.

Lavin, Chad and Chris Russill. "The Ideology of the Epidemic." *New Political Science*, vol.32, no.1 (2010): 65–82.

Le Guen, Jean-Marie and Jean-Pierre Door. *Le H5N1: une menace durable pour la santé animale*. Paris: Rapport de l'Assemblée Nationale, vol.2, no.2833 (2006).

Lem, Stanislaw. *Imaginary Magnitude*. New York: Harcourt Brace, 1984.

Lemieux, Cyril. *Mauvaise presse. Une sociologie compréhensive du travail journalistique et de ses critiques*. Paris: Métailié, 2000.

Lemke, Thomas. *Biopolitics: An Advanced Introduction*. New York: New York University Press, 2011.

Leng Haiyue. "Hai 'zaolian' yige yuanshai: zaolian taolun de jieshu yu" ["The Positive Side of 'Premature Love'"]. *Hao fumu*, no.11 (2003): 10–11.

Lévêque, Sandrine. *Les journalistes sociaux. Histoire et sociologie d'une spécialité journalistique*. Rennes, France: Presses universitaires de Rennes, 2000.

Levine, Philippa. "Modernity, Medicine and Colonialism: The Contagious Diseases Ordinances in Hong Kong and the Straits Settlements." *Positions*, vol.6, no.3 (1998): 675–705.

———. *Prostitution, Race and Politics: Policing Venereal Disease in the British Empire*. New York: Routledge, 2003.

Li Guofang. "Guanyu zaolian yu zhongxuesheng weifa fanzui de diaocha" ["An Investigation of Premature Love and Crime among Secondary School Students"]. In *Zhongguo Qingshaonian fanzui yanjiu nianjian* [*Yearbook of Chinese Juvenile Delinquency Studies*]. Beijing: Chunqiu chubanshe, 1988.

Li Yanfeng. "Dusheng zinü de 'du'" ["'Only' as in Only-Child"]. *Shidai*, no.6 (1988): 21.

Lifton, Robert Jay. *The Nazi Doctors: Medical Killing and the Psychology of Genocide*. New York: Basic Books, 1986.

Lin Xi. "Zaolian de houguo" ["The Consequences of Premature Love"]. *Kewai yuedou*, no.3 (2008): 28.

Lippens, Ronnie. "Viral Contagion and Anti-Terrorism: Notes on Medical Emergency, Legality and Diplomacy." *International Journal of the Semiotics of Law*, vol.17, no.2 (2004): 125–139.

Lombardi-Nash, Michael A. *Sodomites and Urnings: Homosexual Representations in Classic German Journals*. London: Harrington Park Press, 2006.

Lombroso, Cesare. "Introduction." In *Criminal Man*. Translated and with an Introduction by Mary Gibson and Nicole Hahn Rafter. Durham, NC: Duke University Press, 2006.

Löwy, Michael. *The Theory of Revolution in the Young Marx*. Chicago: Haymarket, 2005 [2003].

Luhmann, Niklas. *The Reality of the Mass Media*. Translated by Kathleen Cross. Stanford: Stanford University Press, 2000.

Lynch, Michael. "'Here is Adhesiveness': From Friendship to Homosexuality." *Victorian Studies*, vol.29, no.1 (1985): 67–96.

Machen, Arthur. *The Three Imposters.* London: John Lane, 1895.

MacPherson, Kerrie L. "Conspiracy of Silence: A History of Sexually Transmitted Diseases and HIV/AIDS in Hong Kong." In *Sex, Disease, and Society: A Comparative History of Sexually Transmitted Diseases and HIV/AIDS in Asia and the Pacific,* ed. Milton Lewis, Scott Bamber, and Michael Waugh. Westport, CT: Greenwood Press, 1997.

Madden, Frederick and David Fieldhouse, eds. *The Dependent Empire and Ireland, 1840–1900: Advance and Retreat in Representative Self-Government.* Westport, CT: Greenwood Press, 1991.

Manceron, Vanessa. "Les oiseaux de l'infortune et la géographie sanitaire: La Dombes et la grippe aviaire." *Terrain,* no.51 (2008): 160–173.

Mankowitz, Zeev. *Life Between Memory and Hope: Survivors of the Holocaust in Occupied Germany.* Cambridge: Cambridge University Press, 2003.

Mann, Thomas. *Buddenbrooks.* Translated by Helen T. Lowe-Porter. New York: Vintage, 1984.

———. *The Magic Mountain [Der Zauberberg].* Translated by Helen T. Lowe-Porter. New York: Vintage, 1969.

Mao Yuyan, "Dushengzi yu fan dushengzi zai ruyuan shiying fangmian de bijiao yanjiu" ["A Comparative Study of the Adaptive Behavior between the Only-Child and the Non-Only child"]. *Xinli xuebao,* no.3 (1984): 240–249.

Marchetti, Dominique. *Contribution à une sociologie des transformations du champ journalistique dans les années 80 et 90. A propos d'"événements sida" et du "scandale du sang contaminé."* Paris: EHESS, 1997.

———. *Quand la santé devient médiatique: les logiques de production de l'information dans la presse.* Grenoble, France: Presses universitaires de Grenoble, 2010.

Marcus, Sharon. *Apartment Stories: City and Home in Nineteenth-Century Paris and London.* Berkeley: University of California Press, 1999.

Markowitz, Gerald and David Rosner. *Deceit and Denial: The Deadly Politics of Industrial Pollution.* Berkeley: University of California Press, 2002.

Marx, Karl. *Capital: A Critique of the Political Economy,* Vol.1. Translated by Ben Fowkes. Harmondsworth, UK: Penguin, 1990.

Matsumoto, Katsumi. "Asbestos Litigation in Japan: Recent Trends and Related Issues." In *Asbestos Disaster: Lessons from Japan's Experience,* ed. Kenichi Miyamoto, Kenji Morinaga, and Hiroyuki Mori. Tokyo: Springer, 2011.

McCarthy, Cormac. *The Road.* New York: Vintage, 2006.

McCarthy, Tom. *Remainder.* New York: Vintage, 2005.

McLean, Angela, Robert M. May, John Pattison, and Robin A. Weiss, eds. *SARS: A Case Study of Emerging Infections.* Oxford: Oxford University Press, 2005.

McCloud, Scott. *Understanding Comics: The Invisible Art.* New York: Harper, 1994.

Meillassoux, Quentin. *After Finitude: An Essay on the Necessity of Contingency.* Translated by Ray Brassier. New York: Continuum, 2008.

Metzel, Jonathan M. and Anna Kirkland, eds. *Against Health: How Health Became the New Morality.* New York: New York University Press, 2010.

Michaels, David. *Doubt Is Their Product: How Industry's Assault on Science Threatens Your Health.* Oxford: Oxford University Press, 2008.

Milburn, Colin. "Science from Hell: Jack the Ripper and Victorian Vivisection." In *Science Images and Popular Images of the Sciences,* ed. Peter Weingart and Bernd Hüppauf. London: Routledge, 2011.

Mohammed, Marwan. "Youth Gangs, Riots and the Politicisation Process." In *Rioting in the UK and France, 2001–2008: A Comparative Analysis,* ed. David Waddington, Fabien Jobard, and Mike King. Cullompton, UK: Willan, 2009.

Mori, Hiroyuki. "Asbestos Disaster and Public Policy: From the Prewar Era through the Postwar Economic Boom." In *Asbestos Disaster: Lessons from*

Japan's Experience, ed. Kenichi Miyamoto, Kenji Morinaga, and Hiroyuki Mori. Tokyo: Springer, 2011.

Morinaga, Kenji, I. Hara, S. Yutani and Yoshizumi Sera. "Use of Population-Based Cancer Registration in Occupational Epidemiology: Experience in Osaka." *Journal of the University of Occupational and Environmental Health*, vol.5 (1983): 215–223.

Morinaga, Kenji, Kunihiko Yokoyama, Satoshi Yamamoto, Yoshinobu Matsuda and Yoshizumi Sera. "Mortality and Survival of Workers Receiving Compensation for Asbestosis in Osaka, Japan." In *Proceedings of the 6th International Pneumoconiosis Conference*. Geneva: International Labor Office, 1984.

Morinaga, Kenji, Takumi Kishimoto, Mitsunori Sakatani, Masanori Akira, Kunihiko Yokoyama and Yoshizumi Sera, "Asbestos-Related Lung Cancer and Mesothelioma in Japan." *Industrial Health*, vol.39, no.2 (2001): 65–74.

Mosse, George. *Toward the Final Solution: A History of European Racism*. New York: Harper, 1980.

Mucchielli, Laurent and Véronique Le Goaziou. *Quand les banlieues brûlent . . . Retour sur les émeutes de novembre 2005*. Paris: La Découverte, 2007.

Mukharji, Projit Bihari. "The 'Cholera Cloud' in the Nineteenth-Century 'British World': History of an Object-Without-an-Essence." *Bulletin of the History of Medicine*, vol.86, no.3 (2012): 303–332.

Munn, Christopher. *Anglo-China: Chinese People and British Rule in Hong Kong, 1841–1880*. Richmond, UK: Curzon, 2001.

———. "William Caine." In *Dictionary of Hong Kong Biography*, ed. May Holdsworth and Christopher Munn. Hong Kong: Hong Kong University Press, 2012.

Munro, Robin. *China's Psychiatric Inquisition: Dissent, Psychiatry and the Law in Post-1949 China*. Hong Kong: Simmonds & Hill Publishing, 2007.

Muntean, Nick. "Viral Terrorism and Terrifying Viruses: The Homological Construction of the 'War on Terror' and the Avian Flu Pandemic." *International Journal of Media and Cultural Politics*, vol.5, no.3 (2009): 199–216.

Nau, Jean-Yves. *Journal de la vache folle*. Paris: Georg, 2003.

Nead, Lynda. *Victorian Babylon: People, Streets and Images in Nineteenth-Century London*. New Haven: Yale University Press, 2000.

Nerlich, Brigitte and Christopher Halliday. "Avian Flu: The Creation of Expectations in the Interplay between Science and the Media." *Sociology of Health and Illness*, vol.29, no.1 (2007): 46–65.

Niehoff, Debra. *The Biology of Violence: How Understanding the Brain, Behavior and Environment Can Break the Vicious Circle of Aggression*. New York: The Free Press, 1999.

Nossack, Hans Erich. *Der Untergang*. German: E. Kabel, 1981.

Ofer, Dalia. "Another Glance through the Historian's Lens: Testimonies in the Study of Health and Medicine in the Ghetto." *Poetics Today*, vol.27, no.2 (2006): 331–351.

Oikawa, Fujio, Kōsuke Ōta, Keinosuke Kaburagi, Kikuji Kimura, Hiroyuki Sakabe, Shōgo Shima, et al. *Nihon no jinpai taisaku*, vol.4. Tokyo: Chuô rôdô saigai hôshi kyôkai, 1985.

Oosterhuis, Harry. *Stepchildren of Nature: Krafft-Ebing, Psychiatry, and the Making of Sexual Identity*. Chicago: University of Chicago Press, 2000.

Otis, Laura. *Membranes: Metaphors of Invasion in Nineteenth-Century Literature, Science, and Politics*. Baltimore: Johns Hopkins University Press, 2000.

———. *Networking: Communicating with Bodies and Machines in the Nineteenth Century*. Ann Arbor: University of Michigan Press, 2001.

Parsons, Talcott. *The Social System*. New York: The Free Press, 1951.

Peckham, Robert. "Economies of Contagion: Financial Crisis and Pandemic." *Economy and Society*, vol.42, no.2 (2013): 226–248.

———. "Infective Economies: Empire, Panic, and the Business of Disease." *Journal of Imperial and Commonwealth History*, vol.41, no.2 (2013): 211–237.

———. "Ghosts in the Body: Infection, Genes, and the Re-Enchantment of Biology." In *The Ashgate Research Companion to Paranormal Culture*, ed. Olu Jenzen and Sally R. Munt. Farnham, UK: Ashgate, in press.

Peiris, Malik, Menno de Jong, and Yi Guan. "Avian Influenza Virus (H5N1): A Threat to Human Health." *Clinical Microbiology Review*, vol.20, no.2 (2007): 243–267.

Pelling, Margaret. *Cholera, Fever, and English Medicine, 1825–1865*. Oxford: Oxford University Press, 1978.

Perechodnik, Calel. *Am I a Murderer? Testament of a Jewish Ghetto Policeman*, ed. and trans., Frank Fox. Boulder, CO: Westview, 1996.

Pick, Daniel. *Faces of Degeneration: A European Disorder, c.1848–c.1918*. Cambridge: Cambridge University Press, 1989.

Poovey, Mary. *Making a Social Body: British Cultural Formation, 1830–1864*. Chicago: University of Chicago Press, 1995.

Poston, Jr., Dudley L. and Tony Falbo. "Academic Performance and Personality Traits of Chinese Children: 'Onlies' versus Others." *American Journal of Sociology*, vol.96, no.2 (1990): 433–451.

Proctor, Robert. *Racial Hygiene: Medicine Under the Nazis*. Cambridge, MA: Harvard University Press, 1988.

———. *The Nazi War on Cancer*. Princeton: Princeton University Press, 2009.

Rabinbach, Anson. *The Human Motor: Energy, Fatigue, and the Origins of Modernity*. New York: Basic Books, 1990.

Rafter, Nicole H. *Creating Born Criminals*. Urbana: University of Illinois Press, 1997.

———. *The Criminal Brain: Understanding Biological Theories of Crime*. New York: New York University Press, 2008.

———. "Criminology's Darkest Hour: Biocriminology in Nazi Germany." *Australian and New Zealand Journal of Criminology*, vol.41, no.2 (2008): 287–306.

Reynolds, Simon. *Retromania: Pop Culture's Addiction to Its Own Past*. New York: Faber and Faber, 2011.

Rice, James. "The Global Reorganization and Revitalization of the Asbestos Industry, 1970–2007." *Occupational and Environmental Health Policy*, vol.41, no.2 (2011): 239–254.

Robinson, Matthew. "No Longer Taboo: Crime Prevention Implications of Biosocial Criminology." In *Biosocial Criminology: New Directions in Theory and Research*, ed. Anthony Walsh and Kevin M. Beaver. New York: Routledge, 2009.

Roland, Charles. *Courage Under Siege: Starvation, Disease, and Death in the Warsaw Ghetto*. New York: Oxford University Press, 1992.

Rosario, Vernon A. *The Erotic Imagination: French Histories of Perversity*. Oxford: Oxford University Press, 1997.

Rose, Nikolas. *The Politics of Life Itself: Biomedicine, Power, and Subjectivity in the Twenty-First Century*. Princeton: Princeton University Press, 2007.

Rosenberg, Charles E. *The Cholera Years: The United States in 1832, 1849 and 1866*. Chicago: University of Chicago Press, 1987.

———. "Introduction—Framing Disease: Illness, Society, and History." In *Framing Disease: Studies in Cultural History*, ed. Charles E. Rosenberg and Janet Golden. New Brunswick, NJ: Rutgers University Press, 1997.

Rosental, Paul-André. "Health and Safety at Work: An Issue in Transnational History—Introduction." *Journal of Modern European History*, vol.7, no.2 (2009): 169–173.

Rosner, David and Gerald Markowitz. *Dying for Work: Workers' Safety and Health in Twentieth-Century America*. Bloomington: Indiana University Press, 1987.

———. *Deadly Dust: Silicosis and the Politics of Occupational Disease in Twentieth-Century America*. Princeton: Princeton University Press, 1991.

———. "The Trials and Tribulations of Two Historians: Adjudicating Responsibility for Pollution and Personal Harm." *Medical History*, vol.53, no.2 (2009): 271–292.

Rowbotham, Judith and Kim Stevenson, eds. *Criminal Conversations: Victorian Crimes, Social Panic, and Moral Outrage*. Columbus: Ohio State University Press, 2005.

Rowe, David C. *Biology and Crime*. Los Angeles: Roxbury Publishing, 2002.

Royle, Nicholas. *The Uncanny*. Manchester: Manchester University Press, 2003.

Safrian, Hans. *Eichmann's Men*. Translated by Ute Stargardt. Cambridge: Cambridge University Press, 2009.

Sarat, Austin and Stuart Scheingold, eds. *Cause Lawyering: Political Commitments and Professional Responsibilities*. Oxford: Oxford University Press, 1998.

———, eds. *Cause Lawyering and the State in a Global Era*. Oxford: Oxford University Press, 2001.

———, eds. *Cause Lawyers and Social Movements*. Stanford: Stanford University Press, 2006.

———, eds. *The Cultural Lives of Cause Lawyers*. Cambridge: Cambridge University Press, 2008.

Scheffer, Thomas. "Knowing How to Sleepwalk: Placing Evidence in the Midst of an English Jury Trial." *Science, Technology, & Human Values*, vol.35, no.5 (2010): 620–664.

Schmidt-Macon, Klaus F. *Aschenspur. Gedichte. Trace de Cendres. Poems*. Wörthsee bei München: Groh, 1988.

Schrader-Frechette, Kristin. *Environmental Justice: Creating Equity, Reclaiming Democracy*. New York: Oxford University Press, 2002.

Sebald, Winfried G. *On the Natural History of Destruction*. Translated by Anthea Bell. New York: Modern Library, 2004.

———. *Campo Santo*. Translated by Anthea Bell. New York: Modern Library, 2005.

Sedel, Julie. *Les médias et la banlieue*. Lormont, France: INA/Le bord de l'eau, 2009.

Sellers, Christopher. *Hazards of the Job: From Industrial Disease to Environmental Health Science*. Chapel Hill: University of North Carolina Press, 1997.

Seltzer, Mark. *Serial Killers: Death and Life in America's Wound Culture*. New York: Routledge, 1998.

———. "Die Freie Natur." In *Gefahrensinn: Archiv für Mediengeschichte*, ed. Lorenz Engell, Bernhard Siegert, and Joseph Vogl. München: Wilhelm Fink, 2009.

———. "Parlor Games: The Apriorization of the Media." *Critical Inquiry*, vol.36, no.1 (2009): 100–133.

———. "The Official World." *Critical Inquiry*, vol.37, no.4 (2011): 724–753.

Sera, Yoshizumi, et al. "Haigan o gappei shita sekimenhai no 1 bôkenrei." *Sangyô igaku*, vol.2, no.4 (1960): 326.

———, et al. *Sekimenhai to haigan no kanren ni kansuru ekigakuteki linshôteki byôri soshikigakuteki kenkyû "Jinpai no byôri soshikigakuteki kenkyû" hôkoku* [*Research on the Relationship between Asbestosis and Lung Cancer: Epidemiology,*

182 Bibliography

Clinic, and Histopathology, "Histopathology of Human Lung" Report]. Tokyo: Kankyôchô kôgai chôsa kenkyû itaku jigyô, 1973.

Shanghai shi ertong jiaoyu yanjiu shi [Shanghai Municipality Office for Child Education Research]. "Tantan dusheng zinü de jiating jiaoyu" ["Discussing the Family Education of Only-Children"]. *Zhongguo funü* [*Chinese Women*], no.5 (1980): 16–17.

Shortland, Michael. "Courting the Cerebellum: Early Organological and Phrenological Views on Sexuality." *British Journal of the History of Science*, vol.20, no.65 (1987): 173–199.

Siegel, Greg. "The Similitude of the Wound." *Cabinet*, vol.43 (2011): 95–100.

Siegert, Bernhard. "There Are No Mass Media." In *Mapping Benjamin: The Work of Art in the Digital Age*, ed. Hans Gumbrecht and Michael Marrinen. Stanford: Stanford University Press, 2003.

Simon, Jean, ed. *Le camp de concentration du Struthof. Konzentrationslager Natzweiler. Collection documents-tome III*. Schirmeck, France: Essor, 1998.

Sinn, Elizabeth. "Chinese Patriarchy and the Protection of Women in 19th-Century Hong Kong." In *Women and Chinese Patriarchy: Submission, Servitude and Escape*, ed. Maria Jaschok and Suzanne Miers. Hong Kong: Hong Kong University Press, 2001.

———. *Pacific Crossing: California Gold, Chinese Migration, and the Making of Hong Kong*. Hong Kong: Hong Kong University Press, 2013.

Smail, Daniel Lord. *On Deep History and the Brain*. Berkeley: University of California Press, 2008.

Smith, Andrew. "The Whitechapel Murders and the Medical Gaze." In *Jack the Ripper: Media, Culture, History*, ed. Alexandra Warwick and Martin Willis. Manchester: Manchester University Press, 2007.

Sontag, Susan. *On Photography*. Harmondsworth, UK: Penguin, 1978.

Spark, Corey S. "Violent Crime in San Antonio, Texas: An Application of Spatial Epidemiological Methods." *Spatial and Spatio-temporal Epidemiology*, vol.2, no.4 (2011): 301–309.

Stark, Andrew. *The Limits of Medicine: Cure or Enhancement*. Cambridge: Cambridge University Press, 2006.

Terry, Jennifer. *An American Obsession: Science, Medicine, and Homosexuality in Modern Society*. Chicago: University of Chicago Press, 1999.

Teyssot, George. "Norm and Type: Variations on a Theme." In *Architecture and the Sciences: Exchanging Metaphors*, ed. Antoine Picon and Alessandra Ponte. New York: Princeton Architectural Press, 2003.

Thébaud-Mony, Annie. *La reconnaissance des maladies professionnelles en France. Acteurs et logiques socials*. Paris: La Documentation Française, 1991.

Thévenot, Laurent. *L'action au pluriel. Sociologie des régimes d'engagement*. Paris: La Découverte, 2006.

Thomann, Bernard. "L'hygiène nationale, la société civile et la reconnaissance de la silicose comme maladie professionnelle au Japon (1868–1960)." *Revue d'histoire moderne et contemporaine*, vol.56, no.1 (2009): 142–176.

———. "Yoroke: la silicose au Japon." In *Santé au travail: approches critiques*, ed. Annie Thébaud-Mony, Véronique Daubas-Letourneux, Nathalie Frigul, and Paul Jobin. Paris: La Découverte, 2012.

Thomas, Nicholas. *Colonialism's Culture: Anthropology, Travel and Government*. Cambridge: Polity, 1994.

Tsing, Anna Lowenhaupt. *Friction: An Ethnography of Global Connection*. Princeton: Princeton University Press, 2005.

Tweedale, Geoffrey. *Magic Mineral to Killer Dust: Turner & Newall and the Asbestos Hazard*. Oxford: Oxford University Press, 2001.

Van Pelt, Robert Jan. *The Case for Auschwitz: Evidence from the Irving Trial*. Bloomington: Indiana University Press, 2002.

Vidler, Anthony. *The Architectural Uncanny: Essays in the Modern Unhomely.* Cambridge, MA: MIT Press, 1992.
――――. *Warped Space: Art, Architecture, and Anxiety in Modern Culture.* Cambridge, MA: MIT Press, 2001.
Villa, Renzo. *Il deviante e i suoi segni: Lombroso e la nascita dell'antropologia criminale.* Milan: Franco Angeli, 1985.
Villeneuve, Gaël. *Faire parler le public. Une ethnographie comparée des débats politiques à la télévision.* Unpublished PhD thesis, Université de Paris 8, 2008.
Vogl, Joseph. "Becoming-Media: Galieo Telescope." *Grey Room,* vol.29 (2007): 14–25.
Von Foerster, Heinz. *Observing Systems.* Seaside, CA: Intersystems Publications, 1981.
Walby, Kevin and Nicolas Carrier. "The Rise of Biocriminology: Capturing Observable Bodily Economies of 'Criminal Man.'" *Criminology & Criminal Justice,* vol.10, no.3 (2010): 261–285.
Wald, Priscilla. *Contagious: Cultures, Carriers, and the Outbreak Narrative.* Durham, NC: Duke University Press, 2008.
Wallis, Patrick and Brigitte Nerlich. "Disease Metaphors in New Epidemics: The UK Media Framing of the 2003 SARS Epidemic." *Social Science and Medicine,* vol.60, no.11 (2005): 2629–2639.
Walsh, Anthony and Kevin M. Beaver, eds. *Biosocial Criminology: New Directions in Theory and Research.* New York: Routledge, 2009.
Wan Chuanwen, Fan Cunren, and Lin Guobin. "Wu sui dao qi sui dusheng he fan dusheng zinü moxie gexing tezheng de bijiao ji xingbie chadao de yanjiu" ["A Comparative Study on Certain Differences between Five to Seven Year Old Onlies and Non-Onlies"]. *Xinli xuebao,* no.4 (1984): 383–391.
Wang Caiping, et al. "Jiu dusheng ertong xingwei wenti tan yousheng youyu" ["Discussing Good Pre-Natal Education with Regard to Behavioural Problems among Only-Children"]. *Renkou yanjiu [Population Research],* no.2 (1991): 47–50.
Wang Le. "Buxu chaochao mumu, zhiqiu cengjing yong you." *Hao fumu,* no.11 (2003): 10.
Wang Xiaoling, "Zhongxuesheng lianai qingkuang de diaocha" ["An Investigation of the Situation of Love Affairs among Secondary School Pupils"]. *Shanghai jiaoyu,* no.2 (1986): 12.
Warren, James Francis. *Ah Ku and Karayuki-san: Prostitution in Singapore, 1870–1940.* Singapore: Singapore University Press, 2003.
Warwick, Alexandra. "The Scene of the Crime: Inventing the Serial Killer." *Social Legal Studies,* vol.15, no.4 (2006): 552–569.
Warwick, Alexandra and Martin Willis, eds. *Jack the Ripper: Media, Culture, History.* Manchester: Manchester University Press, 2008.
Washer, Peter "Representations of SARS in the British Newspapers." *Social Science and Medicine,* vol.59, no.12 (2004): 2561–2571.
Watson, Katherine D. *Forensic Medicine in Western Society: A History.* London: Routledge, 2011.
Watters, Ethan. *Crazy Like Us: The Globalization of the American Psyche.* New York: Free Press, 2010.
Weindling, Paul. *Health, Race and German Politics Between National Unification and Nazism, 1870–1945.* Cambridge: Cambridge University Press, 1989.
Weiner, Marc. *Richard Wagner and the Anti-Semitic Imagination.* Lincoln: University of Nebraska Press, 1995.
Werner, Michael and Bénédicte Zimmermann. "Beyond Comparison: Histoire Croisée and the Challenge of Reflexivity." *History and Theory,* vol.45, no.1 (2006): 30–50.
Wetzell, Richard F. *Inventing the Criminal: A History of German Criminology, 1880–1945.* Chapel Hill: University of North Carolina Press, 2000.

Whyte, Martin King and S. Z. Gu. "Popular Response to China's Fertility Transition." *Population and Development Review*, vol.13, no.3 (1987): 569–571.

Winick, Myron, ed. *Hunger Disease: Studies by the Jewish Physicians in the Warsaw Ghetto.* Translated by Martha Osnos. New York: Wiley, 1979.

Wise, Sarah. *The Blackest Streets: The Life and Death of a Victorian Slum.* London: The Bodley Head, 2008.

Worboys, Michael. *Spreading Germs: Disease Theories and Medical Practice in Britain, 1865–1900.* Cambridge: Cambridge University Press, 2000.

Wu Fan. "Institutional Roots of Ageism and Public Policy Reconstruction for the Elderly in China." *Chinese Journal of Sociology*, vol.31, no.5 (2011): 190–206.

Xin Yang, ed. *Zhongguo banzhurenxue* [*Chinese Class Teacher Studies*]. Changchun: Jilin jiaoyu chubanshe, 1990.

Xu Ming, Chu Xian, Song Defu and Qiang Wei, eds. *Sixiang zhengzhi gongzuo daoxiang* [*Guidance in Ideological-Political Work*]. Beijing: Kexue chubanshe, 1990.

Yang Chengpu. "Dusheng zinü de xianzhuang ji jiaoyu duice" ["The Present Situation among Only-Children and Its Educational Countermeasures"]. *Rensheng*, no.7 (1988): 3–5.

Young, Alison. *Imagining Crime*. London: Sage, 1996.

Yuan Jinhua. "Qingshaonian fanzui yu xuexiao jiaoyu de guanxi de diaocha" ["Survey on the Connection between Juvenile Crime and School Education"]. *Jiaoyu yanjiu*, no.11 (1986): 4.

Yuoka, Kazuyoshi. "Kakusareta higai no genba o aruku" ["Walking around the Site of Hidden Damages"]. In *Asubesuto sanka o kuni ni tou* [*Questioning the State about Asbestos Disasters*], ed. Osaka jinpai asubesuto bengodan [Osaka Attorneys' Group on Asbestos Silicosis] and Sennan chiiki no sekimen higai to shimin no kai [Asbestos Victims' and Citizens' Association for the Region of Sennan]. Kyōto: Kamogawa, 2009.

Zhang Jian and Zhang Wenbang. "Dui Zhejiang sheng nü fanzui fuxing qijian de tuanhuo huodong fenxi" ["Analysis of the Gang Activities of Female Prisoners in Zhejiang Province during the Period of Incarceration"]. In *Zhongguo qingshaonian fanzui yanjiu nainajian 1987*. Beijing: Chunqiu chubansje, 1988.

Zheng Yunzhen. "Xing fanzui nü qingshaonian de gexing pianqing he tiaozheng" ["Individual Character Deviation and the Correction of Young Sexual Criminal Girls"]. *Jiaoyu lilun yu shijian*, no.1 (1986): 61–63.

Zhonghua renmin gongheguo gonganb [The PRC Ministry of Public Security]. "Zhongguo qingshaonian fanzui de qushi he yufang" ["Trends of Chinese Juvenile Crime in China and Their Prevention"]. In *Zhongguo qingshaonian fanzui yanjiu nianjian 1987* [*Yearbook of Chinese Juvenile Crime Research 1987*]. Beijing: Chunqiu chubanshe, 1988.

Zhou Lishun, "Dusheng zinü jiaoyu zhong jiedai jiejue de wenti" ["Pressing Problems in the Education of Only-Children"]. *Shanghai jiaoyu keyan*, no.4 (1988): 55–56.

Zola, Emile. "The Experimental Novel." In *Documents of Modern Literary Realism*, ed. George J. Becker. Princeton: Princeton University Press, 1963.

Contributors

Børge Bakken is Associate Professor in the Department of Sociology at the University of Hong Kong. He has written extensively on crime, deviance, and social control, as well as on the history of crime and punishment, with a particular focus on the People's Republic of China. Publications include *The Exemplary Society: Human Improvement, Social Control, and the Dangers of Modernity in China* (2000) and the edited volume *Crime, Punishment, and Policing in China* (2005).

Chiara Beccalossi is Lecturer in the History of Medicine at the Centre for Health, Medicine and Society: Past and Present (Department of History, Philosophy and Religion) at Oxford Brookes University. She works on the history of sexuality, medicine, and human sciences in modern Britain and Europe, with a special focus on comparative and transnational history. She is the author of *Female Sexual Inversion: Same-Sex Desires in Italian and British Sexology, ca. 1870–1920* (2012), as well as a number of articles on the history of medicine and sexuality.

Michael Berkowitz is Professor of Modern Jewish History in the Department of Hebrew and Jewish Studies at University College London. He is the author of *Zionist Culture and West European Jewry before the First World War* (1996), *The Jewish Self-Image in the West* (2000), *Western Jewry and the Zionist Project, 1914–1933* (2003), *The Crime of My Very Existence: Nazism and the Myth of Jewish Criminality* (2007), and co-editor of the volume *We Are Here: New Approaches to Jewish Displaced Persons in Postwar Germany* (2010).

Paul Jobin is Director of the French Centre for Research on Contemporary China, Taiwan Branch (CEFC Taipei) and Associate Professor at the University of Paris Diderot. His research focuses on industrial pollution and social movements in Taiwan and Japan, a subject on which he has published widely. He is the author, among other work, of *Industrial Diseases and Labor Union Revival in Japan* [in French] (2006) and co-author of *Health at Work. Critical Approaches* [in French] (2012).

Frédéric Keck is Researcher at the CNRS, based at the Laboratoire d'anthropologie sociale in Paris. He has conducted research on the history of social sciences and on the social aspects of avian flu. His publications include *Claude Lévi-Strauss: An Introduction* [in French] (2005), *Lucien Lévy-Bruhl: Between Philosophy and Anthropology* [in French] (2008), and *A Fevered World* [in French] (2010). He has also contributed to the collections *Biosecurity Interventions: Global Health and Security in Question* (2008) and *Food: Ethnographic Encounters* (2011).

Robert Peckham is Co-Director of the Centre for the Humanities and Medicine at the University of Hong Kong, where he teaches in the Department of History. His current research focuses on histories of infectious disease and epidemic control, technologies of biopower, and the modern state's role in the supervision of public health. He is the author of numerous journal articles and book chapters and co-editor, among other works, of the volume *Imperial Contagions: Medicine, Hygiene, and Cultures of Planning in Asia* (2013). He is currently completing the monograph *Infective Economies: Plague and the Crisis of Empire*.

Mark Seltzer is Evan Frankel Professor of Literature at the University of California at Los Angeles. His work explores the social, artistic, and technological forms of a modern world. His recent work focuses on the cultural techniques that organize collective life and art in the epoch of social systems—in particular, the demarcation zones that epitomize what he terms "the official world." He is the author of *Henry James and the Art of Power* (1984), *Bodies and Machines* (1992), *Serial Killers: Death and Life in America's Wound Culture* (1998), and *True Crime: Observations on Violence and Modernity* (2006). The piece included in this volume is part of a forthcoming book, *The Official World*.

Carol C. L. Tsang teaches in the Department of History at the University of Hong Kong, where she completed her PhD in 2011 on the history of medicine. She is currently preparing the manuscript *Women's Health in Modern Hong Kong* for publication as a monograph.

Index